Turning to Christ

URBAN T. HOLMES, III

TURNING TO CHRIST

A Theology of Renewal and Evangelization

THE SEABURY PRESS·NEW YORK

1981
The Seabury Press
815 Second Avenue
New York, N.Y. 10017

Library of Congress Cataloging in Publication Data

Holmes, Urban Tigner, 1930-
Turning to Christ.

Includes bibliographical references.
1. Church renewal—Episcopal Church.
2. Evangelistic work. 3. Episcopal Church—
Missions. 4. Episcopal Church—Doctrinal and
controversial works.   I. Title.
BX5930.2.H64   269   81-8939
ISBN 0-8164-2289-3   AACR2

In Memory of
ROBERT GILDAY
1925–1980

Contents

Foreword

An earlier form of some of the material in this book was presented at the annual meeting of the Network of Episcopal Clergy Associations in May, 1979, at St. Christopher's Conference Center of the Episcopal Diocese of Oklahoma. These lectures were reported in the professional supplement of *The Episcopalian* in July, 1979.

Still more of the material was used in the Francis X. Cheney lectures at Yale's Berkeley Divinity School in October, 1979. I am very grateful to the Very Rev. Charles Clark for the invitation to give those lectures and for the hospitality extended me at that time.

The New English Bible (NEB) is used in quotations throughout this book, except where a particular reading of the Greek text was lacking. In such instances, I have made my own translation, which I have indicated (UTH).

As always, I am indebted to friends and colleagues who have read and criticized portions of the manuscript. It goes without saying that they are not responsible for any of the ideas expressed in this study, but I am most grateful to them for their willingness to collaborate with me. Arthur Zannoni, John Westerhoff, and Gray Temple, Jr., have been of particular help.

The manuscript was typed and retyped by my secretaries, Mary Lynn Floore and Patricia Smith. I greatly appreciate their patience.

This volume is dedicated to the memory of Robert Gilday, who died while it was being written. Bob invited me to become a published author over ten years ago. From that initial contact he became a close friend and critic, who encouraged me and shared my desire to state to the church a reasoned Anglican theology on a variety of issues, a theology faithful to both the Anglican tradition and to our times. This is the first book I have written that I have not discussed with Bob. I have missed him. I hope that the dedication in some small way expresses my sense of loss and love.

URBAN T. HOLMES

The Feast of William P. DuBose, 1980

Introduction

In the fall of 1978 Charles Price of the Virginia Theological Seminary was lecturing at the University of the South on the occasion of the centennial of the School of Theology. His subject was the relevance of the Anglican Communion to Christianity in the last two decades of this century. His talk began with a catalogue of Anglican worthies—Cranmer, Hooker, Taylor, Baxter, Wesley, Wilberforce, Pusey, Gore, Temple, and many more. It may strike one as a rather prosaic beginning, yet I unexpectedly found myself swallowing a very large lump in my throat, tears running down my cheeks. Other than feeling a bit foolish, I wondered why.

Upon later reflection, I recalled a story that I was told many years ago about John Rathbone Oliver, a pioneer in American psychiatry. I do not know whether or not the story is true, but it does not matter. Oliver was brought up in the Episcopal Church and was even a choirboy for a time. Then he left the church and pursued his medical and psychiatric studies. Years later he was walking down a Baltimore street on his way to lunch and saw a sign outside an Episcopal Church announcing that confessions were being heard. Drawn by a power greater than himself, he stumbled into the church, wandered into the confessional, and pressing his face against the screen, he sobbed, "I want to come home."

I do not think that I am all that unique among Episcopalians over the last ten to twenty years. Amid the spasms of our country's struggle for self-understanding, Anglicanism in this country has experienced a continuing trauma. Our response to national and world crises has been necessary and, I think, often prophetic. The fight over the ordination of women to the priesthood and the episcopate has left many of us, while in favor of the action, feeling somewhat remote from our fore-bears. Prayer book revision has been a necessary process, and I judge it to be a far greater good than evil. But in all the turmoil there has been a loss of our sense of place.

For myself, the 1960s was not a good time. Ten years of university ministry based upon an inherited model of the Anglican priest seemed to vanish far more easily than it came. Theological education went a bit crazy, and we forgot what we should have known. We lost a wisdom that comes with perspec-tive. We fell too easily into models of priesthood that were helpful, but inadequate to the profound nature of our calling. We looked for direction from the human sciences, forgetting their secular presuppositions. For many of us, all this was followed by a search in other traditions for some clearer perception of what God wanted of us, sometimes with good effect.

While this may sound something like a confession, it is more than that. Bad times can be the occasion of discovery and growth, and for me this was the case. But there was also a sense of being away. A novel that has meant so much to me is Robert Penn Warren's *A Place to Come To*. The hero is the son of very humble parents from a small town in Alabama. He leaves home to become a distinguished university professor only to discover his need to return, symbolized in the visit to his parents' graves. Standing in the cemetery the hero says of himself:

> I had a wild impulse to lie on the earth between the two graves [of his parents], the old and the new, and stretch out a hand to each. I thought that if I could do that, I might be able to weep, and if I could weep, something warm and blessed might happen. But I did not lie down. The trouble was, I was afraid that nothing might happen, and I was afraid to take the risk.[1]

The Episcopal Church has become increasingly aware of what it has forgotten to do over the last twenty years. Princi-pally, it has failed to attend to mission, and now on all sides we are calling ourselves to recover our ministry of mission, with all that implies for evangelization and renewal. No observer of the contemporary religious scene can have failed to observe the various movements that have caught the imagination of many church people both within and without the Anglican tradition. I have no desire to make a sweeping or generalized condemnation of any of those movements, and I am wholeheartedly in support of the emergence of the spirit of mission that is inherent in many of them.

But before we can do the things we have forgotten to do, we need to take the risk and remember who we are. "Something warm and blessed might happen." We need to do our "root work." This is what my surprising reaction to Charles Price's catalogue of Anglican worthies has brought vividly to my attention. There is no general "Christian ministry." We each work out an effective ministry through the eyes of our particular tradition, and we need to know what that ministry is before we can get about God's business in this world. To me it is clear that many Episcopalians have little, if any, sense of what it is to be an Anglican, and this shows in our attempts at mission, renewal, and evangelization. We often produce an inept imitation of what is natural to other traditions, rather than doing what flows naturally from our own.

Occasionally we are brought up short by the people in the pews. Not so long ago I was leading a discussion with members of a parish on *Christian Believing,* the first volume in the new Church's Teaching Series, written by John Westerhoff of Duke University and myself. Suddenly they demanded to know why the Episcopal Church was not behaving according to its own tradition, but seemed to be pursuing methods of evangelization that were imitative of denominations that they had left. To a person, these questioners were converts to the Episcopal Church. Their question was neither petty nor without affection for what they had left. It was just that they had *expected* something different.

Since the nineteeth-century churchmanship controversies, there has been a strong tendency to disclaim anything unique to the Anglican Communion, except its "incomparable liturgy" and its comprehensiveness. But our converts do not see it this way. Stephen Sykes of Durham University in England has done a good job of calling that assumption into question in a deceptively small book, *The Integrity of Anglicanism*.[2] Despite the fact that he forgets, like many other English church people, that the Anglican Communion is far bigger than the Church of England (there are more black Anglicans than white), Sykes well documents the Anglican unwillingness to wrestle with the hard issues and the consequent escape into an endemic vagueness. However, we are *more* than the Tory or Republican parties at prayer.

This book is written in the belief that the Anglican Communion is unique—not just comprehensive—and in refutation of the notion that "anything goes" in evangelization and renewal. I believe there is an Anglican theology within the mainstream of the tradition that must express itself in our theology of mission. This book is intended to define and illumine that theology. I do not claim the *magisterium* of the church for my opinion, but I offer a point of view aimed toward the goal of reclaiming our heritage and explicating its implications for ministry.

Anglican authority is threefold: Scripture, tradition, and reason. Although this "three-legged stool" is not original with Richard Hooker, who was the first to speak of it after Canterbury's separation from Rome in the sixteenth century, or even with Anglicanism, it is a guiding principle that we need to recall and hold dear. I suspect that many Episcopalians are unaware of this pivotal point of our heritage. In what follows I have made a conscious effort to be true to Scripture, tradition, and reason in developing an understanding of evangelization and renewal. One needs only to recall that a three-legged stool topples if any one of its legs is removed. I intend to keep all three legs operative.

In this light, it might be helpful to outline briefly the place of Scripture in the Anglican tradition, since the Episcopal Church is experiencing some conflict over this issue. To begin with, the canon of Scripture—i.e., the particular books within the Bible—is the canon because the church says it is. Other reasons, for instance, the familiar one of explaining that all the books of the New Testament were written by eyewitnesses to the Resurrection, do not pertain. Scripture must be taken as a whole. Recognizing that there are differing theologies and contradictions within the Bible, we do not choose sides, but work through the conflicts that address us in holy writ to a coherent perception of God's action in his world.

The Scriptures have an independent authority that confronts us and calls us into judgment. But the chief value of the Bible is that it illumines our life. It is not to be read for its own sake or as an "answer book." The worst example of this is bibliomancy. (I sometimes suspect that my first name, Urban, was chosen by my Methodist great-great-great grandparents for their twenty-first child by letting the Bible fall open to Romans 16:9.) Consequently, the Scriptures must always be exegeted or interpreted. This requires us to be cognizant of the culture within which the Scripture was written, the bias of the author(s), and the language and religious tradition available. The Scriptures are not to be read out of context or without an awareness of our own tendency to use them to justify our own culture, bias, or tradition.

Having said all this, we must recognize that the Scriptures have a life of their own, independent of their authorship. They belong to the church at every period in history and speak for themselves. There may be truths in them that never occurred to those who first uttered the words or placed them upon the page. Like a great work of art, but infinitely more than just a great work of art, the Scriptures are the medium for God's disclosure of himself to us. But it should be noted that as Anglicans we are to teach nothing *contrary* to the Bible, which is *not* the same thing as saying everything we teach must be explicitly "proved" by the Bible.

An implication of the Anglican doctrine of authority is the centrality of the Incarnation to its thought. Paul Tillich once described the Incarnation to me as "the Anglican heresy." Despite my admiration for Tillich, *he was wrong*. The Incarnation is not heresy, but the ground for our conviction that there is a continuity, as opposed to a radical discontinuity in some reformed theology, between nature and supernature. This becomes the source of a Christian humanism, where the study of humanity informs our understanding of God's ways with humankind. It is a sad day when Episcopalians find themselves joining forces with traditions alien to their own in the blanket condemnation of "humanism." To deny the possibility of a Christian humanism is to repudiate our own heritage.

A threefold authority and the centrality of the Incarnation are two important parts of any answer to the question of the nature of Anglicanism. Undoubtedly, throughout any reading of this book, the meaning of what I call "mainstream Anglicanism" will arise. The book itself is an explication of the term.

The churches of the Anglican Communion are not confessional churches, as the Lutherans are with the Augsburg Confession or the Presbyterians with the Westminster Catechism. Also it is clear that Anglicanism does not vest authority in the hierarchy in the same way as the Roman Catholic Church. Much of what we identify with the Anglican ethos is often more *English* than anything else. There is a feminine or receptive consciousness in Anglicanism, which is sometimes described as a pastoral sensitivity, and other times as fuzzy thinking. The Anglican fondness for historical theology rather than analytical theology is a symptom of this. Also the honor accorded conciliar authority and the Vincentian Canon—i.e., the Catholic faith is what has been believed in all places at all times—despite the obvious problems with both notions, is another indication.

Since the sixteenth century, conformity in the outward pattern of worship has contributed to the idea that belief grows out of our corporate worship: *lex orandi lex credendi* ("The principle of praying is the principle of believing"). Worship is primarily an act of receptive consciousness. The commitment to the priority of worship undergirds an Anglican emphasis upon the experience of God as prior to its meaning and, consequently, a suspicion of theological imperialism. Anglicans tend not to write *systematic* theologies, but our style does breed mystics and poets. This corresponds to a strong undercurrent of corporate introversion, as opposed to extroversion. Introverts are sometimes seen to be cold or unfriendly, although we all know that this can be a misperception.

Everyone needs both structure and freedom. They go hand in hand. In Anglicanism the structure is *doing* things in "decency and order." This is not just a petty preoccupation with appearance. It is more often the establishment of a framework for the mind and heart to *be* free. Anglicans tend to be outwardly conforming and inwardly independent. Consequently, one should not expect a concern in Anglicanism for a detailed conformity to theological notions of any particular school, as long as they do not do obvious violence to the history of the tradition, to reason, to the centrality of Christ's Incarnation, or to the life of the church.

No explanation of mainstream Anglicanism is going to please everyone—and it certainly won't please all Anglicans. I have written this book, however, out of a desire to reflect on the mission of the church from a conscious sense of the Anglican heritage. But I do not believe what I have to say is narrowly provincial. It has much in common with Roman Catholic, Eastern Orthodox, and Lutheran thought, as well as with some Presbyterian and Congregationalist theology. Methodists who consciously follow in the tradition of John Wesley should find themselves at home. Those from a more pietist or radical Protestant background will, I hope, discover an alternative to their traditional position and an opportunity for dialogue.

One of the problems we meet in discussing evangelization and renewal is vocabulary. My experience has been that discussions in this area are often like *Alice in Wonderland;* we make up the meanings of the words as our fancy directs, without bothering to communicate them to anyone else. I have made a particular effort in this book to define the meaning of **mission, evangelization,** and **renewal.**

Contrary to fairly wide usage, it should be carefully noted that I do *not* use **renewal** to mean ministry directed within the church and **mission** for ministry directed outside the church. This distinction seems to imply too sharp a division between the church and the world, which is inconsistent with Anglicanism's perception of discipleship. We are better off acknowledging that evangelization is in the service of renewal and that our mission is to all humankind, baptized or not.

The approach of this book to mission, renewal, and evangelization is primarily phenomenological. I am trying to raise the questions of what these processes look like when they are happening and to work toward a critical distance on our claims to be doing them. Far too much ministry in the church lacks an explicit pastoral theology. We are the victims of our feelings and of a subtle secularization of our values. We should not congratulate ourselves when large numbers of people appear on parish rolls who are there primarily because we offer them a release from the pain of guilt and make them feel good. But we often do.

The Episcopal Church has for generations been accused of being the church for the upwardly mobile. I suspect my grandparents, at least in part, joined it in 1907 for those social and economic reasons. Perhaps the prestige of the Episcopal Church is not what it used to be, or so our *downward* growth would perhaps indicate. In fact, people become church members for a variety of reasons, and motives will never be pure. But we do need to be as clear as we can about our complicity in the less than edifying reasons for coming to the church. In this way we can begin to chasten our claims and to shape our ministries so as to act for the Kingdom of God.

CHAPTER ONE

Beginning with Renewal

The wholeness of humanity is the objective. Mission is the mobilization of the church in the cause of Christ. Renewal is the strategy. Evangelization is the tactics. In the cosmic struggle for the fulfillment of God's purposes, it is essential that we be clear about these distinctions. As one committed to mission, I choose to begin with a discussion of renewal. And before moving to evangelization, it will be necessary to speak of the objective: humanity united with God.

The metaphor I am using is from military usage. For example, William Manchester, in his description of Douglas MacArthur's plan for the liberation of Luzon in the Philippines during World War II, states that, while MacArthur left the matter of tactics to his generals, he controlled the strategy. Strategy has to do with large-scale, long-range planning; tactics involves the immediate use and deployment of troops in combat. Without careful attention to the relation of tactics to strategy, no war could be won—much less the war against sin and evil.

Military analogies are certainly biblical (see, for example, Ephesians 6:10–20, Revelation 8:6–13:18), and they abound in Christian spiritual classics. In this case, a military analogy helps us make an important distinction. There is a tendency to claim too much for evangelization, as if it were the *whole question,* or to discuss evangelization without careful attention to its relationship to a larger understanding of an intentional ministry. This error needs to be avoided and, therefore, we look first at renewal, the *strategy* of the church's mission.

Renewal is the church's only strategy or long-range plan. This is not to say that Christians won't divide themselves on the issue of renewal. From New Testament times we have chosen sides: "'I am Paul's man', or 'I am for Apollos'; 'I follow Cephas', or 'I am Christ's'" (1 Cor. 1:12; NEB). But as Paul spoke out against this misunderstanding, saying that Christ's purpose is one, so must we. As we shall see, renewal, *properly understood,* is the community's response, in grace, to the Gospel, the proclamation that God's reign is upon us. Renewal is God shaping our vision and action. For the people of God, renewed by the Spirit of Christ, their world is turned upside down. The renewed community no longer constitutes its world of meaning as the society closed to God. It "marches to the sound of a different drummer."

If we hear the Gospel, we have no choice but to be renewed. But that does not mean that everyone "wrapping about them-selves the mantle of renewal" has indeed *heard.* It is important, therefore, to seek some criteria of effective renewal, which we can describe and perceive in the life of a people. Granted, the ultimate judgment of true renewal lies in the mind of God; nevertheless, we have the responsibility to make a penultimate judgment, lest we be misled into inappropriate tactics.

The Response to the Gospel

"Jesus came into Galilee proclaiming the Gospel of God: 'The time has come; the kingdom of God is upon you; repent, and believe in the Gospel" (Mk. 1:14–15; NEB). These very familiar words are the central theme of Jesus, attested to by no less than five different New Testament sources. They sum up his message in a very few words. The life, death, and resurrec-tion of Jesus sought to enable God's reign to break in upon humankind. That was the objective. The key to his strategy was the call to *repentance.*

It is important that we understand the meaning of repen-tance. The original Greek word, *metanoia,* unlike some other important words in the New Testament, is a common word, found in Greek literature for many centuries. From the time of the Maccabees in the mid-second century B.C., the Hasidim, the "pious ones," in the Jewish community preached *metanoia* in preparation for the end time. Later, as Jewish apocalypticism with its message of the immanent dawn of a new aeon developed, its proponents called for *metanoia* as well, in anticipation of the final event. *Metanoia* literally means a change of mind and heart.

It follows that when we change our minds we reflect on the past in a negative light; so *metanoia* has as well a derivative meaning of *repentance, regret,* or *remorse.* We think of remorse for sins. John the Baptist, a prophet of woe, particularly emphasizes this dimension of *metanoia.* The relationship between remorse and a change of mind works both ways. Paul, in writing the Corinthians, notes that his earlier letter to them caused them hurt, but does not regret this because "the wound led to a change of heart [*metanoian*]" (2 Cor. 7:9; NEB), which enables them to perceive the Gospel of salvation.

Our problem is that we tend to think of repentance *more* in terms of the hurt, remorse, or wound, than in terms of the change of heart or mind. Repentance is a turning away from our sins, which stand in the way of God's reign, and toward God. The author of the Letter to the Hebrews tells his readers that, having repented from the deadness of their former ways, they need to advance toward maturity (Heb. 6:1–3). Repentance is not concerned with a perpetual reflection upon our sins or our sinfulness. Luke in the Acts of the Apostles uses *repentance* as an appositive for *faith.* Here Luke speaks of Paul "testifying as under oath to both Jews and Greeks of repentance that leads to God and the faith that leads to our Lord Jesus" (Acts 20:21; UTH). These two clauses, joined by "and," appear to me to be a parallel structure, conveying with great force the emphasis of what Luke wants us to understand.

We are conditioned to equate repentance with feeling sorry for our sins. This is a skewed perception, rooted in misconceptions of the last few centuries of our Western religious heritage. The important thing for us to grasp now is that this emphasis upon the pain of sin prevents our fully understanding the strategy of renewal. A synonym for *repentance* is *conversion,* which is derived from a Latin word meaning "to turn around." *Conversion* is another word we need to understand differently than most people do today. But for the moment the important thing is to consider the image of repentance as a turning to see things differently, to look and move toward God. In this way we may overcome the exclusive association of repentance with sin.

In the Gospels, John the Baptist calls people to a "baptism of repentance for the purpose of a remission of sins" (Mk. 1:4; UTH). The witness to a change of mind or repentance by baptism is an effective sign of a turning from sins to God. When Jesus receives the baptism of John, he consciously identifies his mission with John's preaching; but, at the same time, he points the significance of baptism in a new direction. It is not just an effective acknowledgment of our sin, but also an anticipation of the rule of God. This is what is in the evangelist's mind when he puts in the mouth of John the words: "I have baptized you with water; he will baptize you with the Holy Spirit" (Mk. 1:8; NEB).

In the baptismal service in the Book of Common Prayer, this significance of Christian baptism is enacted. The priest, after the three renunciations of sin (personal, social, and cosmic), asks the candidates, "Do you turn and accept Jesus Christ as your Lord and Saviour?" The word *turn* recalls the action in the early church, when the candidates facing west spit upon Satan and then actually turned to face the east, the dawning of the light of Christ. Their "conversion," their turning *away* from sin *to* the kingdom of God, is dramatically portrayed, as are important moments in any good ritual.

This brief reflection upon repentance as a *turning* should focus two things in our thoughts. The first is that what we turn *toward* is more important than what we turn *from;* what we turn toward lies in our future and shall determine who we shall be. It gets us away from an excessive preoccupation with the past, without denying the past. The second is to remind ourselves that baptism in the Scriptures and in the life of the church is the effective sign of our repentance. To be baptized is to be one who is in the *process* of turning to repent. We are reminded of our intention in baptism, and we are supported by God's power in acting upon that intention, which is what an "effective sign" means.

To be a Christian is to be in a continuing state of repentance, to be in the process of renewing our minds. It helps to develop our understanding of what this means if we look in the New Testament at the word for "renewal" itself. It is found in various forms—*anakainoō, ananeoomai*, and *anakainizō*—in the Hebrews, Titus, and Pauline letters. Paul writes, "But be you transformed by the renewal of the mind" (Rom. 12:2; UTH). The mind pertains to the inner person. Paul says elsewhere that renewal has to do with a change within (2 Cor. 4:16). How does this change occur? One answer is given by the author of Titus, who writes that Christ has saved us "through the bath that brings about regeneration and through the renewal by the Holy Spirit" (Tit. 3:5; UTH). It is the same point made by the Fourth Evangelist (Jn. 3:5). Baptism is the effective sign of renewal, if not the exclusive occasion of the continuing gift of the Spirit.

Renewal is associated in the New Testament with the images that are evoked by repentance. To repent is to be renewed, and, as Paul and his followers saw it, to be renewed is to experience all that is involved in repentance. It is to have a new mind and heart, a new way of seeing things. It is to be baptized, and to live in the light of that baptism. If one is to respond to the good news that the reign of God is at hand, then the mind must be transformed, so that we are open to the Spirit, who teaches us the truth in Christ—the truth that will make us free.

The Transformation of the Mind

We live in a time and culture that puts a great deal of value upon the identification and sharing of feelings. We tend to believe that if we feel something strongly it is right, and that positive feelings are important. The quality of a sermon is often judged on how it makes us feel; human relationships are frequently evaluated upon our positive or negative feelings about them; and the presence of God, many people feel, should make us feel happy.

The ancient world was not like this at all. Romantic love, for example, was considered a disease. Tears were considered an authentic sign of holiness, but an absence of strong feeling was even more important. One did not base actions upon feelings, but upon wisdom. "Do not let your passions be your guide," writes Jesus ben Sirach, "but restrain your desires" (Ecclesiasticus 18:30; NEB). To be guided by one's emotions was to be less than human, as far as the ancients were concerned. There was no disagreement in this matter between Hebrew and Greek thought.

There are two Greek words for feeling: *aisthēsis,* from which we get the word "aesthetics," and *pathos,* as in "sympathy" or "pathology." *Aisthēsis* has more to do with moral understanding or an intuitive grasp through the senses, like the German *Gefühl,* than it does with emotion. *Pathos,* which is related to *passio* and, thereby, to the English "passion," is intense emotion. *Aisthēsis* appears once in the New Testament, and is usually translated as "insight" or "discernment" (Phil. 1:9). *Pathos* appears three times in the New Testament, all in Paul's letters, and each time in a negative sense (Rom. 1:26, Col. 3:5, 1 Thess. 4:5).

Some might reply to this that the very common word in the New Testament for "heart," *kardia,* speaks of the importance of emotion. "How blest are those whose hearts are pure" (Mt. 5:8; NEB) would rank high among the familiar texts that come to mind. But the evidence indicates that to the ancient Jew the heart was the center of physical, spiritual, and intellectual life; it had little to do with the emotional life. As Kierkegaard has said, to be pure in heart is to *will* one thing.

The fact is that the New Testament world saw little value, if any, in feeling per se. Knowledge that came through thinking —including intuition as well as reasoning—illumined by God and action based upon that knowledge were tantamount. It follows that the path to renewal lay in the transformation of the mind, understood as *more* than reason or logic.

But there are two ways of thinking about the mind. What we must realize is that what humanity has in common, what is universal to us all, is the *process* of thinking, not the particular content of the thought. To be human *is* to think. The content of our thought is conditioned by our particular cultural and historical world. It is imperative to understand this if we are to grasp the meaning of the renewal of our minds.

Humans cannot help thinking, whether they do it poorly or

well. As thinking creatures we make our world. This is part of
the universal process of creating a culture. The world-as-we-
know-it is not something we perceive "out there" as a camera
takes a picture. Our world is a product of our thinking selves
looking at or attending to the flow of experience about us and
making something of it in terms of the images in our memory
and environment. No two people live in exactly the same world,
although people in the same culture and time in history will
have worlds more similar than those who do not.

In understanding this crucial point, it might help to reflect
on an experience common to all of us; namely, the awareness
that no one sees us as we see ourselves. We play a different role
in our own world compared to the roles we play in other
people's worlds. I see myself as a nice, rather bright, intuitive,
vulnerable person, who longs to help other people and wants to
be supported; but who is more judged than loved for reasons
beyond my understanding. Some students in the seminary of
which I am the dean apparently see me as a formidable,
compulsive authority, given to unreasonable expectations and
devious hidden plans for them. I am certainly, they feel, not
helping them be ordained. Some faculty see me as someone
with excessive control needs; a person who needs no support,
and for whom they have respect mixed with some apprehen-
sion born of an occasional confrontation. They are really not
quite sure I have the best interests of the seminary at heart. It is
not a matter of anyone being correct and others in error; it is
just that we build different worlds in which each person
occupies a different relationship within the field of meaning.

Another illustration of the different worlds we build on a
corporate level would be that of the impasse between Iran and
the United States in 1979 and 1980. The Ayatollah Khomeini
believed himself to have a direct "pipe line" from God and that
the only explanation possible of American behavior was that
President Carter was Satan. The world of the United States,
built at least ostensibly upon international law and a sense of
fair play, could only conceive of Iranian behavior as fanatical,
deranged, and immoral. We wondered how all those people in
the streets could get off work to demonstrate—a typical

northern-European view shaped by the work ethic. We literally
were acting out of two different worlds.

These worlds are of immediate concern to us because they
have different capacities for being open to divine illumination.
If the Spirit is to move in our lives, there must be room or space
in our worlds of meaning. The possibility of renewal depends
on the room for repentance.

There is a fascinating image of room for repentance in the
Wisdom of Solomon. The author is explaining why the Israelites conquered the inhabitants of the Promised Land slowly. It
was, we are told, to give the Canaanites "space for redemption"
(*topon metanoias*), room to turn around and welcome God. But
the author goes on to point out that there really was no
possibility of such space, "for there was a curse on their race
from the beginning" (Wisdom 12:11–12; NEB). The author
probably had in mind the Greeks then ruling Judea more than
the ancient Canaanites. Whether or not the Canaanites or the
Greeks had space, the image is a good one.

Why did some people in the New Testament hear Jesus while
others did not? This is a question of space for repentance as
well. The Fourth Evangelist explains by citing Isaiah, "He has
blinded their eyes and hardened their heart, in order that they
may not see with their eyes and apprehend with the heart and
turn" (Jn. 12:40; UTH; see Is. 6:10). A "hardened heart"
describes a world of meaning with no space for seeing God and
turning to him. One cannot repent. The world of the little child
has more space (see Lk. 18:17). In the ancient world of the
Near East where God was seen as the immediate cause of
everything, the hardened heart or closed world was believed to
be caused by God for his own hidden purposes. We today can
acknowledge the reality of a spaceless world, but understand
that it exists because of our own lack of faith and our own
failure to build a world of meaning with space in it. Our spaceless worlds have a lot to do with sin.

The call to repentance is a summons to change our world, to
open it to God so that he may illumine our thinking. Paul says,
in writing the Corinthians, that the idea of the crucified
Messiah, is a "stumbling-block to the Jews and folly to the

Greeks" (1 Cor. 1:23; NEB). He is speaking of the world of the Jews and the world of the Greeks: their respective perceptions of the role of God in relation to matter and the human condition. There was no space in either world for a God who so loved us that he would die for us, and so they could not respond to the Gospel, repent, and be renewed. The Jews knew that they were the chosen people and had Abraham for their father. The Greeks knew that the gods did not care and it was all a matter of living out one's fate. There were no loose ends, no unanswered questions allowed to exist. Jews and Greeks both lived in the closed worlds of their own rigid systems.

If renewal is to take place, it has to begin by finding even the smallest crack in our self-centered worlds, if that is all there is, so that the living water of the Gospel may leach a cavern in our stony hearts—a place where we may repent and turn to God. It is not so much our feeling as our thinking that must become new if we are to build worlds that have space for God in them. When this happens, then our lives will change in what we do, because we have been renewed in what we think.

Thinking and Acting

There are times in which we all want to be "mind readers," but no one really knows what another person is thinking. In fact, there is a sense in which the individual's consciousness of his own world of meaning is not complete. Images function within each of us in ways of which we are not aware. We all make strange slips of the tongue and wonder why we said what we did. Some time ago I moved from one house to another house several houses up the street, and for months I consciously had to override the unconscious world of meaning that told me the former house is where I should be going.

The primary access we have to the world of meaning of others and ourselves is our actions. However, we are more likely to judge ourselves by our intentions, and to judge others by their behavior. Jesus in speaking of false prophets reminds us that we "will recognize them by their fruits" (Mt. 7:20; NEB). *Action* is a special word. It means more than our behavior; but also what we do based upon our world of meaning. An action involves in some sense—not always conscious or deliberate—a decision on our part. We are responsible for our actions, because we are responsible for what we think.

If we are going to understand why we have access to what we are thinking by looking at what we are doing or not doing, it is necessary that we look at the nature of an action. To do that we have to look at the word *intention*. In a sense, our intention is our world of meaning, but it is an operative description of that world. By "operative" I mean the way in which the world of meaning *works*.

Intention can be understood spatially. Our intention is the structure of meaning within our consciousness. Even when we try to do this in meditation—"to pray with empty hands," as some spiritual guides would suggest—there are always a few images floating around in the focus of our consciousness. We identify what is happening in terms of those images. Language is within our intentionality. Events from the past are there. Perhaps there is some primordial human memory that transcends our individual life and occupies our consciousness as it focuses within the space around us.

An example of how intentionality operates spatially is found in the account of the time when Jesus came with his disciples to the territory of Caesarea Philippi. He asked them, "'Who do men say that the Son of Man is?'" (Mt. 16:14; NEB). In the very act of posing the question, Jesus is making a claim. In his thinking he is, at least, the "Son of Man"—an ambiguous term from Jewish memory, but one with considerable power. The answers Jesus gets from his disciples are, as we would expect, in reference to the common images to be expected to be in a first-century Jewish intentionality. They experienced Jesus, and this is the image they attach to him from their conscious memory. "'Some say John the Baptist, others Elijah, others Jeremiah, or one of the prophets'" (Mt. 16:14; NEB).

The story is told for the sake of Peter's confession of faith: "'You are the Messiah, the Son of the living God'" (Mt. 16:13–17; NEB). While this response is only possible as the result of divine intervention, as Jesus says, it is nonetheless based upon the imagery of a Jewish intentionality of the age. The "Messiah" is the annointed one to whom faithful Jews looked for salvation, and "Son of God" means to a Jew of that time the anointed king. It is an appositive for "Messiah." The inspiration comes with Peter's openness to the possibility of Jesus of Nazareth being this divinely anointed savior.

Our intentionality is expanded as we engage the flow of experience around us. The extent of this expansion depends upon our willingness to reflect intuitively, looking for new insights through new images and relationships of images. Peter possessed this imagination and could see in a way most of his contemporaries could not see. A rigid intentionality sees little more than it has inherited, and therefore is not open to the new. Such rigidity would contradict the vocation of the Christian, if we are indeed people who "have his promise, and look forward to new heavens and a new earth, the home of justice" (2 Pet. 3:13; NEB).

Intentionality has not only a spatial quality, but also a temporal dimension. It is by our intentions that we live consciously and with decision into the future. How does this happen? The answer to that comes from reflecting upon what goes on in our minds, in our intentions, in the process of an action. What we do is we build an image or constellation of images from our world of meaning and we *project* into the future. This is how an objective is created. I have a son who wants to be a doctor. He has an image of what a doctor is, and he is moving toward that image *in time*. As he moves, he continues to elaborate the image by observing and asking questions, which is part of the continual building of the projected image. The image itself is, grammatically speaking, in the "future, perfect." He is in his intentionality saying, "I *will have* become a doctor by [in his case] 1987."

We cannot project an image or a constellation of images of that which is not already in our world of meaning or our intentionality. We cannot have an objective that we cannot picture. My son knows about doctors. It never occurred to him to aspire to be a Huichol *mara 'kame,* about whom he knows nothing. Intentional invention is a possibility only to the extent that our imagination can play with new arrangements of the images available to us. When integration was first ordered in the South, there was no way a great many people could conceive of it as anything but a force that would destroy their way of life. Their ability to rearrange the images, to conceive of or imagine the new, was severely limited. It was the rare prophet, like Martin Luther King, Jr., who had this ability, this "vision."

For most of us who are not prophets, encounters with new and future meanings and worlds can only come as surprises, startling encounters. We call the Christian season that takes us into the future "Advent." The Latin word *adventus* from which it is derived connotes a sudden encounter. It calls to mind the possibilities that come not from our reflections upon past experience, but those that meet us from out of the future. God is a God of surprise, who "had made a better plan" (Heb. 11:40; NEB). It is appropriate that the New Testament all but ends with the words of God, "'Behold! I am making all things new!'" (Rev. 21:5; NEB). Our intentionality must be evaluated by the power of its imagination, and also by its openness to surprise.

If we recall again the scene at Caesarea Philippi, Jesus says to his disciples "that he had to go to Jerusalem, and there to suffer much from the elders, chief priests, and doctors of the law; to be put to death and to be raised again on the third day" (Mt. 16:21; NEB). This is a temporal, intentional statement. It projects a constellation of images into the future, and states a decision to act as well. There is an objective, and a decision to pursue it. Peter's reaction was to say this would never happen; in reply to which Jesus calls him "'Satan,'" and adds, "'You think as men think, not as God thinks'" (Mt. 16:21–23; NEB). It is a question of the intentionality of Peter, which is not open to insight or surprise, as compared to that of Jesus, which is in accord with God. The wonder is that years later Peter's world of meaning is changed. He will later intend his own martyr's death. There was space in Peter's mind for repentance.

Acting depends upon thinking. We decide upon what to do based upon an objective projected into the future, which is constructed out of our world of meaning. This is what intention means. The freedom within our intentionality depends upon both our own willingness to imagine new possibilities and to be open to the surprises of God. Without doubt, the possibility of repentance, of renewal for each of us, depends upon an intention that possesses this imagination and openness to surprise.

There is one more way in which we might consider our understanding of intention and its relation to renewal and, ultimately, evangelization. An objective is the statement of an intended action in the future perfect tense. The final test of our action and the intention out of which it emerges is the consequences or the *outcome*. I will use the word *outcome* to signify "the consequences of an action." *Outcome* may refer to an objective projected and achieved; or it may refer to the result of an ill-considered action, which was not sufficiently calculated in relation to a clearly understood objective; or it may be the product of fortuitous or *graceful* circumstances.

The outcome as opposed to the objective may be illustrated this way. Peter at Caesarea Philippi understood Jesus to be the Messiah. Although we are not told by the evangelist, we may readily assume that he perceived the objective of Jesus' ministry in terms of the usual Messianic expectations of the Jews of his day, which certainly ruled out the notion of a crucified, risen Lord. Hence the evangelist, quite appropriately, pictures Peter as protesting Jesus' prediction of his Passion. The outcome, as we know, was quite different from Peter's intentionality. As Jesus had just said, he was to go to Jerusalem, suffer, die, and be raised, rather than save Israel through political or divine means. Peter is rebuked by Jesus for failing to have God's intentionality, including God's objective for Jesus.

In all probability, however, the evangelist is describing an outcome and relating it as if it were an objective. He is standing on *this* side in time of the suffering, death, and resurrection of Jesus, looking at it as an outcome and assuming that it was an objective in the mind of Jesus. There are New Testament scholars who believe that in fact Jesus had no such objective, and was just as surprised on Easter morning as anyone else. This would be more consistent with the Incarnation. The perfection of Jesus' humanity lay in his willingness to explore new possibilities for his ministry and to be open to that surprise which is the characteristic of the renewed intentionality of the Christian person. It is for this failure of perception and vision that Peter would have been appropriately rebuked by the historical Jesus.

It is important here to grasp the difference between the outcome and the objective. Even though one needs to act in terms of an objective, the parameters of that objective must never so tyrannize the intention that one is not capable of accepting a different outcome.

Indications of Renewal

Our world of meaning and its operative intention is largely a product of our enculteration. What we make of our experience is what the society and culture tell us it means. There are those who believe that the self is nothing more than the reflection of the social meaning or the vortex of a field of collective forces impressed upon a passive mind. Some scholars suggest that what we call meaning is the rationalization of behavior rooted in our genes or in our conditioning. In this system, the individual is a self-conscious focus within a collective meaning, whose objective is survival and whose strategy is equilibrium.

For the person with this kind of understanding, religiousness is a tactic on behalf of equilibrium, that is, a preservation of the status quo. This is what Karl Marx meant when he wrote that religion is the "opiate" of the people. It keeps the oppressed quiet amidst the pain of slavery under the bourgeoisie. Religious ritual legitimates the norms of the society, while providing a controlled outlet for the pent-up emotions of those who suffer under the system. American slaves in the first half of the nineteenth century were, in fact, encouraged to attend emotional church services as a means of keeping them docile. Preaching and teaching support the morality of the prevailing culture with threats of sanctions. Adultery, from this viewpoint, is wrong because it threatens to confuse kinship and lines of inheritance, but ostensibly it is condemned because it will result in eternal hellfire for its perpetrators.

There is a good deal of truth in all of this. William Clebsch, a historian of religion at Stanford University, has shown in his book, *Christianity in European History*, that the accounts of the experience of the post-resurrection Christ—what he calls "Christophany"—take on the forms of that human sensibility current at a given time in history. He identifies five such epochs: the pagan Roman Empire, the chaos of the Heroic Age, the renaissance of the High Middle Ages, the rise of nationalism, and the modern concern for human and cultural autonomy. In each age there is a distinctive understanding of Christ: the martyr's companion, the incarnation of reason, the heavenly bridegroom and pedagogue-savior, the exemplar of perfect piety and morality, and the autonomous god-man conferring human authenticity.

The function of religion as the highest legitimization of the social system and its equilibrium is not unknown in New Testament Christianity. Paul tells the Romans to "submit to the supreme authorities" (Rom. 13:1; NEB). The author of 1 Timothy asks that his readers pray "for kings and all in high office, that we may lead a tame and quiet life in piety and probity" (1 Tim. 2:2; UTH). Whoever wrote 1 Peter tells us: "Love the brotherhood, fear God, honor the emperor (1 Pet. 2:17; UTH). Even Jesus' words, "'Then pay Caesar what is due Caesar'" (Mt. 22:21; NEB), have been used to justify the exactions of the IRS. None of these texts is a call to demonstrate against injustice, and there was a great deal of injustice in the Roman Empire of the first century.

Anglicans need to keep in mind that our whole ethos contributes to the equilibrium function of Christianity within society and culture; we may be inclined, at least subliminally, to find genuine renewal uncomfortable. The coronation of the English monarch has been considered a sacrament of the church, and from the time of Elizabeth I the monarch has been the head of the church in England. Notions of social evolution are only about a century old. Before that, the church was believed to have the solemn duty to uphold the state, which means to maintain the status quo. It is no wonder that in England in the eighteenth and nineteenth centuries Anglicanism lost the working classes; in America it never won them.

These four indications of the existence of renewal are controversial. There is no guarantee that by virtue of their presence what is happening is "of God"; but it is true that *without* their presence there may well be no renewal happening.

While this may appear to be a strong claim, it is justified; these indications are an explication of the belief that renewal is a change of mind and, consequently, a redirecting of our actions. Renewal involves "marching to the beat of a different drummer" than that to which the secular world marches. The particular manifestations of this may be discovered if one looks at the history of renewal movements within the church. The evangelical awakening of the twelfth and thirteenth centuries, usually known as the Gregorian Reform, is a vivid example of renewal in action.

A Spirit of Risk

Paul often describes himself and his fellow Christians as fools or ignorant persons, sometimes in the spirit of irony (1 Cor. 3:18, 4:10; 2 Cor. 11:16–21). A fool in this sense is one that does not follow that universal axiom of human common sense: "Look out first for number one!" It is elaborated by such principles as: one should not risk what he has unless there is probability that in so doing he can get more; or one should not serve his ideals unless it has the promise of a personal payoff; or, again, only bet on a sure thing. A fool is one who in the eyes of the world appears to take risks for which he has not reasonably calculated the cost against the reward.

In renewal, the transformation of our world meaning carries with it no assurance that our vision is correct. The only sign Jesus would give was Jonah's call to repentance, and we cannot expect anything more (Mt. 12:39). Although faith may not be blind, it is built upon intuition, not certainty. Any action proceeding from such an intentionality will be seen as a stupid risk or will be interpreted as having some hidden, ulterior motive.

It is unfortunate that from our hindsight of six to eight hundred years, with its negative judgment of "holy wars" and its cynical appraisal of motives inaccessible to our own entrepreneurial interests, we see the Crusades in such a bad light. If we could stand inside the intentions of the people, beginning with Urban II at Clermont in 1095 and all that followed for the next two hundred years, we might view this monumental effort as the result of the reawakening of Christian discipleship. The Crusades were an incredible risk to life and property in the pursuit of a dream of Christendom, as foolish or misguided as we might now judge that particular dream to have been. There are all kinds of sociological reasons why a sudden openness to a new vision would focus, at the end of the eleventh century, on the wresting of the Holy Land from the infidels—i.e., the Moslems—but the point is that hundreds of thousands of European Christians did respond to the vision and at a "foolish" cost.

Such risks have always characterized the renewed Christian. There is Paul's response to the vision of the Macedonian (Acts 16:9–10), Anthony's acceptance of the challenge of the desert, Boniface's mission to the Germans, Francis Xavier's trip to India and Japan, and Bonhoeffer's attempt to overthrow Hitler.

The Confrontation of Society

Genuine renewal cannot help but call into question the common sense assumptions—i.e., "what everyone knows is true"—of the society in which we live. Ruben Alves, a Brazilian "third-world" theologian, calls this the "contemporary illusion." The only alternative to confrontation is to assume that the world of meaning within a given society is identical with the mind of God. When pressed, there are those who will claim this identity for themselves. Hitler told Germany that he was the Holy Spirit. There have been preachers in the American religious tradition who have implied that Jesus was the first capitalist.

If we look at the evangelical awakening of the twelfth and thirteenth centuries, we notice that it is dominated politically by the investiture controversy. The issue of who bestows the insignia of office upon a bishop, a king, or the pope may not strike us today as all that important—but it actually was vitally important. It was a question of the supremacy of the temporal or spiritual values within European society at that time. Although Gregory VII's triumph over the Holy Roman Emperor, Henry IV, at Canossa was only a Pyrrhic victory, it heralded the unwillingness of a renewed church to let the state dominate. The greatest victory in the investiture controversy was won with a martyrdom, that of Thomas à Becket at the hands of Henry II of England. It is not surprising. For it is a supreme Christian value that there is strength in weakness (see 2 Cor. 12:10).

The cynics among us can always point out the flaws in the appeals of Christians to divine will. Thomas à Becket was not altogether a laudable character; his near contemporary, Richard I, the Lion-Hearted, who went on the Third Crusade, was undoubtedly irresponsible. Today the witness of Martin Luther King is frequently challenged by allusions to problems in his personal life. All this is beside the point. There is no claim here that renewal is the same as perfection, however one might describe the latter.

If we are truly open to the Spirit, we will probably find ourselves in conflict with many well-meaning people about us. Christians were martyred in Rome by people earnestly concerned for the public good. Thomas More can be admired for his resistance to Henry VIII—even by Anglicans. It was church-going folk who turned the dogs on the blacks demonstrating in Birmingham. The issue is the effect on renewal and the inevitable result of seeing our world as we have never seen it before.

Every revolutionary or social reformer is not of God. But those who unqualifiedly affirm the status quo do thwart God's purpose. For creation is not complete. We have not arrived. We are called to live so that the approaching rule of God may be present in all its meaning. As the juxtaposition of phrases within the Lord's Prayer implies—"Your kingdom come, your will be done"—the doing of God's will is related to the approach of the Kingdom. Confrontation is a part of this action. Cardinal Suenens is correct when he writes:

As Christians, we have to face the world. . . . We have to
confront the world; and this means confronting imperialist
oppression, economic domination, military might, religious
conformism, state bureaucracy, and a continuing temptation to violence in support of causes, good as well as bad.[1]

An Emerging New Order

This is a delicate point. I would not want the reader to reflect
on "order" without always qualifying it with "new." Genuine
renewal brings us into an awareness of the experience of God
for which the *old* order cannot account. Renewal is not nostalgia, much less a desperate struggle for control. It is a journey
that risks *chaos*—in itself not a negative word, but connoting
power for good or evil—in the quest of a vision. Renewal is a
movement out of the old comforts of Harran, as with Abram,
into the wilderness in quest of the land that God will show us
(Gen. 12:1).

In *The Structures of Scientific Revolutions,* Thomas Kuhn describes a process of scientific model-building. As Kuhn understands it, a scientific paradigm—i.e., description of reality—
serves until it can no longer account for the data. A pressure
builds as a result of this increasing surd within our experience,
until the old paradigm must be cast aside and a new one
constructed. An illustration would be the effect of the discovery
of the uncertainty principle in quantum theory upon classical
Newtonian physics. Another illustration would be in the contrast between the subjective style of leadership to be found in
Paul's letters (as in 1 Cor. 12:4–11) and the emerging new
order in the next generation, as found in 1 Timothy (as, for
example, 1 Tim. 3:1–16).

In the evangelical awakening in the twelfth and thirteenth
centuries, there is both the birth of canon law and the theological system of the Schoolmen. Our tendency is to look upon
these phenomena as sources of intellectual tyranny. The truth
is quite the opposite. The freedom of the Gospel is always
within a context. Experience without thought, which begets
form, is the worst kind of despotism. Whereas in later centuries
both canon law and scholastic philosophy became idols, in their

inception they were instruments of liberation from superstition, immorality, and confusion.

A Cultural Renaissance

Culture in this sense is the human equivalent of the genetic, intraspecific behavior of the lower animals. It includes the language, actions, and artifacts of humankind that make possible the acquisition and transmission of knowledge. It is the product of thought, and gives expression to vision. It is difficult to understand how humanity can perceive its world anew without the eventual revitalization of culture.

"Eventual" is an important qualification; there is an element in some renewal that retards cultural renaissance. If there is, as was the case often in the New Testament, a strong apocalyptic, world-denying dimension, then there is a resistance to the rebirth of the arts and the empowering of the language. The arts and language are seen as worldly. (Sometimes a cultural renaissance happens, despite religious beliefs to the contrary, within a theoretically resistant community. The Shaker communities in America exemplify this.) The persecution of the church in the first three centuries worked against the development of the cultural implications of Christian discipleship. It was not until the fourth century that Christian culture blossomed, even though there were intimations before.

The twelfth-century renaissance was a remarkable time for new expression in literature, architecture, sculpture, and music. Perhaps the Gothic cathedral is what comes most immediately to our minds, but there was much more to the cultural awakening of the period. It was the time of the birth of the French, Italian, and Spanish languages, followed within a century or so by English. The creative spontaneity, which was embodied in the "courts of love" and devotion to the Blessed Virgin, gave a vitality and tenderness to what had been for centuries a brutish existence (although one must not caricature the Heroic Age as the so-called "dark ages").

The indication of cultural renaissance is, undoubtedly, the most subtle of the four indications of renewal. In many ways it is the premier test, since it is indicative of the comprehensive outreach of renewal to the wholeness of person and society. If our minds are truly transformed, then we can only expect that transformation ultimately to find expression in every aspect of human thought that touches our environment and shapes the pattern of our lives.

CHAPTER TWO

The Biblical Objective

My younger son attended an Episcopal high school and played on its varsity basketball team. Each year one of its opponents was a conservative Baptist school. I always knew when the game was coming up. My son would ask me the day before, "Dad, what do you say when someone asks you, 'Are you saved?'" What particularly irritated him, aside from the question itself, was that the Baptist boys seemed totally unimpressed with the fact that my son's school was an Episcopal institution—coupled with the fact that the Baptists always won. The question, their indifference, and their ability all three conspired together to disturb him.

The answer to the question "Are you saved?" has to be another question: "What does it look like when you are 'saved'?" One could answer with the historical fact of Jesus' Passion and argue that, since this act was for the salvation of all humanity, he was indeed "saved." This is, of course, to avoid the point of the inquirer, which can only be resolved by appealing to the objective of God for humankind and its outcome in each of us. It is *not*, however, an adequate answer to appeal to our inner feelings. The question "Are you saved?" requires a knowledge of the objective, as well as the ability to judge its outcome in each of us by some criteria.

The New Testament verb for being "saved" is *sōzō*, whose non-New Testament meaning relates to the preservation of life and health. It has physical connotations. We are still breathing and the heart is beating; we feel well. We are "saved," to judge from the outcome of being alive and/or healthy.

In the New Testament, *sōzō* clearly has this meaning as well (e.g., Mk. 3:4, Lk. 18:42), but it also means more. One might say it has a spiritual dimension. "For whoever would wish to save his soul, he shall lose it; whoever would lose his soul for the sake of me and the gospel, he shall save it" (Mk. 8:35; UTH). But what is this "spiritual dimension"? Some would answer by saying the spiritual dimension of salvation is "the acceptance of Jesus Christ as our Lord and Savior." But this misses the point. Such acceptance is not an objective, much less an outcome, but a tactic. The tactic and its strategy have to be judged on the basis of the projection of the objective and its outcome.

The fundamental flaw in so much discussion of renewal and evangelization is the failure to examine the issue of objectives and outcome. What is the spiritual equivalent of physical life and well-being? What does it mean to be a whole person? Renewal and those tactics that carry out renewal are only of value if they produce that outcome of wholeness, whatever it may be. So it makes no sense to look at evangelization until we have explored in some depth what could be the anticipated outcome of evangelization, just as my son cannot answer the question "Are you saved?" until he knows what outcome the inquirer has in mind.

It is not an easy study. Definitions of wholeness or the outcome of the Gospel are historically conditioned. This is evident if we look at the Scriptures. We can hope to perceive within the various conceptions some common thread. It will be of the utmost importance to understand to what extent the biblical images support the more recent understandings of the objective of Christian discipleship and to what degree the latter carry on the common biblical thread, if one exists at all.

The People of the Covenant

The notion of the *covenant* catches up the fundamental concept of the objective of the relationship between God and man to be found in the Old Testament at almost every point in its history. The word itself connotes a firm guarantee of a relationship between two parties in matters affecting their common life. The Hebrews of the early monarchy, eighth century B.C. and before, believed themselves to be in such a covenant relationship with God. It was fundamental to their self-understanding.

There are in these early Hebrews two recollections of the establishment of their covenant with Yahweh. There is the covenant with the patriarchs. This first covenant is said by an early tradition (the Yahwist, tenth century B.C.) to be with Abraham (Gen. 15:18), although a later tradition (the Priestly writers, beginning early seventh century B.C.) knows of a covenant with both Abraham (Gen. 17:2) and Noah (Gen. 9:8–17). The sign of the covenant with Abraham, according to the Priestly writers, is circumcision; with Noah, it is the rainbow. The former sign is undoubtedly an explanation told after the fact of the Semitic practice of circumcision. It is fascinating to see how by the time of King Solomon in the tenth century notions of the covenant common to the Hebrews of Solomon's time were skillfully embedded in the telling of the story of the patriarchs.

The covenant with the patriarchs seems to have been retrojected upon Noah and Abraham without any option for acceptance or rejection on their part. Yahweh calls them out and tells them that this is the agreement. He promises them land and fertility. The Law is not at issue here. The Priestly writers tell us that Yahweh told Abraham to "live always in my presence and be perfect" (NEB) ["walk before me and be blameless" (RSV)] (Gen. 17:1–2). It is a call to a moral life, which is directed not only to Abraham as an individual, but to Israel, which Abraham represents. By the time we come to the covenant at Mt. Sinai, it is clearly based upon the giving of the Law (Torah). In the work of one editor (the Elohist, ninth century B.C.), the covenant is established by the free assent of the people. "The whole people answered with one voice and said, 'We will do all that the Lord has told us'" (Ex. 24:3; NEB).

The Law, which in Hebrew theology is the expression of God's will or his loving self-disclosure, becomes the description of the perfect or blameless people. The fruits of living by the Law are the blessings of Yahweh. The "blessing" is conceived in two ways in the early Old Testament. First, it can account for the success at war, as the nomadic Hebrews progressively conquered the land of the Canaanites and became settled city-dwellers. In other words, the covenant relationship becomes, on God's part, the guarantee of victory in battle. Or the covenant can be quite the opposite: the vision of peace, *shalom*, as one finds described in several passages.

> Then the wolf shall live with the sheep,
> and the leopard shall lie down with the kid;
> the calf and the young lion shall grow up together,
> and a little child shall lead them;
> the cow and the bear shall be friends,
> and their young shall lie down together.
> The lion shall eat straw like cattle;
> the infant shall play over the hole of the cobra,
> and the young child dance over the viper's nest.
> (Is. 11:6–8; NEB)

This description, which is probably a later insertion into the prophecy of Isaiah, is of the peaceable kingdom.

Three things need to be said about the notion of covenant being evolved here. First, the relationship between Yahweh and the Israelites is clearly *not* one that exists by nature. Yahwism is a patriarchal religion, whose masculine God *calls* a relationship into being. He is not an intrinsic dynamic within the ebb and flow of the seasons of the year. Yahweh is initially distinct from and over against his people and chooses to come to his people, and, in the case of the Elohist, they can choose to respond. This concept exists, of course, in opposition to the nature religion of the Canaanites and others, who include the feminine principle in deity and all that it implies for the identification of the processes of existence with the divine life.

Second, it follows from this, even before the monarchy arises in the eleventh century B.C., that for Israel, God is king. The nomadic tribes that give themselves to the covenant at Sinai know no king. They are a loose confederation, united in their common allegiance to this covenant, and the earthly king readily becomes a mediator of the covenant. In fact, during the period of the monarchy the king was considered Yahweh's vice-regent.

Finally, there is *no* correlative concern along with the covenant relationship between Israel and God for personal salvation in the early monarchy. The outcome expected is the wholeness of the people, Israel. The objective is the supremacy or the peace of Israel. Individuals either died and they were no more, or they existed in Sheol, a place of shadows and wraithlike existence. A person lived on in his children; which is the reason why Deuteronomy provided for a man to marry the wife of a deceased brother, who died without children (25:5–10). The fact that one needed children to live on in them is also an explanation for the lack of respect for virginity in Hebrew thinking.

The Prophetic Protest and Reform

It is very easy for a people to conclude that if they are "chosen" of God, their style of life must be congruent with God's will. From the very beginning of the establishment of the covenant at Mt. Sinai, such spiritual pride afflicted the Hebrews, as well as the constant temptation to follow the religions of the cultures they were assimilating. King David's (c. 1000–961 B.C.) seduction of Bathsheba, murder of Uriah, and confrontation by Nathan is an account of such spiritual pride (2 Sam. 11:1–12:25). The apostasy of Ahab, king of Israel (c. 869–850 B.C.), through his marriage to Jezebel (who worshiped the Canaanite god, Baal) is an example of the appeal of the more feminine fertility cults. The lament of the Prophet Elijah, escaping from Ahab and hiding in a cave on Mt. Horeb, is indicative of what happened, "'The people of Israel have forsaken thy covenant, torn down thy altars and put thy prophets to death with the sword. I alone am left, and they seek to take my life'" (1 Kings 19:10; NEB).

It is essential to recover the objective of Yahwism. But as in all such "recoveries," the vision was never the same as before. The intention of the people had been changed and enriched by their history. In the Northern Kingdom, the Prophet Amos emerged in the mid-eighth century. He preached judgment. Israel was to be punished for its sins; it would be wiped out by a military conquest. The terrible "day of the Lord" would descend upon the Israelites

> because they sell the innocent for silver
>   and the destitute for a pair of shoes.
> They grind the heads of the poor into the earth
>   and thrust the humble out of their way.
> Father and son resort to the same girl,
>   to the profanation of my holy name.
>   (Amos 2:6–7; NEB)

It is not a happy picture of the future.

> She has fallen to rise no more,
>   the virgin Israel,
> prostrate on her own soil, with no one to lift her up.
>   (Amos 5:2; NEB)

It is essential that we not see the condemnation by Amos and others of the prophets as merely an exposé of the moral depravity of Israel. This would make the prophets nothing but teachers of ethics, and they were much more than this. They were agents of God's revelation. What the prophets were attacking was the loss of the sense of the immediate presence of God among the people and the abandonment of God's sovereignty over their lives, of which the moral life was an expression. Social justice for Amos is built into God's law.

Amos' contemporaries, Hosea and Isaiah of Jerusalem, joined with him to develop a vision of Yahweh—his abundant love and his ethical majesty—that came to transcend the narrow concept of a national deity, assuring his worshipers of regional hegemony. They too predicted the Day of Yahweh, when judgment shall be visited upon the people. The possibilities for the notion of covenant and the outcome of faith in Yahweh were greatly developed in these prophets. Whereas all three interpreted the destruction of Israel—Isaiah even names the instrument of Yahweh in this destruction: Assyria—they also spoke of the "saved remnant" (Amos 9:9–15, Hos. 14:1–8, Is. 37:31–32). It would appear that this remnant, according to

Isaiah, is those who have a "firm faith" in Yahweh as he himself is faithful (Is. 7:9). The notion of the "remnant," which strikes one as an afterthought and may literally be a later addition to the texts, is not well-developed in any of these three prophets and does not ameliorate the grim picture of the future of Israel.

The hope for the future and a happy outcome lies in Isaiah's sense of history. Yahweh was the lord of creation. He was the universal God. He summoned the Assyrians to punish Israel and would, in turn, punish the arrogance of the Assyrians. For Isaiah, God was just, and he prevailed.

> Round his waist he shall wear the belt of justice,
>   and good faith shall be the girdle round his body.
> (Is. 11:5; NEB)

But Isaiah did not tell us where history is going, which is always a problem for a people for whom the outcome is not the recovery of a known past, but the anticipation of an unknown future.

Israel, the Northern Kingdom, did indeed fall to the Assyrians in 722/1 B.C.; Judah, the Southern Kingdom, which was for a period in vassalage to Assyria, was to last another 134 years. The seventh century, once Judah had survived the cruel reign of Manasseh (687–642 B.C.), was marked by an effort at cultic purity and national expansion. The strategy was recovered. The record of this effort first appears in the Book of Deuteronomy, a collection of addresses written in the sermonic style of the period; Deuteronomy was intended to make the old cultic and legal traditions relevant for their time. The preachers of a renewed covenant, as found in Deuteronomy, are utopian. "If you will obey the Lord your God by diligently observing all his commandments which I lay upon you this day, then the Lord your God will raise you high above all nations of the earth, and these blessings shall come to you and light upon you" (Deut. 28:1–2; NEB).

The preachers believed that through obedience to the Law, the Northern Kingdom would be restored and reunited with the Southern Kingdom. It is noteworthy that the theology of Deuteronomy understood Yahweh as a God of love and the Hebrews as called to love and reverence him in response to his great goodness. "Hear, O Israel, the Lord is our God, one Lord, and you must love the Lord your God with all your heart and soul and strength" (Deut. 6:4–5; NEB). There is a perceptible movement to the God found within the person.

The vision of the preachers of Deuteronomy, which was possibly written down and possibly presented to King Josiah (640–609 B.C.) in 621 B.C.—this is a very disputed point—failed to capture the imagination of Judah. Among the problems of Deuteronomic objective was a simplistic interpretation of history. If one obeyed the Law, it seemed to say, all would be well. This "bargain-counter" notion of divine rewards and punishments, with its very naive concept of humanity and society, is always doomed to bring disappointment. The Prophet Jeremiah (626–587 B.C.) had apparently supported the Deuteronomic renewal of the covenant in his early days, but he himself became disillusioned as it failed to accomplish the promised outcome of the chosen people, living in love, fear, and obedience to Yahweh. Jeremiah, after telling them it is a lie to trust in the Temple in Jerusalem to save them, addresses the people of Judah:

> How can you say, "We are wise,
> we have the law of the Lord",
> when scribes with their lying pens
> have falsified it?
> (Jer. 8:8; NEB)

Jeremiah, like all the other true prophets, assures Judah that destruction awaits her. The only hope is to obey his command: "Deal justly and fairly, rescue the victim from his oppressor, do not ill-treat or do violence to the alien, the orphan or the widow, do not shed innocent blood in this place" (Jer. 22:3; NEB). But Jeremiah knows that such repentance will not happen in his day, and he awaits the fall of Jerusalem to the Babylonians. Yet he is not without hope. He shares the vision of

an everlasting covenant that God will make with Israel when it
is restored.

> Although they broke my covenant, I was patient with them,
> says the Lord. But this is the covenant I will make with Israel
> after those days, says the Lord; I will set my law within them
> and write it upon their hearts; I will become their God and
> they shall become my people. No longer need they teach one
> another to know the Lord; all of them, high and low alike,
> shall know me, says the Lord, for I will forgive their
> wrongdoing and remember their sin no more. (Jer. 31:32–
> 34; NEB)

The covenant of which Jeremiah dreams is a sophisticated
vision of a people who live with a sense of God's presence
within them. He seems to move deeper into an understanding
of the objective of God's mercy and the bond of love between
Yahweh and his people. The knowledge of God rises up as a
consequence of self-knowledge. The people live not by an
imposed set of ordinances, but by a moral vision that follows
because they think as God thinks.

The Post-Exilic Covenant

When Jerusalem fell in 587/6 B.C., it marked the end of
an independent Jewish state, save the brief semiautonomous
existence of Judah under the Maccabees in the mid-second to
early first centuries B.C.—until the modern establishment of
Israel in 1948. Three successive peoples ruled the Jews until
the coming of the Christ: the Persians, the Greeks (first under
the relatively benign Ptolemies and then under the aggressively
Hellenistic Seleucidae), and the Romans. Consequently, several
cultural streams met in Palestine, with the inevitable influence
they had upon all theological reflection, including the images
of the destiny of humanity.

We would expect that when the cream of Jewish society was
carried away into Babylon in 597 B.C., with the initial conquest
of Jerusalem, and then 587/6 B.C., with the final fall of the Holy
City, that a longing for a return to Jerusalem would thrive. The

outcome of a renewed, penitent Israel would be a restoration to the covenantal community in the Holy City. This was, in fact the case. The Prophet Ezekiel (593–573 B.C.), once Jerusalem had fallen, began to promise the return. He even described in detail the purified cult, the expression of the renewed life of the people with Yahweh. His most powerful expression of the objective of this return is found in the vision of the valley of dry bones.

> These are the words of the Lord God: O my people, I will open your graves and bring you up from them, and restore you to the land of Israel. You shall know that I am the Lord when I open your graves and bring you up from them, O my people. Then I will put my spirit into you and you shall live, and I will settle you on your own soil, and you shall know that I the Lord have spoken and will act. (Ezek. 37:12–14; NEB)

It is obvious that the objective is the covenant community. It is important to note, however, that in Ezekiel's theology the individual figures more prominently than ever before in Hebrew imagery. It is not that the individual is totally absent before, but he is very much in the background until now. Once the question of the individual begins to receive attention, however, then new issues are raised for the objective of life in obedience to God.

A little after Ezekiel's time (about 539 B.C.) an unknown prophet emerged who is now called "Second Isaiah," because his writings are appended to those of the eighth-century Isaiah, beginning with the fortieth chapter. The importance of Second Isaiah is immeasurable, as he gives a deeper nuance to the Jewish expectation of the future: the projected outcome of the faithfulness to Yahweh. Second Isaiah speaks in magnificent poetry of the restoration of the covenant community.

> Awake, awake, put on your strength, O Zion,
> put on your loveliest garments, holy city of Jerusalem;
> for never shall the uncircumcised and the unclean
>   enter you again.

> Rise up, captive Jerusalem, shake off the dust;
>   loose your neck from the collar that binds it,
>   O captive daughter of Zion.
> (Is. 52:1–2; NEB)

The fact that this interpretation was proven false over and over again does not gainsay its beauty or, for our purposes, the vision.

The God of Second Isaiah is a universal God, a figure emerging over the preceding two centuries in the theology of the prophets. The objective of this prophet is, therefore, Yahweh's world sovereignty achieved not by military conquest, but by the suffering of Israel corporately and by its representative, the savior-king. The enigmatic figure of the suffering servant, which made such a profound impact upon the Christian understanding of Jesus, by the very fact of his affliction opened the hearts and minds of Israel to God's word. The suffering servant became the herald of the divine covenant. "In the furnace of affliction; there I purified you," says Yahweh (Is. 48:10; NEB). Now Yahweh says, "I will make you a light to the nations" (Is. 49:6; NEB). The mystery of suffering became the instrument of the fulfillment of God's creative vision. "So the Lord's people shall come back, set free, and enter Zion with shouts of triumph" (Is. 51:11; NEB).

What was begun in Ezekiel continued to develop in Second Isaiah. The individual, as a member of the restored Israel, emerged more clearly. The promise of forgiveness was extended, at the same time being tied to obedience to the Law. "I will make a covenant with you, this time forever, to love you faithfully as I loved David" (Is. 55:3; NEB). "Maintain justice, do the right; for my deliverance is close at hand" (Is. 56:1; NEB).

The mention of King David in Second Isaiah pointed to a developing eschatological expectation, beginning in the theology of the suffering servant. The restored Jerusalem found here is the center, however, of a world-wide community, existing under God's sovereign rule, and it shall be like the idealized Davidic kingdom.

The objective of both Ezekiel and Second Isaiah began to be realized in the return from Babylon of a portion of the exiled Jews and the building of the second Temple (finished 515 B.C.). At this time the restored covenant community was seen in terms of a purified temple worship, guaranteed by the leadership of a true high priest and of someone in the line of King David. The outcome is to be the restoration of the Davidic covenant, conceived religiously more than politically. The Hebrew-derived word, "Messiah" (in Greek, *christos*), meaning the "anointed one," is not yet used. Rather, this precursor of the "golden age" is called the "branch" of King David.

> I will now bring my servant, the Branch. In one day I will wipe away the guilt of the land. On that day, says the Lord of Hosts, you shall all of you invite one another to come and sit under his vine and his fig-tree. (Zech. 3:9–10; NEB)

The historical figure to whom Zechariah is referring is Zerubbabel, the civil servant who accompanied those Jews who returned to Jerusalem.

The establishment of the second Temple is an important foundation for the realization of the first promise of the restoration of the Davidic covenant community. There had been intimations in the earlier prophets—Isaiah 11:1, Micah 5:2, and Jeremiah 23:5—of a recalling of the Davidic golden age by a ruler who harks back to him. The words they use, which later become a technical term for the eschatological prophet or Messiah, include "a shoot from the stock of Jesse," "one whose roots are far back in the past," and "a righteous Branch from David's line," respectively (NEB). As tempted as we are to see in such words a developed eschatological hope, if not Christian implications, we need to avoid such an interpretation.

This foundation of the dream of a recovery of the "golden age" of David—which, in fact, as we know was no "golden age" at all—was laid higher by the work of Nehemiah and Ezra in the latter half of the fifth century and, possibly, the early fourth century B.C. Judah was not a sovereign nation. It was a religious community under Persian rule. Nehemiah was the local governor, serving at the will of the Persian king. He did a great deal to bind the Jewish community together with the Persian Empire. In order to accomplish this purpose, Nehemiah advocated a very isolated Jewish community, forbidding marriage with "foreigners." This had its narrowing effect on some visions of the future.

Ezra, whose chronological relationship to Nehemiah is unclear, was a priest of the Temple, who published the Law and made it the operative expression of Yahweh's will for the people (Neh 8:1-8). Rabbinic Judaism really starts with Ezra, as the covenant is renewed with the canonical text of the Law and the worship of the Temple as its symbols.

The Law that Ezra read was probably the first four books of the Old Testament, compiled from all the sources (the Yahwist, the Elohist, and the various Priestly writers) and, in addition, Deuteronomy. But the Law or Torah was not a source for the Davidic covenant, but rather it described it in 2 Samuel 7. Obviously there is an interpretation of the Law that is functioning in the Jewish community which is outside the letter of the Law. The concern of the Priestly writers has to do with the purity of the cult and its moral implications. The intent is in the restoration of the Davidic covenant, and King David is seen as the principal guide. For example, in Nehemiah the order for the service of the Levites in the Temple is said to follow "according to the commandment of David the man of God" (Neh. 12:24; NEB), as if David were the head sacristan or chief liturgist. The commandment of David seems to have been found not in the Torah but in the Psalms of David.

Cult is an essential part of all religion. One should not read the Old Testament as if there were a sharp antagonism between priests and prophets. They are sometimes the same persons and are both products of the cult. But inasmuch as Judah was now a religious community and not the ruler of its own destiny, the cult becomes an intensive concern for energies of the people; and, at the same time, the focus of the Jewish theologians begins to turn inward. As this is happening, an intellectual ferment surrounds and eventually washes over Palestine.

Four Options

We do not know a great deal about Judah in the third and fourth centuries B.C. This should not lead us to conclude that it was an isolated community. Quite the contrary. It was a crossroads for the passage of armies, commerce, and ideas. This rich flux of peoples and their thoughts about the destiny of humankind left an impact that was varied and incapable of neat resolution. We are its heirs today.

The Persian Empire, which freed the Jews to return to Jerusalem, had its own religious heritage. Whereas it is hard to trace the complicated beliefs of the Iranian people, we know that their religion as represented in their kings focused on a great cosmic struggle between the god of light and the powers of darkness. To what extent the prophet Zarathustra, who may have been roughly contemporary with Jeremiah or Ezekiel, actually shaped the theology of Zoroastrianism or what is sometimes called Mazdaism (after the worship of Ahura Mazda) we do not know. The fact of the matter is that Persian religion, with its elaborate cosmology, its astrologers (called Magi), and its fascination with numbers was a part of the great syncretistic mix of which Judaism was a part.

The degree of Persian influence upon Jewish thinking is greatly debated. Undoubtedly there was some. Satan as personified evil is taken from Mazdaism. (This is not the Satan of Job.) The word means the "adversary." The Book of Tobit, a didactic romance advocating faithfulness to the Law, dating from this period, has explicit Iranian influence. The "magi" in Matthew 2:1 do not have to be Persian. Astrology was common in all religion, including Judaism, at that time. But Persian religion is part of the cultural milieu.

The Persian Empire fell to Alexander the Great in 330 B.C. Alexander had, among other purposes, the objective of bringing Greek culture to the civilized world. He had been a pupil of Aristotle. Socrates was contemporary to Nehemiah and, if one accepts one possible chronology, Plato was contemporary with Ezra. Greek philosophy could not help but have a profound influence upon the cultural world, even of Judah, particularly in its exported form called Hellenism.

Although the rise of the individual cannot be attributed to any one source—as we have seen, it was already implicitly apparent in Ezekiel—it certainly received intellectual support in the Greek notion that to be human is to be a rational creature. Reason draws our attention inward and sets the individual off from the collective.

In very simple terms, Jewish, Persian, and Greek ideas, with the infinite varieties within each culture, percolated in the ancient Near East and left an indelible imprint upon the thought of Western humanity. This is as true concerning the objective of the religious life for Jews and Christians as anything else. It is possible to identify four distinct images from second and third centuries B.C. on.

The Jewish Sage

Jewish wisdom literature (Proverbs, Job, Ecclesiastes, Ecclesiasticus, and Wisdom) is the particular expression of the common theological preoccupation of the next thousand years: the relation of knowledge to the union with God. It begins in a sense with Ezekiel's claim that an individual is responsible for his sins, works through the doubt of Job (written somewhere between the fifth and third centuries B.C.), and "comes a cropper" with the religious skepticism of Ecclesiastes (probably third century B.C.). The anticipated end of humanity in Ecclesiastes is, as most of us recall, death. The dream of the covenant does not appear in this writing. "Emptiness, emptiness, says the Speaker, all is empty" (Eccles. 12:8; NEB) is what he tells us is our destiny. In the face of this, the only advice the Preacher of Ecclesiastes can give is, "Fear God and obey his commands" (Eccles. 12:13; NEB).

The canonization of the Pentateuch gave the Jewish sage the material for his quest of wisdom. Perhaps the epitome of the sage is Jesus ben Sirach, the author of Ecclesiasticus (written in the third century B.C.). For ben Sirach to medidate upon the Law is to acquire Wisdom:

> All this is the covenant-book of God Most High,
> the law which Moses enacted to be the heritage of the
>   assemblies of Jacob.

He sends out wisdom in full flood like the river Pishon
or like the Tigris at the time of firstfruits . . . .
(Ecclesiasticus, 24:20-25, NEB)

For ben Sirach, when a man dies, he dies:

When the dead is at rest, let his memory rest too; take
comfort as soon as he has breathed his last. (Ecclesiasticus
38:23; NEB)

The principal goal is to be wise:

Wisdom is fitting in the aged,
and ripe counsel in men of eminence.
(Ecclesiasticus 25:5; NEB)

Ben Sirach, as the other Jewish sages, was a man of profound
moral concern. Wisdom begets a sense of right and wrong. Ben
Sirach was not totally devoid of a notion of individual existence
after death, despite his admonition to forget the dead. He even
offers a slight suggestion of rewards and punishment after
death. There had emerged in Jewish theology a notion of a
shadowy existence, known as Sheol, perhaps in the later
monarchy or at least by the time of the Exile. The Jewish sage
built upon this image. Ben Sirach suggests that death and
existence in Sheol can be a happy release for the destitute
(Ecclesiasticus 41:2). But he also suggests that it is a place of
"fire and worms" for the impious (Ecclesiasticus 7:17). Yet one
gets the impression that ben Sirach really believed that the wise
and moral life this side of the grave is its own reward.

The Jewish sage contributes much to New Testament and
later Christian thought, particularly in the Fourth Gospel. The
love of wisdom or, as it comes to be in the early church,
knowledge, is bound in the Christian tradition to the sage and
his love of wisdom. In the New Testament the images of Word,
logos, and Wisdom, *sophia,* are confused. We think of the Word
as Christ and Wisdom as the Holy Spirit, two separate persons
of the Trinity; but the apostolic church made no such clear
distinction and drew for their understanding of Word and
Wisdom upon the literature of the Jewish sage, as much or

more than they drew on parallels in Hellenistic thought. He who possesses eternal life is he who is possessed by Wisdom.

The Messianic Expectation

The continuation of the expectation of the sovereignty of God over the world carried more of an impact on Christian thinking in regard to the objective of the religious life. This continuation depended not so much on the canonization of the Pentateuch as the expectation of the restoration of the covenant community in Christ. The individualism of the times was not as prominent as the longing for redemption of Israel. When things looked most bleak for those of the Jewish faith, an eschatological theology developed, associated in some quarters with an apocalyptic hope. This was particularly true after 167 B.C. and the desecration of the Temple by the Seleucid king, Antiochus IV.

The difference between an eschatological hope and an apocalyptic expectation is this. An eschatological hope can be no more than the belief that at some time in the future Israel will be restored as an independent nation under a great king, perhaps descended from King David. An apocalyptic expectation is the belief that a new aeon will come from outside this present age that will replace the present aeon. Apocalypticism presumes a dualism of the cosmos, in which the evil world is destroyed and the new world established by divine intervention. In the messianic expectation of late Jewish times and the early Christian era, the eschatological hope and the apocalyptic expectation, while not necessarily identical, possessed an overlapping imagery.

The continued cross-fertilization of ideas particularly confused the notion of the eschatological prophet, as I shall call him here, variously described among other terms as the "Messiah" (a term that originally referred to the kings of Israel), the "Son of Man" (again a term originally meaning "humankind"), the "Branch of David," or the "Heavenly Man." In the apocalyptic sense, the terms "Messiah" and "Son of Man" appear in the Old Testament only in Daniel (7:13, 9:25–26), an apocalyptic book written after 167 B.C. By this time the eschatological prophet has taken on the quality of a Persian subdeity.

It is hard to say just what the precise Jewish expectation was of the eschatological prophet, but generally it was that he would by some means—natural or supernatural—destroy the enemies of Judah, abolish the sinners from Jerusalem, and establish a theocratic kingdom like unto that of King David. It was with this expectation that the Jews greeted Jesus on the Sunday before his crucifixion. The Psalm (118:26) that they sang as he entered Jerusalem was one of the Messianic Psalms: " 'Hosanna to the Son of David! Blessings on him who comes in the name of the Lord' " (Mt. 21:9; NEB).

The fact that Jesus came preaching repentance in preparation for the eminent coming of the Kingdom of God "triggered" these expectations in the Jewish people. Without doubt the place of Jesus' birth, "the city of David," in both Matthew and Luke, as well as Matthew's genealogy of Jesus showing him as a descendant of David, is a post-resurrection commentary on the Gospel story reflecting the Davidic interpretation of the Christ event. This objective, the restoration of the covenant community, seemed to have been in the mind of Jesus before his Passion, whether or not he was literally of the lineage of David. The utterly strange aspect of behavior was, however, that he did not seek to bring it about either by natural, military, or political means, or even by some supernatural sleight-of-hand. He sought to prepare humankind for the Kingdom, which God would initiate, by teaching in parables, proclaiming in miracles, and by enacting in his own person the ethical quality of the Kingdom. There is no question as to what the outcome of Jesus' ministry was to be: the reign of God over the world.

The Beatitudes, particularly in their reference to the poor, the hungry, and those who mourn (assuming that Luke 6:20–22 is a more primitive version than Matthew 5:3–11), strike the keynote of the moral character of God's sovereignty. The presence of love and justice as the character of the Kingdom prevailed throughout Jesus' teaching.

Jesus saw himself as the eschatological prophet. He is the host at the messianic banquet. Jesus felt more at home in the apocalyptic language of the two worlds—the old, evil aeon, and the new, divine aeon—than he did in the anticipation of the restoration of the ancient Davidic kingdom; although he is not an apocalypticist in the strict sense. He and his disciples pick up the vocabulary of the apocalyptic expectation of the coming of the Kingdom to indicate an expectation of the breaking-in of God's rule. An example of this would be his answer to the Pharisees, who ask him when the Kingdom shall come. Jesus responds in terms of the "days of the Son of Man" (Lk. 17:20–37; NEB), a conflation of the ancient prophetic day of judgment with the messianic, apocalyptic image.

The ultimate New Testament apocalyptic vision appears in Revelation, in which the "new heaven and the new earth," "the holy city Jerusalem" (Rev. 21:1, 10; NEB), is seen to descend and replace Death and Hades, "flung into the lake of fire" (Rev. 20:14; NEB). This objective of Christian discipleship, following upon the suffering of the martyrs, is thoroughly Jewish in its spirit, as is the prevailing picture of Jesus' expectations of the result of his life and teaching. If it is true that Jesus did not anticipate his own resurrection, it is nonetheless true that following his resurrection his disciples continued to conceptualize the objective of their faith as the coming of the Kingdom; his resurrection was seen as anticipating that event.

The Resurrection of the Body

There is a new line of thought introduced into Jewish theology about the second or third centuries B.C. It involves the resurrection of the dead as the outcome of a faithful witness to God. By the time of the Gospels, while there is disagreement within the Jewish community on the subject, this new line of thought has been incorporated into the much older Jewish expectation of the reign of God.

We do not know where the notion of the resurrection of the dead entered Jewish thought. For thousands of years those nature religions that encircled the Hebrews had taught of the god who dies and rises, a mythological rationalization of the cycles of the seasons and the lowering and rising of such rivers as the Nile. But this mythological image is not the same thing as this later belief that the dead shall be awakened and the just shall be with God and the evil shall either remain dead or shall suffer torment.

The only reference to anything like the resurrection of the dead in the Protestant canon before the New Testament appears in Daniel. There Michael, who is apparently a Jewish modification of a Persian semideity, appears at the time of the end and:

> many of those who sleep in the dust of the earth will wake,
>> some to everlasting life
> and some to the reproach of eternal abhorrence.
>
> (Dan. 12:2; NEB)

There is an extended witness to the belief in the resurrection of the dead, more literal than found in Daniel, in the account in 2 Maccabees of a woman and her seven sons, who were tortured to death because they refused to eat pork (2 Maccabees 7:1–41).

It is impossible to generalize about what was believed to be the nature of the resurrection. There is no clear evidence as to whether it was universal or just for the elect, whether it was to a life of immortality or to a new created world. It should be noted that resurrection to immortality in Daniel is called "everlasting" or "eternal life" (the Greek Old Testament reads *zōēn aiōnion*). Those words appear again in the New Testament, particularly in the Fourth Gospel.

Attached to the notion of the resurrection of the dead is the image of personal judgment. Throughout the Old Testament there is salvation and judgment, but it is a judgment of nations, not individuals. However, as early as the Prophet Malachi (early fifth century B.C.) there is a change, and individuals are said to face the day of the Lord (Mal. 4:1–3). By the time of Hellenism it is an event for some that takes place after our death. We are awakened to be judged.

Where did the notion of resurrection and judgment come from? No one is sure. It appeared in Persian religion, but there are many who doubt a direct influence. The Persian practice was to expose the dead to the air. Their theory was that at the last day the bodies of the dead were reassembled from the elements of the ether. This is obviously not the same scenario as being raised from the earth. The resurrection of the dead was not Greek, although sometimes Greek vocabulary slipped into its development. Perhaps the belief in the resurrection of the dead, as ambiguous and uncertain as it was, was an image that evolved out of the interaction of a number of cultures and a continuing expansion in the religious consciousness of some Jewish theologians.

Certainly by the time of Jesus, it was a firmly held belief of some Jews, particularly the Pharisees, and an explicitly rejected belief of other Jews, the Sadducees (Mt. 22:23–30). Jesus obviously sided with the Pharisees. Jesus appeared to have taught not only the resurrection of the dead, but also the Evangelists attribute to him a belief in a judgment in which one option is hell-fire (Mt. 25:31–46). Whether or not Jesus actually spoke of hell-fire or the apostolic church picked it up from Jewish sources other than Jesus, there was an obvious commitment of the early Christians to the imagery of the resurrection of the dead and a final judgment. It is significant that the passage from Matthew 25 is a judgment of nations, not individuals.

Three things need to be said in regard to the resurrection of the dead. First, the belief in the resurrection of the dead is not a result of the resurrection of Jesus. It is the other way around. Whatever was the hope that the image of the resurrection gave some first-century Jews, Jesus' resurrection was a sign that the hope would be fulfilled at some time and in some manner. The resurrection of Jesus is seen within the wider belief as a promise of the new creation to the faithful. Paul speaks of this, declaring that Christ is "the firstfruits, and afterwards, at his coming, those who belong to Christ" (will enter into the new life). Paul adds, "Then comes the end, when he delivers up the kingdom to God the Father" (1 Cor. 15:23–24; NEB).

This leads to a second point. There is no agreement in the New Testament as to what the dead are raised. Paul speaks of being raised so that we might "possess the kingdom of God" (1 Cor. 15:50; NEB), which is very much like a new created world or the "holy city." The Fourth Evangelist speaks of "eternal life" (John 3:15 is one of many examples). There is also a story that appears in all three synoptic Gospels that makes the reference to "eternal life," along with a few uses of the term in Paul himself. "Eternal life" (*zōēn aiōnion*) is a "catch phrase," as we have already seen, for union with God, which is purposely ambiguous. It is not necessarily the same thing as the Kingdom of God or a "new heaven and a new earth." The New Testament reflects the ambiguity of the times.

Third, there was obviously a disagreement about the nature of the resurrected body. Paul would not have written his long argument for a noncorporeal resurrection if some Christians had not taught a corporeal resurrection (1 Cor. 15:35–49). He also taught that some would not have to undergo resurrection (1 Thess. 4:13–18). It is important that we not try to press the image too far.

Beyond the objective of the resurrection of the dead and final judgment, another image needs some thoughts: heaven and hell. They very likely come into Jewish and Christian thought from Mazdaism. The problem of heaven will be discussed in more detail later, but notice needs to be made of the word "paradise," a possible synonym for heaven, which appears three times in the New Testament (Lk. 23:43, 2 Cor. 12:4, Rev. 2:7). Briefly, it is derived from a Persian word meaning a "wooded park," and by New Testament times had come to mean the abode of the righteous awaiting or after resurrection. It is an image in advance of the previous murky abode of the dead, Sheol.

Hell or Gehenna (the name of a valley outside Jerusalem where, during the monarchy, infants were passed through fire in fertility rites) is a place of punishment by means of eternal fire. Whereas there are a few references to punishment through conflagration in earlier Old Testament writings, the specific belief of a fiery hell arises in later Judaism. It would appear to be related to the Persian teaching that the evil shall be punished by burning in molten metal.

There are no consistent images of heaven or hell in the New Testament. The contemporary reader needs to know this and avoid, particularly, attributing to the words ideas inherited from two thousand years of Christian tradition, especially those from Dante's *Divine Comedy*. At the same time, if the objective of the religious life is a moral life rewarded by God and that outcome is obviously not achieved within this life for the individual (the problem with which Ecclesiastes and Job struggled), and if the individual has come to achieve a new importance, then notions of rewards and punishment beyond the grave appear to offer a solution. No wonder by the time of Jesus many Jews had picked up on the metaphors of Persian religion.

The Immortal Soul

This final option for an objective of the religious life needs only to be mentioned briefly here, but it will be developed later in our study. It comes to us from Greek thought and is based upon the belief that the human person is by some happen stance a union of the soul, which is the real, immortal self, to the corruptible body. The dualistic understanding of the person was not taught by all Greek philosophers by any means, it was not held as naively as some of its contemporary detractors suggest, and even its attributed originator, Plato, did not provide a consistent doctrine of the soul.

As this teaching developed, the essence of man, the rational part, is perceived as being contained in the mind, which is, in turn, part of the life principle, the soul (*psyche*). The soul, according to this school of thought, is eternal. This can be very confusing for two reasons. But the word *soul* does not always mean this in ancient authors. And in a revision of this doctrine in the second century A.D. the rational part of humanity is perceived as residing in the spirit (*pneuma*), and the soul is seen as mortal just as the body is mortal.

The only place this teaching appears in the Bible is in the Book of Wisdom, whose author is influenced by Hellenistic thought. "But the souls of the just are in God's hands," he writes, "and torment shall not touch them" (Wisdom 3:1; NEB).

Wisdom implies further that the soul of the individual is preexistent ("a noble soul fell to my lot" [8:19; NEB]), and that it survives after death (16:14). The body, the author tells us, is a burden to the soul (9:15). Wisdom, on the other hand, is an attribute of the soul (7:27).

If one followed the teaching of the Book of Wisdom, the objective of the religious life would be the cultivation of the soul principally by the acquisition of wisdom, manifested by the just life, so that once the soul was rid of the body it could be joined to God. As such, this notion does not appear in the New Testament. In fact, the word *immortality* is used in the New Testament only twice. Once we are told that God alone is immortal (1 Tim. 6:16). The other time Paul says that the mortal person in the resurrection of the dead is "clothed" with immortality (1 Cor. 15:53).

Paul is struggling in this passage to make sense of the resurrection of the dead. If we look at what he says closely, we will, I believe, discover the "beachhead" for the objective of Christian discipleship contained in the notion of the immortal soul. In all honesty, this objective has been the basis of almost all Christian thinking since the early church. For Paul in this same passage tried to make the distinction between the two bodies: the earthly and the resurrected. The language he uses becomes by the next century the technical vocabulary of the current religious philosophy. As Paul said, there are two kinds of body: the natural (*psychikon*) and the spiritual (*pneumatikon*) (1 Cor. 15:44). It meant for Paul that on an *ethical* level there are two kinds of people. A hundred years later it meant for some philosophers that *by nature* there are two (or even three) kinds of people.

There also crept into Paul's thinking another image. In 2 Corinthians he justified himself to his readers by listing his credentials. In one place he coyly writes, "I know a Christian man who fourteen years ago . . . was caught up as far as the third heaven" (2 Cor. 12:2; NEB). What is the meaning of the "third heaven"? It was a commonly held belief in the Judaism of Paul's time that there were three levels to heaven. Yahweh lived in the third level, above the stars. There was a corresponding pagan belief that above us lay a series of astral spheres. The objective for the human soul was to ascend through the heavens to union with God. Taught by pagans and Christians alike, it became our fervent hope after death to "go up to heaven"; but apparently a few, such as Paul, received something of a foretaste. (This is what lies behind the imagery of 1 Thessalonians 4:17.)

In Paul the resurrection of the dead began to be cast into Hellenistic thought forms. When we read the word *heaven* we can expect that the current notions widely associated with that word may well apply, and that there is no pure Hellenistic or Jewish imagery intended. The author of 2 Peter, for example, described the Day of the Lord in terms of a classic Greek conflagration of the "heavens" while he promised a Jewish "new heavens and a new earth" (2 Pet. 3:10–13; NEB). The author of Hebrews appears to make a distinction between *soul* and *spirit* (Heb. 4:12) from which later Christians probably drew a Greek point of view. Actually, Hebrews is more rabbinic than Hellenistic, and probably had something else in mind.

The notion of the immortality of the soul focused on the disembodied individual after death. Contemporary theology, for the last generation or so, has been blaming Greek thought for this. Actually, Hellenistic culture was not all that narrow-minded. It understood the importance of the body to the soul and believed the human to be a political creature. It was the erection of a gymnasium in Jerusalem in the early second century B.C. where people appeared in public in the nude in quest of the sound body that made possible the healthy soul, which initially angered the Jews and, in turn, provoked the desecration of the Temple. Furthermore, the Greek concept of the *polis* or city as essential to being human fit very well into the anticipation of the heavenly Jerusalem in Revelation. If we are honest with ourselves, we will realize that the resurrection of the dead was an ambiguous metaphor, which needed Greek philosophical clarification if it were to be lifted above Jewish and even Persian eschatology and made understandable to educated citizens of the Roman Empire. Paul's work is the first example of the effort to do that.

Analysis and Summary

This has been a relatively long recounting of the biblical metaphors for the objectives or hope of salvation. It is necessary to wrestle with the question of the end for which we as Christians pursue renewal and seek to evangelize the world. The basic conclusion must be that in the Bible there is no one comprehensive, clear objective of discipleship, and that as the story unfolds the options increase and interact in a variety of ways. Furthermore, the objective of the immortal soul has, practically speaking, no more basis in biblical theology than many other scriptural metaphors.

But there are certain "threads" that run through the exploration of the biblical story. I want to identify five.

First, the objective is always union with God. It may be union of the community, irrespective of the individual who must die; or the union may be one of the individual and community beyond the grave, although this is not as universal as one might expect. There is no clear way in which such a union is described except to say that God is our creator and ruler. There are many metaphors: the Garden of Eden, the back of Yahweh on Mt. Sinai, Elijah on Mt. Horeb, Isaiah in the Holy of Holies, the Mount of the Transfiguration, or Paul caught up in the third heaven. But without a doubt, the biblical longing is to be with God, just as Jesus called his disciples first of all "so that they might be with him" (Mk. 3:14; UTH). To be human is to be in relation with God and fellow priests.

Second, no one ever seems to "arrive." The objective remains, it changes, it challenges, but it is always just beyond us. It never becomes an outcome. The Bible thinks in the future perfect tense, never in the perfect. This is another way of saying that biblical theology is historical in scope, and that as all history is the story of salvation, history is still going on. In the fourth century A.D., Gregory of Nyssa put this insight very succinctly: "This truly is the vision of God; never to be satisfied in the desire to see him."[1] History is not ended. Consequently, to quote Gregory again, "The perfection of human nature consists perhaps on its very growth in goodness."[2]

Third, *almost* without fail it is impossible to conceive of the objective without imagining a community. To be human is to live together, and to be a whole human being is to live in perfect togetherness. There is very little sense in the Scriptures of the individual and God together alone. There is no doubt this comes later in Christian spirituality, but it is not biblical. Even the Greek Jew who wrote Wisdom, after describing the souls of the just, says "they will be judges and rulers over the nations of the world, and the Lord shall be their king for ever and ever" (Wisdom 3:8; NEB). The author of Hebrews declares that God has prepared for the faithful a city, a city to come, a "city of the living God" (Heb. 11:16, 12:22, 13:14). It is hard not to see in these words the image of that perfect human community, with God as its judge, of which the Greeks believed the cities on earth were a shadow. The Bible teaches that human wholeness requires human community as of its very essence.

Fourth, whatever is the nature of the restored or achieved union with God, it always has a moral component. Israel cannot fulfill the covenant and live unjustly. It is only the just that are raised from the dead into the holy city or eternal life. The wise man is the one who lives justly. Even the person who ascends through the heavens to be illumined by God does so only to live the just life. Above all, Jesus not only taught the impending arrival of the reign of God, he acted on that basis. "The blind recover their sight, the lame walk, the lepers are made clean, the deaf hear, the dead are raised to life, the poor are hearing the good news" (Lk. 7:22; NEB)—all the time-honored signs of the breaking-in of the Kingdom.

Fifth, a period of testing, even suffering, precedes the achievement of the anticipated union with God. In order for the Hebrews to come into the Promised Land they had to undergo the trials of the wilderness. The scourge of the Assyrians and Babylonians was necessary before the covenant of David would be restored. Martyrdom is the frequent lot of those who look for the resurrection. The very expression "to take up your cross" is a Semitic saying before the time of Jesus. It seems possible that the church's reflection upon the experi ence of Calvary and its relation to Jesus' resurrection can very well have shaped its interpretation of the objective of the religious life and the meaning of the Cross for Christian discipleship. It could be argued that there is a more persistent, clearer case for an expectation of a period of purgatory in the biblical objective than there is for a blissful abode, where we all become like angels, and loved ones are reunited.

CHAPTER THREE

Sharpening the Strategy

There is good evidence for saying that more people have died for the cause of Jesus Christ in the twentieth century than all the previous nineteen centuries combined. Ours is an age of martyrs. I knew one: Janai Luwum, the Archbishop of Uganda. We spent ten days in Dublin together in 1973. He was a large, quiet black man, with a gentle, unassuming presence. I had no premonition of one who would soon "have come through the great tribulation" (Rev. 7:14; UTH). He was almost ordinary—but not quite! What was it that brought him knowingly to give up his life for Christ in a world where most people live only for the moment and for themselves? Unlike the author of Revelation, we have not seen the outcome of his witness. We can only look at what preceded his decision.

I know that Janai Luwum came to his death knowingly, because one of the priests close to him was a student of mine. My student had fled Uganda at the urging of the church there, so that in more peaceful times he might return to lead the Ugandan Christians. He has described for me the last days of the Archbishop and of his own escape literally minutes ahead of those who came to claim his life also. It is strange to hear one discuss his thoughts when he knew that his own Christian witness might at any moment require his violent death. What is it that sustains us in those moments?

There is no doubt that in the church of the first three centuries, where martyrdom was always a possibility even in times of relative peace, the character of discipleship, renewal, and evangelization was shaped by an immediate sense of the end and a vivid remembrance of the objective of the Christian life. The vision of John of Patmos in Revelation, the only apocalyptic book in the New Testament, sought to instill hope in a persecuted church. The frequent appeals to singleness of mind the great fear was of becoming literally "double-souled" or double-minded—by leaders among early Christians is indicative of that purity of intention for which they sought. The imagery of their appeal to renewal was supported by the common vision of Christian and non-Christian alike, that the true end of humanity was union with its creator by means of a spiritual ascent of our minds to the mind of God. How is it that we are not led astray?

I would think that the strength of God comes to someone like Janai Luwum as he sees the future as God sees it: the promise of a life in the community that God rules and where justice prevails. The reality of this vision so excels anything that the world offers that there is very little that can deter us from its pursuit, even death itself. I have no doubt that Janai Luwum and I would describe the details of that vision differently. As I have said repeatedly, time and place shape the details of our objective for the Christian life. But that is not the issue. The issue is that, first, the hope each of us has for the future be so vivid that we are free to bet our life on it, and second, that our objective be consistent with that guiding image that Jesus laid before us in his historical witness.

In this chapter we will identify elements in a strategy of renewal that, when we continue to look to the example of our Lord, lead us to live for the objective that we might be true to Jesus' witness. These elements are constants or intermediate objectives within the repentant intentionality that serve as instruments of transformation and direction. Christian theology quite rightly speaks of Jesus as the primal sacrament of God to the world. But this Jesus is operative in our consciousness only as Christ is able to address us in a manner not solely dependent upon our inner feelings. The very nature of a sacrament is *outward* and *visible,* and so we need to look for concrete constants or identifiable, intermediate objectives in the renewal process that lie outside a personal solipsism.

There are at least seven intermediate objectives that lie within a Christian strategy of renewal that we need to identify and nurture. There is nothing sacred about the number "seven," nor are these objectives exclusive of other possible intermediate objectives. These constants within the repentant intention are drawn from the observation principally of the evangelical awakening of the twelfth and thirteenth centuries, which on the basis of the four indications of effective renewal listed at the end of the first chapter I judge to be a prototypal renewal movement in Christian history. I do not mean to imply that the twelfth and thirteenth centuries were a "golden age." Far from it, they were a time of recurring chaos and confusion, bitter conflict, and sin—just like any other time. The ideals of the Gregorian Reform were only partially realized, but the movement itself did leave its profound imprint upon the evolving consciousness of Western humanity.

It would also be an exaggeration to insist that for true renewal these seven intermediate objectives needed to be equally present to some degree. The measurement of effective renewal has to be left to God, who alone knows the outcome. The purpose here is to give us a measure of distance or objectivity in analyzing effective renewal.

The question is: how does a person come to be so inflamed with the love of God that he or she knowingly *and wisely* risks their life for the sake of the Gospel? The answer lies in the perfection of desire which enables one to look briefly and partially at the world through the eyes of God, to think as God thinks. It is not enough to have the desire. One must persist, possess a singleness of mind, and cultivate a sense of discretion. Otherwise our desire may destroy our freedom and, for that reason, our humanity. A true martyr is not one who enjoys dying for Christ, but one who is willing to die because it is the wiser course of action, even though he prefers to live. " 'Father, if it be thy will, take this cup away from me,' " Jesus prayed. " 'Yet not my will but thine be done' " (Lk. 22:42; NEB).

The Extraordinary within the Ordinary

It is obvious that for us to believe that God shapes our thinking we believe as well that God is present to us. This is easy to say, it is not easy to argue convincingly. I think occasionally of the contest between the prophets of Baal and the Prophet

Elijah on Mount Carmel, where Elijah sets up a test to see whose sacrifice God will call fire to consume. There is the dramatic picture of Elijah mocking the prophets of Baal, " 'Call louder, for he is a god; it may be he is deep in thought, or engaged [possibly a euphemism for being in the act of defecation], or on a journey; or he may have gone to sleep and must be woken up' " (1 Kings 18:27; NEB). What would it be like as a Christian to be put in the same position as Elijah placed the prophets of Baal?

One way we sometimes squirm out of this challenge is by suggesting that our God is present to us in an extraordinary way, not susceptible to common, everyday kinds of observation. God does not light "real fires," only "inner fires." We perceive him with a special faculty—a sixth sense, if you will—or he makes himself known in a different context, perhaps in our dreams as opposed to our reason. In the early nineteen fifties, a British philosopher and agnostic told what came to be called "The Parable of the Gardener." It reduced to absurdity those cosmological arguments for God that defined the "orderer" as one unsusceptible to any kind of verification of existence. There is the easy temptation to divide the world into a sacred realm and a secular realm, as if to say: Christ is lord of salvation history, but not ordinary history; or Jesus is present in our prayers, but not our sex life; or God is interested in speaking to our spiritual feelings but not to the family budget.

The Bible with pretty fair success resists the temptation to divide the world into two: the ordinary and the extraordinary. It reminds us again and again that God is the creator of all and present in all. The familiar words of the psalmist remind us of this fact.

> Where can I escape from thy spirit?
>   Where can I flee from thy presence?
> If I climb up to heaven, thou art there;
> If I make my bed on Sheol, again I find thee.
> If I take my flight to the frontiers of the morning
>   or dwell in the limit of the western sea,
> even there thy hand will meet me
>   and thy right hand will hold me fast.
>   (Ps. 139:7–10; NEB)

No more telling image of Jesus' rejection of the common human tendency to confine the presence of God to "sacred" objects, people, or events is the fact that he ate with sinners, meaning people who did not observe the Law—possibly because they could not afford the leisure it took (e.g., Mt. 9:10– 13). Sinners are just as much a part of God's purpose as anyone else. "God has no favourites" (Acts 10:34; NEB).

This quotation—"God has no favourites"—comes from the story of Peter and the Roman centurion, Cornelius. In the account we are told of Peter's vision, where he is told to eat what the Jews considered unclean. Three times he is told, " 'It is not for you to call profane what God counts clean' " (Acts 10:15; NEB). There is a constant struggle in the New Testament to follow through the implications of the Incarnation and what it says for God's immediate presence to the entire created order.

The church has always had to fight against a false "spiritualism." Certain trends within Hellenism lead us to deny the value or even the reality of the physical world. This has cut the Christian off from his community and his body, and created a spirituality that is an affront to a genuine Christian mysticism, rooted as it must be in the created order. No century, including our own, is exempt from this temptation. While subject to great abuse, one great potential gift of medieval persons was their belief that the created order was translucent. Life was short, brutish, and often cruel; yet amid all of it, the eternal was perceivable in the temporal, the extraordinary within the ordinary.

Richard of St. Victor (d. 1173) had one of the keenest minds of the twelfth century. He spoke of his times. "Through the appearance of visible things she [reason] rises to the knowledge of invisible things, as often as she draws a kind of similitude from one to the other."[1] Even the obscene becomes a cause for vision. For example, the word "monster," describing a distortion of nature, comes from the Latin *monstrare*, meaning "to show" the hand of God. This is quite different from today, when physical abnormalities are often regarded as "proof" that God is dead!

An Institutional Carrier

Schism and sectarianism are the enemies of renewal. Jesus was not a schismatic nor was he a sectarian. Institutions that *transcend our enthusiasm* not only keep us honest, they provide a freedom that avoids the pitfalls of license or tyranny. Freedom is the function of a defined space. It is that "room for repentance," of which the author of Wisdom spoke, where we do not have to be "everybody," but we have space to be "somebody else." The temptation of the person who believes himself filled with the Spirit is either to lapse into a religious psychosis (as with the cult of Jim Jones in Guyana in 1979), the dissolution of the conscious self evoked by anomie; or, far more likely, it is a temptation before the threat of anomie, to be tyrannized by the need for absolute control. This is why most sects seek to regulate every aspect of life. One cannot be free because there are no identifiable borders at which, if we let go, our freedom would stop. The fantasy is that we will "fall over the edge" and God will not stop us.

The borders within an institution are more than the experience of its members, they are the memory of that institution. They provide a context where the meaning of the presence of Spirit can exist without our direct effort. We are liberated from the fear that a loss of control will end in the dissolution of the integrity of that meaning. The individual or the group of like-minded individuals is not solely responsible for the knowledge that God speaks to us, but can enjoy a collaborative, evolving perception of his Word.

For Jesus, the institution that carried his movement was the Jewish cult, the synagogue, and the Temple. We have no reason to assume that he was not regular in his attendance at both. The centuries of Hebrew learning that formed the memory of the synagogue and Temple and enriched the lives of their participants made possible the preaching of Jesus and the initial expansion of the church in a way that fulfilled humanity's longing and spoke to their expectations. There was much debate in the early church as to how important the Jewish Law was to the Christian community. The account in Matthew 5:17–19, which is the strident voice of the Jewish Christian church in opposition to the Greek gentile church, is more theologically interesting than the debate in Acts 15:4–21—but there is no doubt that the church is a child of the Jewish cult, whatever account you read.

What the institution carries, which is more important than conceptual systems and ethical prescriptions, is the symbolic life of a people. The Word of God is first verbalized in this deep language, ambiguous and subtle, yet powerful. It is this symbolic world that shapes the intention of our minds in much larger ways than the fine point of any system (with all apologies to Matthew's Gospel and its obsession with every letter and stroke of the pen of the Law [Mt. 5:18]).

This point is well, if subtly, made by the Fourth Evangelist when he puts in the mouth of Jesus these words: "The wind, where it wills it blows, and the sound of it you hear, but you do not know whence it comes and where it goes" (Jn. 3:8; UTH). The verse is meant to be an enigma, particularly when Jesus goes on to say that this mysterious experience of hearing the Word and being free is characteristic of those born of the Spirit (or wind). It puzzles Nicodemus; and yet Jesus chides him for not understanding, saying, "You are the teacher of Israel" (Jn. 3:10), you above all should be steeped in the symbolic memory that gives you a way of comprehending.

Another analogue for this point is an electrical transformer. The energy generated by the Spirit in the church needs to be transformed into a visible form of energy *throughout* the ecclesiastical system. Otherwise such energy "overloads" parts of the system and there is a breakdown. The Church of England in the eighteenth century is a sad example. The institutional carrier is the "transformer" of the energy of the Spirit.

The institution is necessary. From the end of the tenth century until the beginning of the fourteenth, the carriers of renewal in the Western church were the religious orders. They were well-fitted for the purpose. Beginning with the Cluniac reform of the Benedictines, which petered out at the end of the eleventh century, followed by the remarkable Cistercian movement that became regrettably engrossed a hundred years later in the wool trade, and ending with the coming of the friars, renewal was protected from the renewers. Their enthusiasm fed the church; it did not spend itself on some lonely mountain of apocalyptic hope or limit itself to the company of a few elect.

Parabolic Language

Jesus lacked common sense, a lack all evangelists should share. Common sense is "what everybody knows." It is the collective intention of a society. The call to repentance, *metanoia,* is, as we have already said, a summons to change our way of thinking, to see our experience in a new way. *Metanoia* is the enemy of common sense. Renewal requires a way of speaking that challenges the old assumptions, cracks open our world of meaning, and enables us to construct a new reality.

A parable is a story with an unusual twist. Most parables surprise us. They subvert our common sense world. They do not fit into our categories. Who is so foolish as to run the risk of losing ninety-nine sheep, just to find one (Lk. 15:4–7)? Who is it that would not feel cheated if he worked ten hours and was paid no more than those who worked one hour (Mt. 20.1 10)? Who is it that would not side with the hardworking elder son, when his father rewards the prodigal son who has gone out and wasted all his money (Lk. 15:11–32)? These illustrate only the more obvious subversions by Jesus' parables of society's time-honored notions of truth. Parables engage us at the level of paradox. Jesus is himself a parable. He does not fit. He keeps us off balance. In so doing he and his parables convey a shock to the imagination, which spurs the intuition into action. The temptation to domesticate the image of God in accordance with the categories of the culture is confronted, and we clutch something different. So much renewal fails in this intermediate objective and consequently is not really renewal.

Paul says, "The crucified Christ is a scandal to the Jews and foolishness or stupidity to the Gentiles" (1 Cor. 1:23; UTH). Somehow, the power of the Gospel lies in appearing a scandal, foolish, or both. It is a test of our preaching.

The twelfth century was a time of literary flowering. The set of the medieval mind was toward the parabolic. It was filled with everything from romantic tales of heroes to scatological

animal stories—a sort of unexpurgated Uncle Remus or Win-
nie the Pooh. Medieval folk never allowed the ideals set forth in
the sagas of Chrétien de Troyes and others to hide from him
the irony of human pretension described in the fabliaux—the
English derivative is "fable"—short, usually comic, frankly
coarse, and often cynical tales told in verse. As the son of an
Old French scholar I was regaled with them in my youth, our
family cats were named after some of the principal characters,
and their moral points were driven home. Human fables were
not side by side with romantic tales of mystical missions. The
total effect was to call into question all pretense to identify our
knowledge with God's wisdom. There was something delight-
fully grotesque about twelfth- and thirteenth-century literature.

Any literature genre that is *grotesque* (i.e., pertaining to
grottoes) in the generic sense—the word comes from the early
observation of paleolithic cave paintings, of fanciful and bizarre
human and animal forms, which appeared to modern eyes as
ugly, even absurd caricatures—has a way of touching the
deeper meaning within the human intention. It not only turns
the conceptual system upside down, it provokes to awareness
the symbolic world that lies unconscious within us. This is why
profound prayer awakens the erotic within us. But the erotic is
finally and fundamentally the longing for God.

Theological Development

Jesus was an eschatological prophet, not a theologian. This is
not to prefer eschatological prophets over theologians. They
need one another. We cannot expect, however, to look at what
we uncover about the life of Jesus and justify the necessity of
theology within the strategy of renewal. Theology was left
to Jesus' followers, and they did not waste any time in getting
to it.

Theology is necessary to make judgments about what is true
and, consequently, how we ought to act. It is the discipline of
thinking consciously about our religious experience, giving it a
rational order, which provides clarification and the possibility
for accurate sharing. Theology frees us from the tyranny of

religious emotion and focuses the diffused vision of religious intuition. It delivers us from the illusion that God reveals himself only to the individual heart (in the modern sense of "heart"). Theology does not prevent the spiritual life, it is the middle term between the imaginative exploration of the data of our senses and the quiet, fixed gaze upon the mystery of divinity.

The first-century church was faced with the question of beginning to understand who the Jesus they experienced was. They did not come to any universal agreement. The Jewish Christians had one idea, the Greek Jewish Christians another, and the gentile Christians a third. We are still arguing today. But the New Testament never suggested it was *sufficient* just to feel good about Jesus or to "say Jesus is Lord," even if we were "under the influence of the Holy Spirit" (1 Cor. 12:3; NEB). Our feelings are readily deceived, and all kinds of people mouth the words *Kyrios Iēsous* who have clearly rejected the Holy Spirit. We have to make reasoned judgments in order that we may discern the truth of our feelings and our confession.

The focus of theology is in *making* the judgments, not in rote memory of past judgments. If the apostolic church had depended upon the previous theories about the eschatological prophet prior to Jesus, it would have been hopelessly bogged down. It had to speak imaginatively and reasonably from its culture to the future. Theology is an ever-continuing collaborative *process*, historically conditioned, which must build on the past and never expect to say the last word.

The fear of theology many people have comes in theology's judgment upon our certainties, its lack of emotional appeal, and the fact that theologians sometimes belie even their best theology. Good theology never lets us rest and never protects us from our own self-doubt. It is rightly suspicious of personal feeling. It makes us "come public" in history and in place. Theology is the enemy of privatism, that pious solipsism that says, "If it makes me feel so good, it must be true." Renewal is not "feeling good." It is being illumined by the *Logos,* "reason," the Fourth Evangelist's word for the Christ. The *Logos* of John 1:1–14 is undoubtedly related to the Wisdom of the Jewish sage, who had no trust of feeling, and perhaps to the Stoic *logos,* the rational principle of the universe.

The twelfth and thirteenth centuries saw the rise of scholasticism, a highly creative theological system built upon the Christian past, with the assistance of Aristotelian philosophy. The early leaders in the evangelical awakening of this time, particularly the hierarchy, were not enthusiastic supporters of the scholastic philosophers. The spiritual masters of the period attacked the Schoolmen. The challenge of reason both to the rationalizations of the people in command and to the unexamined enthusiasm of the pious always evokes a negative evaluation of theology. But the truth is that the energy of the Gregorian Reform would have been dissipated without the clarity and course of action given it by the new theology. The evangelical awakening of this age and every age requires for renewal, new thinking.

The scholastic synthesis lasted very little beyond the thirteenth century. After that it never really expressed *as a system* the horizon of Christian experience. The more it receded into history the "safer" it became. It is fascinating to observe how the heterodoxy of a century or so ago becomes the orthodoxy of today. The church appropriately does build upon scholasticism, just as it built upon the work of Augustine of Hippo and Augustine upon those who preceded him back to the first theologians.

An Ascesis with a Purpose

Ascetical theology as a disciplined body of theory does not emerge in Christian history until the early sixteenth century. The word *askēsis* appears only once in the New Testament (Acts 24:16) in its verbal form. It means "to practice," "to train," or "to exercise." Its obvious application is to the athlete. Paul liked athletic metaphors and, whereas he never uses the word *askēsis,* it is certainly implicit in a passage such as this: "Do you not know that in the stadium all the runners run, but only one gets the prize? Run thus in order that you might win! But the contestant must be disciplined in all things" (1 Cor. 9:24–25; UTH).

The point that Paul is making is that we need so to order our life that we achieve the objective of Christian discipline—what he calls the "immortal crown" (1 Cor. 9:25; UTH). In the speech Luke in Acts attributes to Paul before Felix, the governor, Paul says that he trains to keep an untrammeled consciousness, *aproskopos suneidēsin*. The Greek can mean as well a "clear conscience," but in the sense that moral awareness is the result of a single mind, open to the transcendent reason. The adjective is fascinating. It is built upon a Greek root, *skopos*, meaning a "goal" to which one continually looks. In the fourth century A.D., Gregory of Nyssa uses this word to name the goal of the ascetical life.

The point here is clear. The Christian renewed life is neither one of license nor of discipline for its own sake. What is required is an intention or structure of consciousness that looks steadily toward the goal and, in order to do that, keeps one in spiritual training. The whole history of the church can be written in terms of how this was to be done, which may evoke some regret at rather sad practices that were followed for the sake of the "immortal crown."

In the twelfth century the discussion of ascesis was relatively healthy and clear. We owe this perhaps more than anything else to the Victorines, a group of priests who, while not monastics, lived a common rule at a place named St. Victor, on the edge of medieval Paris. It was they who developed a three-step way to God, of the imagination or the "sensibles," reason or the "intelligibles," and understanding or the "intellectibles," that became the basis of much spiritual theology. It was Thomas Gallus of St. Victor who subtly changed the goal of Christian training from secret "knowledge" (as taught by the fourth- and fifth-century Eastern mystics) to "love." Since all mystic experience imparts knowledge, what Gallus means is more akin to illumination than emotion. The definition of the person contemplating the Truth, which is God, in almost every spiritual writer from the twelfth century depends on the Victorines. Richard of St. Victor described it as that "tranquil stability of mind, when the mind is totally gathered within itself and is unalterably fixed on the one longing for eternity"[2]

It is greatly to be regretted that subsequent centuries either lost the hope of the goal and made the discipline of ascesis an end in itself—a duty to make us "tougher"—or reduced the goal of the disciplined life, love, to a warm private feeling of acceptance by God. What Richard meant by *love* is the "longing for truth and the supreme good" or the "love of justice." Richard was a product of centuries of Christian spiritual thought, which believed that there is a double ascent of the rational soul to God: that as the mind is purified and illumined by the divine wisdom so is it filled with virtue to live the just life.

Moral Seriousness

It is essential that the intermediate objectives of the renewal strategy work together. In particular, it should be obvious that theological clarity and ascetical discipline lead to a moral seriousness. Otherwise we are liable to fall into the trap of moralism. Moralism is the concern for right living that is the result of a fearful attitude toward our own inner world of feelings, symbols, and contradictions. It expresses itself by the need to identify right and wrong in behavioral rather than intentional categories. It fails to distinguish degrees of sin or the orientation of the sinner. It seeks to maintain a rigid control over behavior, rather than to enable people to think clearly and to seek illumination in particular cases (i.e., it lacks a necessary casuistry). It has only a primitive moral theology, if any at all. Moralism suffers from reductionism. It focuses on the "warm sins," those pertaining to sex, eating, drinking, and anger, because such feelings are the most individually threatening and also the most self-evident.

The Pharisees were moralists. Paul never really overcame his Pharisaical training. He is given to easy comments about "the works of the flesh" and sin lists that draw heavily on the warm side (e.g., Gal. 5:19–21). He values control highly. He did not develop his theological and ascetical insights fully to their moral implications.

Jesus in the Gospels comes off better. The focus of moral concern is on the care of the poor, the suffering, and those who mourn, as found in the Beatitudes. It is difficult to tell whether the definition of lust in Matthew 5:27–28 is part of Jesus' thinking or of the Palestinian church in its battle with the Hellenists—the notion that to look upon a woman is equivalent to having actual intercourse is rabbinical in origin—but it does not appear to be central to the concern of Jesus for the impending reign of God. His attitude toward the Sabbath, Luke's story of the words to the penitent thief, and the addition to the Fourth Gospel concerning the woman taken in adultery are more consistent with his preaching of repentance (Mk. 2:27; Lk. 23:39–43; Jn. 7:53–8:11). This fits better with the God who "sent forth his son into the world not in order that he might judge the world, but that the world might be saved by him" (Jn. 3:17; UTH); and it is more congruent with the Lord who feeds the masses from his abundance because they are hungry.

This is not to say the Jesus of the Gospels lacks moral conviction. But it is important to understand the nature of such conviction. Current moral theology makes an important distinction between objective and subjective sin, which is helpful for this discussion. Objective sin is the term applied to individual acts of rebellion against God, which we inevitably commit. Moralism is overly concerned with objective sin; and, because it is inevitable that we commit such sins, it reduces the area of its concern to those that some are fortunate to avoid by trying hard. ("If you are tempted to commit fornication, take cold baths.") Subjective sin is the condition of our intention so that it is directed away from God. This is obviously a much more serious situation and must be the concern of moral thought. Repentance makes sense when related to subjective sin.

The twelfth century saw a concerted effort to overcome the callous sinful intention particularly of the clergy. Simony and concubinage were two particular concerns, although it is doubtful the church had much success in overcoming either until the Roman Catholic Reformation of the sixteenth century. The seven corporeal acts of mercy, the first six of which were derived from Matthew 25:31–46, caught the imagination of the church, judging from the art of the period. The hospital movement took on new life in the twelfth century with the formation of hospital guilds as well as several orders devoted to tending the wounded and ill on the crusades, including the Knights Hospitaller of St. John and the Hospitallers of St. Lazarus.

The notion of chivalry has, unfortunately, been filtered through Don Quixote and the novels of Sir Walter Scott. It was actually an effort promoted by the church to provide some element of compassion, particularly the protection of the poor and the weak, amid the irrationality and barbarism of war. War was the expected, common pastime of medieval man. To temper this endemic disease was the goal of chivalry. It was neither as silly nor romantic an ideal as we sometimes think.

The content that another age gives to justice does not gainsay its belief that spiritual renewal for it, as well as for our age, is evidenced in a moral seriousness or it is not renewal. The issue is never why Paul accepted slavery or St. Louis (IX) killed Moslems to the glory of God. It is a matter of whether a new sensitivity to human suffering arises from our repentance.

Leadership

Pope Gregory VII (1073–1085) was driven from Rome by the Holy Roman emperor shortly before his death. The man who gave his name to the evangelical awakening of the twelfth and thirteenth centuries died in exile. He is reported to have said on his deathbed, "I have loved justice and hated iniquity— and so I died in exile." Gregory had notable precedent. The same thing happened to our Lord. He wept over Jerusalem and died outside its walls.

Many so-called leaders of renewal have been pied pipers, leading people out to some mountaintop in the promise of a peace that cannot be. The appropriate leadership for renewal does not take us "out" at all. It leads us "in" and "against" and "through." New Testament authors pictured the conflict between good and evil all of us have experienced as a great cosmic battle between light and darkness. The imagery came from Persia, no doubt, but the reality is universal. The Cross was to them the critical battle in that cosmic struggle, and Jesus set the Cross as his goal, his *skopos*.

Renewal leadership needs to have all the previous six inter-mediate objectives as part of its equipment and have the courage to live by them, as well as to live through them for the Gospel. We must not pretend that there is no personal appeal in renewal. There obviously is and should be. But personal appeal avoids being a "personality cult" when the leadership risks the hatred of humankind for the sake of the Gospel. Leadership does not entertain, it confronts; it does not seek popularity, it offends the self-righteous; it does not reconcile until we know the seriousness of our sin.

The high point perhaps of the Gregorian Reform is captured in two very different men: Francis of Assisi (1182–1226) and Pope Innocent III (1198–1216). Neither one of them was really a very attractive person. Certainly Francis would be considered a bit "mad," since he took the Gospel quite literally. He was obsessed with the meaning for the world of the Passion of Christ and ended his life, lying on the earth, welcoming "Sister death." His priorities were quite different from those of most of us.

Innocent III was an intelligent, aristocratic power politician in the cause of Christ. The fourth Lateran Council (1215), which he called, was in many ways the most significant council in medieval times. It was an effort to organize the church, to temper superstition, to channel enthusiasm, and to establish ideals of commitment. This is the council that opposed the excessively literal notions of Christ's presence in the sacrament, that stated there would be no more new rules for religious orders, and that required priests to desist from wearing green and red hose. (This should say something about colored clerical shirts in our day!)

The most difficult of the intermediate objectives to describe, much less to achieve, within the strategy of renewal is leader-ship. We caricature those from the past we would love, such as Francis, or hate, such as Innocent III. We look for the clay feet of our present-day leaders. There are many today who aspire to leadership, but seduction comes early. To hark back to the beginning of this chapter, what more difficult decision is there than that Janai Luwum must make. He comes to that moment of decision when he knows either he can live out his life a respected prelate of the church or he can die to be recalled as a martyr—and then realizes, like T. S. Eliot's Thomas à Becket, that he is very likely to be doing "the right thing for the wrong reason." Leadership is not a matter of acting out an intention to do the right thing. It is a matter of guiding the intention of the church so that it may truly look toward the impending reign of God and move toward living in that Kingdom.

A Summary Reflection

A reflection such as this upon the first, twelfth, or any century can be very misleading. We pick and choose what we want to see and leave aside what does not fit our expectations or prejudices. Perhaps the only value in this exercise is that it imparts substance to the point we want to make about our times. But in giving substance we can also make further discovery. One concluding thought along this line is helpful.

The twelfth and thirteenth centuries witnessed a chastened, but real, emergence of the feminine within religious and cultural experience. All the spontaneity, ambiguity, passion, creativity, and risk that is carried by that symbol arose. It gave an energy to the life of that period that was not neat, was sometimes excessive, and created opposing forces of intellectual speculation and repression. This was manifested in two sets of phenomena.

One was the appearance starting in southern France, of the "courts of love." This was a genuine, positive pursuit of romantic love. It marked a pivotal point in the evolution of human consciousness, since previously romantic love had often been considered a form of insanity. And it certainly did not occur to the people of this time that romantic love should be a motivation for marriage. It could be a source of self-discovery. At its roots, it was an earthy, erotic enjoyment of passion. More reflectively, it was celebrated in song, the strange companionship of love and death, as in Wagner's "Liebestod," in *Tristan und Isolde,* and as today in "country music" in America. Passion takes two forms: joy and suffering, redeemed by the Passion of Christ.

The other indication of the evidence of the emergence into consciousness of the feminine symbol was the burgeoning cult of the Blessed Virgin Mary. Cathedrals were named for her, such as Notre Dame (i.e., "Our Lady") in Paris, some of the great Marian hymns date from this time, and the various devotions arose to the Blessed Virgin that became the mark of Roman Catholic piety. Doctrines such as the Immaculate Conception came to be popularly believed at this time, and the relics of the Blessed Virgin attracted attention. There is no reason to take offense at what seems obvious; namely, that the need for divinity to possess those qualities of compassion, nurture, and even seductiveness that we associate with the feminine were projected on the Mother of God. Perhaps she is a fitting carrier of this human need.

It is entirely possible that an intermediate outcome of the strategy of true renewal is an emergence of the feminine symbol into the intentionality of the church. It undoubtedly would take different forms at different periods in history—perhaps there would be examples within radical Protestantism of the sixteenth and seventeenth centuries—but the basic constellation of spontaneity, ambiguity, creativity, passion, and risk will be there, if renewal is genuine.

CHAPTER FOUR

An Anthropology of Renewal

Jeremy Rifkin, a member of the Sojourner community in Washington, D.C., in his recent book, *The Emerging Order*, calls for a "second Reformation" or a "third Great Awakening" in America. He is drawing upon our Protestant memory to challenge us to come into a new consciousness, to repent, to be renewed. His point is that the consumer mentality of America, based upon illusions of infinite supplies of energy and raw materials, can no longer sustain us. We must, Rifkin explains, find a new consciousness of conservation and balance between human desire and distribution of resources.

The hope for such a new consciousness, according to Rifkin, lies in the charismatic movement and the evangelical awakening. Together, he believes, they offer the possibility of the second Reformation. He is cognizant of the fact that the charismatic movement has caught the Spirit and made it manifest in our world, but he also knows that the movement lacks that theological clarity and coherence necessary to shape a different vision of reality that can enable us to live in a world of increasing scarcity without resorting to nuclear holocaust and/ or fascism. As he says, "If the Charismatics are beginning to break the eggs, it is the evangelicals who will have to make the omelet."[1]

There is much in Rifkin's analysis that is convincing, even if the news is grim. His diagnosis of the dilemma that faces the Western world is accurate, despite the "whistling in the dark" of the advocates of unbridled consumerism. The prevailing American consciousness that has grown and deepened over the last two hundred years leads nowhere but to disaster. It is also true that elements within the charismatic movement have recalled Christians to an awareness that the Spirit moves among us. There are problems, however, with Rifkin's unqualified evocation of the images of the Reformation and the Great Awakening from America's Protestant memory. *This is because it is just such images and their poverty in respect to the depth of human consciousness that contributed to the trouble we are in now.* From the sixteenth century, Western Christianity tended, first, to reduce the articulation of the Gospel to rational categories and, second, in reaction supplanted reason with sentiment. There was a consistent retreat from the profundity of the numinous.

Rifkin argues that in times of national growth a culture needs to affirm freedom; in times of national retrenchment it should seek order. We are now entering a time of retrenchment. But what is the nature of order? A clear comprehensive outline of the relationship between God and humanity, together with its implications for Christian living, would be an example of such order. Rifkin believes that reformed Christianity, represented in America by evangelicalism, provides this theological order. Such a theology is to be imposed—the word is mine, but it is hard to escape the impression—upon the American consciousness, once the charismatic movement has made us aware of God's presence among us. The alternatives seem to be: order or chaos. Chaos rises up within, order comes from without. What one should seek as a Christian is a good order.

This is a thoroughly understandable approach to any theory heavily dependent upon the sixteenth century. Whether or not our tradition is Roman Catholic, Reformed, Lutheran, or Anglican, it has passed through that century's inordinate and myopic fondness for reason. Only the radical Protestants in the sixteenth century protested, and they came to a sad end as the result of a very rational suppression. In the sixteenth century we divorced the beautiful from the good, and behaved as if by force of logic we could achieve the knowledge of God and his will. In the nineteenth century, disappointed with the observable results of our rational theology, we strove for assurance through the manipulation of religious fervor in American revivalism. Be it the Reformation or the Great Awakening, we have moved away in the last four hundred years from an appreciation for what truly shapes human consciousness.

Although there is much that Rifkin says well, the unfortunate analogue to his solution and, even more, to those who unthinkingly follow in his train, is the French army at the beginning of World War II. When the Germans surrendered in 1918, the French moved out of their trenches. When the Germans attacked once again in 1930, the French, having mobilized for the same war as before, moved back into their fortified lines on the German border, only to find themselves fighting a different war. Trench warfare had become a thing of the past for the Germans. We know the result: the French were quickly outflanked, and in nine months were defeated.

What is the appropriate strategy of renewal? What is our mission? Our awareness of the nature of human consciousness—of the war we are fighting—is essential to answering these questions. In many ways Rifkin's objective is the Gospel truth; but his strategy fails to take into account, at least to the extent that he would call for a second Reformation or a third Great Awakening, the depth of human consciousness.

The Deep Memory

Why do people behave as they do? So much of what they do does not make sense.

I know a woman, who, when I first met her was married to the most unlikely husband one could imagine. Not only did they have nothing in common, there was no evidence that they lived in the same world. A few months later, she came to me to tell me she was going to seek a divorce. When asked why she had married him in the first place, all she could say was, "I don't know; it doesn't make sense."

Why did Nixon's committee for the election of the president break in at Watergate, committing an illegal act, when to the most casual observer he had the election "in the bag"? No one seems to know; it does not make sense.

Why, in the winter of 1980, did Russia invade Afghanistan, a remote and relatively weak country, costing Russia billions of dollars, a tarnished image, the support of the Moslem world, and the threat of nuclear war? Despite the theories, it does not really make sense—probably not even to the Russians.

None of these actions nor most of our important decisions make sense if we depend for their explanation upon some rational, conceptual analysis. The direction of the momentum of human action is generated and channeled by something other than reason. Reason, by which I mean an ordered, logical appraisal of the situation, the need, the desired objective, and the means necessary to achieve that objective, free from emotion and intuition, has its essential place. This is not an argument for or a description of man's fundamental irrationality. It is to say that the dominant images of our intentionality or directed consciousness and its subsequent behavior does not belong to the upper reaches of our memory.

Picture the memory as a deep, glacial lake. The first few feet of water are warm and filled with the reflected light of day. The deeper one goes into the lake, the colder and darker the water. At these depths there are springs of pure water that feed the lake and impart to it a particular quality. Reason operates at the surface of the lake of our memories. There is a consciousness, however, that draws on the deeper levels of that lake of memories that is quite different from reason, but by no means inferior to it. Behavior that does not seem to make sense at a logical level is not a result of surrendering to chaos, but is the effect of a deeper level of intention than the conceptual constructs with which we think we operate.

A number of therapists—particularly those associated with Virginia Satir and her communication theory—have developed an understanding of the process of therapy that engages people at the level of their *metaphoral* world, not their conceptual world. In other words, they go deep within that glacial lake of memories. While the conceptual world is called the *surface structure,* the metaphorical world is named the *deep structure.* Ultimately, humanity's interpretation of the forces of good and evil within its world and of the action required for

survival and growth stems from this deep structure. Richard
Bandler and John Grinder write:

> Individuals who find themselves in therapy and wish help in
> changing are typically there because they feel that they do
> not have enough choices, that they are unable to behave
> other than they do. Furthermore, however peculiar their
> behavior may appear to us, it makes sense in their model of
> the world.

> When the therapist has succeeded in involving the client in
> recovering the Deep Structure—the full linguistic represen-
> tation [of his experience] the next step is to challenge that
> Deep Structure in such a way as to enrich it.[2]

The deep structure or memory does not refer to the source
or boundaries of a shared memory—i.e., personal, communal,
historical, or archetypical memory—but to the character of the
images within our memory. We know what it means to remember the multiplication tables. Everyone of us complains about
not being able to remember names. Some of us went to Sunday
School where we were required to remember Bible verses in the
theory that this made us better Christians. My wife does not
trust her memory even for cooking recipes she has done
hundreds of times. These all pertain to the surface memory, to
which we have ready access and of whose successes and failures
we are very much aware. The deep is not nearly so ready of
access, and we are generally unaware of how it shapes our
action.

Clues to the deep memory include those with whom we fall
in love. I do not say "with whom we *choose* to fall in love,"
because it is not a matter of rational choice, and for this cause
ancient humanity, who believed that to be human is to be
rational, considered romantic love a disease. When I had been
married less than a year, I cut my finger very badly while
carving some bread. I cried out to my wife, "Quick, Mother, get
a bandage." An understandable association? Maybe. But
twenty-five years later it dawned on me that my wife looked
more like my mother than either of my sisters. I slowly became
aware that much that I had laid on her over the years was really

appropriate for my mother. Of course, sometimes we fall in love with someone the exact opposite of the parent of the opposite sex for the same metaphorical reasons.

Another clue are the things we laugh at or weep over. There is an old story about the man who takes his friend to a jokester's club. During dinner someone calls out "109," and everyone breaks up laughing. Someone else cries "78," and it brings down the house. This is followed by a voice yelling "34," and a sly giggle moves through the room. The friend asks his host, "What is all this about?" "Why," he replies, "we have been meeting for years and we have all the available jokes memorized and numbered. To save time and energy we find it easier just to call out the numbers." His friend pondered this marvel and thought he might try it. "Thirty-six," he called out. There was dead silence. His host turned to his embarrassed friend, "You just never could tell a joke, could you?"

Of course, the humor in this story—if there is any—is that we know that it contradicts the essence of a joke, which is in the telling of a story. The story reaches into the deep memory and touches that which we perceive at that level to be incongruous, best handled by laughter. The alternative response to the incongruity of life's metaphors is horror. In this sense the ghost story has much in common with the joke, and obscene humor is perhaps the most powerful in that it evokes those fundamental incongruities centering in our sexual metaphors.

The metaphors of the deep memory beget stories. They arise in our dreams. I had a recurring nightmare as a young child of an airplane falling on me. It can be related both to an incident in the waking world and in my childhood soul. This nightmare is still part of my story and I dream it once again from time to time, as my own inner journey in dialogue with the external environment seems to require.

Folk tales and fairy stories, of course, are expressions of a communal, perhaps even archetypical, deep memory. Long before they were recorded in writing and gathered by such persons as the brothers Grimm, they were shared as elaborated by the community storytellers. The very process of telling elicited from the people and reinforced the metaphors of their world and enabled them to live them. Foolish third sons, evil queens, lovely princesses, princes changed into beasts, wise kings, and wood sprites of questionable morality all form a part of the metaphorical world of humankind.

Such stories find their profoundest expression in the great myths, the true stories of the relation of God and humanity, which are part of the essential ingredient of religion. One definition of religion is that it is a system of symbols or metaphors that provide a means of so representing the response to the ultimate questions of human nature and destiny that we are able to live with purpose and hope. It is doubtful that most of us are aware of our symbol system, much less its narrative expressions, our myths. But this does not deny their existence, only our control of them.

Freedom is a function of an enriched deep memory. People seek counseling therapy because they feel life provides little room for them. The fact that their options are limited is a result of an improverished deep memory. This point implies that repentance is a change or expansion of consciousness at the level of the deep memory. The truth that is Christ engages our deep memory. He becomes the dominant metaphor. This is one way of understanding those familiar verses, " 'If you dwell within the revelation I have brought, you are indeed my disciples; you shall know the truth and the truth will set you free' " (Jn. 8:31–32; NEB).

The Social Drama

For some generations it has been almost axiomatic in the social sciences that human behavior is a function of societal norms or expectations. Every social system, it is said, seeks to maintain equilibrium and therefore devises means to punish deviations from its norms and to sanction or reward the fulfillment of its expectations. In this view, until recently, culture was considered a servant of society, whose institutions defined human existence. The individual is an expression of the social fact, an empty cipher apart from what society makes him. To be human is to be socialized. The alternative is to be a subhuman, living out one's biologically programed destiny.

Religion, particularly ritual, serves in this theory to legitimate at the highest level the social norms.

This theory has been challenged in recent years. There is evidence that culture is not dependent upon society; there are social systems in which equilibrium does not exist, and they not only survive, but prosper; humanity insists upon living beyond its socialization; and ritual somehow does more than assure the society that it is right in doing what it thinks right. There is a certain effervescence to culture, a humanity that lies outside our institutions. It is seen in times of disaster or is discovered among oppressed peoples. In other words, our experience of the human community cannot be exhaustively explained by a closed social theory, which allows with difficulty for the new. Revelation remains a constant possibility.

One description of this dimension of human life that will not fall within those social norms is called *the social drama.* When an institution, such as a parish church, is in crisis and everything collapses, what happens when as a matter of conscience we can no longer conform to the dictates of normative social behavior? It would appear that our life is a process, a flow of experience, which takes on form at both a surface and a deep level. Societal norms operate at the surface, engaging in various interactions between persons, institutions, and events in a harmonic and predictable fashion. Religion, at this level, does serve to legitimate the expected behavior. These interactions, sanctioned by the civil religion, are called *social enterprises.*

There is, however, a deep level of flow within the process that bears the shape of certain root metaphors. It is the nature of a metaphor, of course, to identify one thing in terms of something else, more immediate to our knowing. For example, "Jesus is Lord." The word we translate "Lord," *kyrios,* was a common Greek word for a person of authority, which came to be a form of respectful address, as the word "sir." At the deep level of the social process, there is an interaction between the terms of a metaphor that generates an energy and motivation that challenges the surface process and never allows the social system to settle into a static equilibrium. In other words, there is a dynamic to the deep flow that channels the movement of the society as a whole. The source of this dynamic flow lies generally beneath the surface of the system.

The interaction within the deep process is the social drama. It becomes evident in the life of a people when the harmonic, normative process within a social system fails. There is a breach in the norm-governed social relations, a crisis supervenes, we fall back on the fundamental metaphors of the deep process for new insight, and then this insight is incorporated in a new set of social norms. The social drama is a reflective process, in which a group takes cognizance and possibly questions its own behavior in relation to its own values. The "rhetoric" of the social drama is drawn from the images and metaphors that make up the cultural resources of the deep memory.

The social drama, a theory that renders operative the notion of the deep memory in our life together, provides a means for looking back at Jeremy Rifkin's thesis in order both to build upon it and to sharpen our criticism. Rifkin is predicting, with the increasing scarcity of energy and raw materials, a breach within our normative process. The social enterprise of production and consumption will collapse. His solution is a revamped normative social process, an order imposed that comes out of Reformed Theology. Even with Rifkin's revision of that theology, however, this will not work. When a conflict situation arises, we will inevitably fall back on the social drama, which is an acting out of the root metaphors or the deep memory of the people. From there will arise a surface process, with different norms and a new social enterprise.

At the same time, I do not have all that much confidence in the deep memory of America as a whole. Whatever our national metaphors may be, they seem to generate a persistent paranoia, a tendency to violence, racism, sexism, countered principally by the liberal illusion. There is a serious unwillingness to look deep within the communal self and confront the dark side of the national consciousness. We behave like embittered adolescents, angered because our idols were found to have clay feet. Our creativity is stifled. We are obsessed with ourselves and our own "authenticity," incapable of really "losing ourselves." We need to attend to our deep memory and its expression in the social drama.

One does not attend to the social drama by ignoring it and shopping for a new system, Evangelical, Lutheran, Roman Catholic, or Anglican. An alternative lies in an appreciation for what is called *performance.* Performance provides a source and reinforcement of those root metaphors that emerge as the rhetoric of the social drama. Performance is a means of making the deep memory available to us for decision and action. It avoids the "dehydration" of life by reducing everything to the surface memory.

> The wishes and emotions, the personal and collective goals and strategies, even the situational vulnerabilities, weariness and mistakes are lost in the attempt to "objectify" and produce an aseptic theory of human behavior modelled essentially on eighteenth century "scientific" axioms of belief about mechanical causality.[3]

Liturgy is a form of performance. It has become almost axiomatic in some circles to disavow the value of liturgy as a tactic of evangelization. Even Roman Catholic scholars remind us that one gathers about the pulpit before one gathers about the font. What is the evidence for this? If we understand evangelization as including the nurturing process, rather than one step along the way, we will see that there can be no sequential, logical pattern established. Furthermore, if we properly understand the function of preaching, we will know that it is an element in performance and speaks to the deep memory. What is important at this point is to see the centrality of performance and the social drama to the strategy of renewal. We need to think about those ways in which the mission of the church can engage the human consciousness at the point of its metaphorical world in order that the social drama may be informed by the Gospel.

One illustration of the social drama from the twelfth century is the martyrdom of Thomas à Becket. Becket was the great hero of the evangelical awakening of the twelfth and thirteenth centuries as it affected England. We may briefly recall that his appointment as archbishop of Canterbury by Henry II of England was a ploy on the part of the king to unify the control of the state and the church in England under his own hand. It backfired in 1164 when Becket refused to go along with Henry's policies as set forth in the Constitutions of Clarendon. The conflict disrupted the normative process in the realm, and Becket's course was set to play out that social drama shaped by the metaphor of the Cross. From 1164 he was destined for martyrdom.

It seems reasonable to say that Henry II's drinking buddy, Thomas à Becket, was seized by the Gospel where it counted: in the deep memory. He was a changed, repentant man. The strategy of renewal that characterized the Gregorian Reform was effective; the royal co-conspirator had become a martyr for Christ. What was it that brought about the change? The performance of the duties of archbishop? The daily performance of the Eucharist? His performance as the reformer from the see of Peter? Perhaps all of these and more touched and transformed the deep memory of Becket. Becket himself may have given us a clue to his conversion. When he was once asked by Henry to account for a public act of penance, Becket explained his new behavior by saying, "I pray that my outward manner might mold my reluctant heart."

The Prophetic Vision

It is important to relate the concept of the deep memory and the social drama to biblical patterns. Walter Brueggemann in an insightful book, *The Prophetic Imagination,* does just this. He describes what he calls the "royal consciousness," arising with the reign of Solomon in the mid-tenth century B.C. Brueggemann says that reality under Solomon was reduced to manageable portions and the culture was "paganized," that is, rendered static and lifeless. The future vision was lost, and only the assurance of God's compliant presence remained. Three dimensions characterize the Solomonic achievement: incredible well-being and affluence ("The people of Judah and Israel . . . ate and they drank, and enjoyed life" [1 Kings 4:20; NEB]); a politics of oppression (as in the use of forced labor [1 Kings 9:15]); and a domestication of God, the Temple becoming God's "house." Brueggemann describes the last mentioned as a religion of immanence and accessibility, but I would prefer to shift the focus away from his Protestant bias of utter transcendence to think more literally of a domestication. It means to locate God in the surface memory.

It is certainly not difficult to find parallels between the royal consciousness with its intolerance of the alternative prophetic consciousness, its banality, its obsession with the past, its non-abrasive God, and its lack of passion and the contemporary outlook. Brueggemann's prophetic comment is worth noting: "Our culture is competent to implement almost anything and to imagine almost nothing."[4] Imagination is the enemy to royal consciousness, because it calls in question the surface equilibrium and its illusion of permanence, and unleashes the deep memory and its challenge to our human presumptions of certitude and control. The artist and his imagination is all a frightening challenge to totalitarianism. The true artist is one who uses our root metaphors to reveal ourselves to ourselves.

The royal consciousness begets a numbness. We cannot know our own experience, because we have abrogated the means to move beneath the surface of our consciousness.

The effect of this is to make us insensitive to the reality of death and the power of sexuality. The Old Testament Israelites were, of course, fighting a constant battle with the fertility religions of Canaan. Consequently, the positive dynamism of eros receives only oblique reference in the Scriptures, as in the analogy of Israel as the bride of Yahweh and in the inclusion of the Song of Songs in the canon. But certainly the prophets were explicit in their willingness to face suffering and death. For our purposes, we need to realize that the denial of death and the trivialization of sexuality are the inevitable character of a surface memory that does not want to know anything more than is necessary to "get by."

The task of prophecy is to give new hope to people by offering fresh metaphors or symbols. Such new symbols provide a vitality throughout the community, opening it to the new future. The prophet by virtue of this fact called for repentance, a new consciousness at the level of the deep memory. Prophecy is poetry, the language of the deep memory. The poetry of prophecy is full of images of new songs, abundant fertility, and fresh bread, all of which can only come from God.

The prophets reflect a social drama that they wanted to share with the people of God. The language of the surface memory, concept and system, was inadequate to the call of Israel. A covenant written on stone is inadequate. Jeremiah had the right idea; write it on hearts. But to write on the heart requires performance, which is why the Messiah had to come and why our performance of his Passion in the sacraments lies at the heart of the new life.

James William McClendon, Jr., a seminary professor in Berkeley, California, brings to our attention what he calls character in his book, *Theology as Biography*. We act, he says, in terms of our character, "and a man's character is formed by the way he sees things." Character constellates about a root metaphor. If we are going to understand the action of another, particularly a prophetic leader, we need to identify the root metaphor within his consciousness.

McClendon presents four case studies in support of his thesis: Dag Hammarskjöld, Martin Luther King, Jr., Clarence Jordan, and Charles Ives. The root metaphors for each are the Cross, the Beloved Community, the Incarnate Presence, and a union of Transcendentalism and Revivalism. It is possible to see the grafting of these metaphors to the deep memory of each man within the social milieu in which he was reared. They were a part of the community's performance. If we read Hammarskjöld's book, *Markings,* particularly toward the end, we can discern his sense of mission that leads to the Cross. Perhaps the high point of King's witness was at his speech before the Lincoln Memorial in Washington, known by the oft repeated refrain, "I have a dream." It was the dream of the Beloved Community. Jordan, the founder of the Koinonia Community outside Americus, Georgia, and the author of *The Cottonpatch Gospel,* lived knowing the Christ is present in his fellow people, even those who harrassed him and his community. Ives, the founder of New York Life Insurance and one of America's great composers, expressed in his music, particularly in the Fourth Symphony, that strange mixture of New England Transcendentalism and frontier Revivalism that was his heritage.

Each of these men—perhaps to a less extent in Ives—was living in a conflict situation. The social enterprise had broken down into a banal interaction, fraught with injustice. They were living out the deep flow of their consciousness, shaped by a primordial community sensitive to the metaphorical meaning of existence. The power of a Hammarskjöld, King, Jordan, or Ives lies in the accessibility of that deep memory and its ability to challenge and, at the same time, illumine our life together. This was the source and the motivation for their prophetic vision.

The person who seeks therapy is the one who, far from being like a Hammarskjöld, King, Jordan, or Ives, does not have that accessibility to a metaphorical interpretation of life that provides even a modicum of freedom. They are captured and victimized by the surface flow of the social enterprise in its most dehumanizing lack of care. They are the casualties of the royal consciousness. If such "dry bones" are to be raised to life, we must prophesy that they may "hear the word of the Lord" (Ezek. 37:1–14). But note carefully, the word must be that of metaphor, making love to the deep memory, and giving new life as a fresh wind moving us to action.

The Point of Engagement

The mission for which the church must prepare depends upon appropriate strategy for the renewal of people's minds. How does God, through us, make people whole? How can we help rather than hinder the process of becoming human.

I have listed in the first chapter four indications of the possible existence of renewal, without which no change in consciousness is really taking place. These indications are a spirit of risk, a confrontation with society, an emerging new order, and an eventual cultural renaissance. Such indications are symptoms of our recourse to the social drama and its impingement upon the societal norms.

In the second chapter we took a brief glimpse at the objective of renewal. The evidence from the Bible would indicate that the objective is not all clearly defined, although we can identify certain threads. These threads are union with God at the end of history, at which time we shall live in a community under the reign of God. The objective includes the resolution of all injustice and must apparently be preceded by suffering.

Furthermore, in the third chapter, I have pointed to those intermediate objectives that need to be achieved if renewal is to be sustained in order that the risk may be supported, confrontation be maintained, order be effective, and culture be reborn to the end that humankind be open to God's gift of the ultimate objective. These seven intermediate objectives are: a sense of the extraordinary within the ordinary, an institutional carrier, parabolic language, theological development, an ascesis with a purpose, a moral seriousness, and leadership.

In this chapter the "terrain" of the consciousness has been described so that we might consider how best to engage humanity to bring about a true repentance, open people to the objective, and begin to establish those constants that sustain such renewal. The question is: how shall we move across that terrain to have the greatest possible effect? The answer lies in the awareness of the deep memory.

My criticism of Rifkin, inspite of my sympathy with much that he says, is that he draws on an understanding of the human consciousness from the Reformation and the Greek Awakening that is deficient. It does not take into account the discoveries of the human sciences over the last century, particularly those of analytical psychology, anthropology, and the history of religions. The human consciousness is more than either univocal categories of common sense and conceptual and systematic thinking or chaos. There is a level of felt intuitive knowing, which is equivocal and metaphoric, and it is here that faith comes alive and commitment finds its primordial expression. Such knowing is characteristic of human love for one another, of poetry, of liturgy, and of play.

If our tactics of evangelization do not take into account the root of faith and commitment in the deep memory of humankind, then the efforts to evangelize are going to be counterproductive of the objective of renewal. The difference between transformation and manipulation lies in the ability of our outreach to achieve its professed purpose by befriending the deep memory of the other, rather than assaulting the surface memory. A great deal of so-called renewal in our time violates the inner self by bombarding the external self with gimmicks that force us to choose between sentimentality or cynicism. There are those of us who need to stand up and say that populist piety—sentimental music, marathon catechesis, instant comradery, and the like—*offend* our religious sensibilities. Yet our offense, far from being an indication of our lack of faith and commitment, is a natural reaction to the trivialization of the deep sense of God's presence in our hearts and minds. Any effort at creating performance needs to honor the deep memory, where death and birth, dissolution and nurture, play out their strange conflicting roles.

There is a passage in Ecclesiasticus of which I am particularly fond.

> Happy the man who fixes his thoughts on wisdom
> and uses his brains to think,
> the man who contemplates her ways
> and ponders her secrets.
> Stalk her like a hunter
> and lie in wait beside her path!
> The man who peers in at her windows
> and listens at her keyhole,
> who camps beside her house,
> driving his tent-peg into her wall,
> who pitches his tent close by her,
> where it is best for men to live—
> he will put his children in her shade
> and camp beneath her branches,
> sheltered by her from heat,
> and dwelling in the light of her presence.
>   (14:20–27; NEB)

It is the imagery that delights me. One acquires wisdom not by gobbling at the trough of facts, but by sitting beside her, attending to her, attaching oneself to her. It is an understanding that we absorb through our pores in the heart of our being. It is not merely a garment with which we are clothed. It is a gentle learning that befits the nature of the deep memory.

God may ravish us, but he does not rape us. To be ravished is to awaken the passion, which lies within our deep memory. To be raped is to be forced into acquiescence without regard for the inner self—in fact, it is to nauseate the soul. I am told of a method of evangelization where one encounters a stranger, perhaps on an airplane, and asks, "If we were to crash in the next few moments, what would you have to offer God as evidence of your right to enter heaven?" The point of the question is to get the poor fool to suggest some things of which he is particularly proud, and having done so, the would-be evangelist then gives him the "zinger." "Don't you realize," one is to say, "that those things have no value before God. All that you have done is worthless. All you can offer is your sorrow for sin and to cast yourself upon the mercy of God." I do not believe this atrocious I-am-nothing-but-a-worm theology. Let us call the method what it is: rape. It is immoral pious entrapment in that it seeks to corner the victim and compel a decision that violates what is God's gift for us: our freedom springing from our deepest sensibilities. The end does not justify the means, because the end is not the Gospel promise: the wholeness of the person.

There is an authentic evangelization, which understands the anthropology of renewal. It engages us at that point where true repentance is possible and avoids the easy promotion of inauthentic repentance. It is our purpose to explore just what that evangelization looks like, but first we need to explicate the meaning of the deep memory by thinking about conversion.

CHAPTER FIVE

Conversion

In a very real sense we have already discussed conversion. Conversion and *metanoia* or repentance, the subject of the first chapter, are both names for a change in perception. Yet there are issues that move about conversion that draw us in a different direction than we have previously taken.

Edward Schillebeeckx, the contemporary Dutch Roman Catholic theologian, makes a convincing case for the heart of the Resurrection experience of Jesus' followers. It is, as he sees it, a conversion experience. On the occasion of Jesus' arrest, he is abandoned, "The disciples all deserted him and ran away" (Mk. 14:50; NEB). Peter, the leader of the apostles, denies him three times (Mk. 14:66–72). We can imagine the intense guilt that our Lord's followers must have felt. It is a feeling that left a profound impression upon the deep memory of the Christians, as they hid within the city while outside the walls their master died on the Cross.

Yet, beginning with Peter, the apostles came to know themselves as forgiven for their breach of faith. Schillebeeckx points out that it was to the *assembled community* that Jesus appeared after his Resurrection, not to a scattered flock. Something had brought them together. He suggests that it was the experience of knowing themselves forgiven that motivated the gathering. Deep within them, they knew that Jesus lived. One is not forgiven by a dead Lord, but by a living Lord.

The Resurrection itself carries with it a sense of forgiveness. Aside from Jesus' assurance of his terrified followers (Mt. 28:10, Mk. 16:8, Lk. 24:5–7), in the Fourth Gospel it is a consciousness of the capacity to forgive sin that accompanies the evidence of the Resurrection (Jn. 20:22–23). Luke says that in the power of the Resurrection the Apostles are to go forth and preach "repentance bringing forgiveness of sins" (Lk. 24:47; NEB). Paul tells the Corinthians that "if Christ was not raised . . . you are still in your old state of sin" (1 Cor. 15:17; NEB). In the Fourth Gospel, when Jesus appeared to the disciples on the evening of the Resurrection, he bestowed the power to forgive sins (Jn. 20:19–23).

What Schillebeeckx perceives is that the Resurrection of Jesus is seen by the first Christians in terms of a Jewish conversion story. Particularly in Hellenistic Judaism, the conversion of a gentile to Judaism is described as *one coming to see.* The convert is illuminated! The conversion of Paul on the road to Damascus (Acts 9:1–9, 22:4–11, 26:12–18) is a classical form of this story, adapted for Christian purposes. Paul sees a great light, he is blind for a period, and then he is cured of his blindness. The restoration of sight, a common theme in the Gospels, generally carries the meaning of a new spiritual vision, inasmuch as the blindness of sin has been forgiven.

The ability to see the risen Lord, to understand the meaning of the empty tomb, is the result of the vision that comes with conversion. Earlier I spoke of renewal as the result of repentance and the emergence of a new vision. Conversion is a way of speaking of the transformation of the mind, of our intentionality, so that we are open to the presence of God's impending reign, of which Jesus' Resurrection is the proclamation. It is repentance that means the power of God to turn *from* our sins *to* the new creation of the risen Lord.

It is important to know that the early church described Baptism as the illumination. Baptism incorporates us into the risen life of Christ (Rom. 6:4). It is no accident that in the first few centuries Baptism was administered at the break of dawn on Easter morning. As we are baptized we become one with the first disciples, Peter and the rest of the Apostles, who experienced the Resurrection in the illumination of the forgiveness of their betrayal. Baptism bestows the gift of vision. Inasmuch as this is true, it would be an error to think of conversion as something qualitatively different from Baptism. Rather, to be converted is to be illumined; to be baptized is to be illumined.

If we are to speak of conversion apart from Baptism, it must be as claiming the vision that is given in Baptism, given by our sacramental participation in the Resurrection experience of Christ.

The Sacramental Base

It is not usual to find a discussion of sacramental theology in an analysis of conversion. Historically, those Christians who have emphasized the sacraments have put very little emphasis upon conversion, and those who have sought conversion have had a weak sacramental theology, if any at all. It is just this dichotomy I wish to attack. For a central clue to the nature of conversion lies in sacramental theology, as the common use of illumination in the Jewish conversion story and the early Christian understanding of Baptism hints.

If we understand the relation of performance to the deep memory, we will begin to see how in fact the transformation of the person in terms of his consciousness of intentionality is effected by the sacramental life. The sacraments are the church's rituals, and as such are to be understood in part as rituals are defined. They are the carriers of the central, powerful symbols of our participation in God, and consequently make those symbols available to us in a way that we can appropriate them. Rituals are a type of performance, whose symbols may be embedded within the deep memory. A ritual is a repetitive performance, the enactment of whose symbols "make present." This is what Paul means when he says that when we share the Eucharist we "proclaim the death of the Lord, until he comes" (1 Cor. 11:26; NEB), that primordial event that constituted the community.

The fundamental sacrament of Christianity is Christ. " 'I am the way; I am the truth and I am life;' " says Jesus, " 'No one comes to the Father except by me' " (Jn. 14:6; NEB). The Church is the sacrament of Christ, broken and sinful as it obviously is. This is the implication of Paul's teaching of the Church as the Body of Christ (1 Cor. 12:12–26). Christ is made present now in the life of the Church and the Church is where Christ is made present. In this sense the ancient saying is true:

"Outside the Church there is no salvation." The sacramental life of the Church is the heart of the Church's performance where the symbols of Christ's Passion reach and touch the deep memory of humankind and transform our vision to our roots. We live by the memory of the death and resurrection of Jesus. It is our root metaphor. It evokes the social drama from which we live as Christians. We become, by our participation, sacraments of Christ.

In such a sacramental theology the corporate nature of humanity is fundamental. We are our community. The subjectivity of the individual and his feelings are not to be understood apart from the social environment. Some sociologists say that the difference between humankind and the lower animals is that we are more than our biology; we are our socialization. If this is true—and I think it is as long as we recognize that socialization is open-ended—then conversion is the result of the community in which we live. It is both inspite of it and because of it: but the community, its rituals and its story, shapes us. God does not move and transform us apart from the deep memory, which carries those metaphors that we have assimilated through the years of participation in the rituals of our culture, as well perhaps through the millennia of humanity's struggle to survive in a world always mysterious and sometimes capricious.

The focus upon Christ, his Church, and the sacraments is compatible to an understanding of a Christianity that knows Jesus as one who transforms culture and proclaims the kingdom of God. It is what the late nineteenth-century German theologian, Ernst Troeltsch, called a "church typology" of Christianity, as opposed to a "sect typology." In the "church typology," Christianity is related to the society as a whole. In the "sect typology," Christianity is over against the society. From the point of view of a church typology, to "get religion" is not like someone on social security suddenly winning a Rolls Royce. It is not a matter of acquiring something one never knew existed. If we can even speak of "getting religion," it is more like a philandering husband awaking to the love of his wife after twenty years of indifferent marriage. One is steeped in a religious tradition, and even if he should break from the authoritative interpretation of that tradition as the first Christians did from Judaism, the tradition still feeds the new insights. Certainly the Jewish tradition has always fed the Christian, as the Hellenistic tradition has also shaped the Christian mind. This acknowledgment of different traditions, as embedded in the deep memory coming together to form our Christian awareness, is a clear difference between Anglicanism and radical Protestantism.

A belief that God is present to us in our community and through our culture finds most important an emphasis upon the Incarnation, the Creation, and the Immanence of God. God is the God of nature, of our bodies, and of the physical environment in which we live. He is the Lord of our pagan roots. We do not understand that God is a spirit (Jn. 4:24) as teaching he is over against the natural world, but that he pervades all his creation and yet is infinitely more. Therefore, Anglicanism does not divide the cosmos into nature and supernature, but believes that grace perfects nature. The absolute separation of God from the world does not fit well in the Anglican mind, which for one thing is why we are at home in a church typology and a sacramental theology.

From this viewpoint, the Gospel does not convert individuals apart from their community. Some teachers of evangelization are fond of pointing out that, after Peter preached following the Pentecost experience, "some three thousand were added to their [the Christians'] number that day" (Acts 2:41; NEB). It is as if Luke was gleefully "toting up" the annual parish report. But this is not how the ancient mind worked, which knew little about bookkeeping (which was very primitive until the sixteenth century). It is more likely that the author was thinking in terms of a collective, a community of three thousand and not three thousand individuals. It needs to be noted that the verse which follows the report of three thousand converts records the life of the community in sacramental terms. "They met constantly to hear the apostles teach, and to share the common life, to break bread, and to pray" (Acts 2:42; NEB).

A Greek Orthodox friend of mine explained to an inquirer that the reason his church was not able to evangelize America was that they had no *community* to send to this place or that. For him the proclaiming of the Gospel is the living of the Liturgy, and that act requires a worshiping community. The sacramental life brings about conversion, because it is the immersion in the total sense experience—the sight, the sound, the smell, the touch, and the taste—that reaches into the deep memory to shape it. Once shaped, the deep memory has a high resistance to change. Anyone who thinks that the apparent atheism of Russia is anything more than an ideological veneer simply fails to understand the way in which the Orthodox faith of Russia as in a Dostoevski, a Peter the Great, or a Theophan the Recluse infects the very soil of the land from which its people spring.

To tie the sacramental life to conversion raises an impediment for those who look for dramatic demonstrable success in provoking conversions. Sectarian religion, with its low doctrine of the sacraments and readiness to evoke an emotional crisis, has had much success in recruiting numbers and in generating enthusiasm. One might ask: to what end? We will return to that question again and again. While I am not saying that the life in the sacraments and conversion are the same thing (as we shall see they are not), I *do* believe the sacramental life is rudimentary to genuine conversion.

The point I want to make is assisted by this analogy. Which is better? To quiet the grief-stricken with a tranquilizer for instant relief, or to support those who mourn through the weeks and months, helping them deepen their consciousness of their ambiguous feelings concerning him who is dead? In our impatient land, where we look for "results," our inclination is to choose the former, not only in ministry to the grieving but in all human relationships. The sacramental life is characteristic of the second option, indicative of our belief that there is more to transformation than head counts and enthusiasm.

The Anatomy of Conversion

The common sense meaning of conversion is a sudden, dramatic change in point of view. William James, the prominent turn-of-the century American psychologist and philosopher, made the distinction between the "once born" and "twice born" Christian, and most people seem to accept the distinction. The "twice born" would be someone who is conscious of a moment of spiritual rebirth, unassociated with joining the church or being baptized. The "once born" would be the person unaware of any life-changing spiritual event in his existence. In looking at conversion here, I want to prescind from the issue of conversion as a dramatic event for the present.

The experience of conversion must in the final analysis be self-reported. Our friends can ask us why we "look different" or note a radical change in action, but only we can confirm the cause. The subject knows whether he looks different because he has taken up jogging or overcome a spiritual crisis, or whether he is giving to the poor for the sake of his income tax or out of love for God. This is regardless of the suddenness of the change. While it is more likely that a dramatic change will be reported, it is the *change* —a turning from and to—that concerns us here. What seems to be associated with this conversion or change?

Research in the field of religious conversion indicates that prior to conversion there is a preconversion experience of an intense intrapsychic conflict. The conflict is between what one is and what one wishes to be. One way of interpreting that conflict is to understand conversion as a means of claiming our identity.

The idea of tension or anxiety, rooted in a personal conflict, as prior to the experience of conversion, is widely documented by persons of varying schools of thought. The degree of tension or conflict is related to the extent of change in outlook and action. This is readily understandable.

It is possible that the source of the identified tension prior to conversion lies in a conflict between either the deep memory and the surface memory or within the deep memory itself. Such a conclusion is supported by the fact that more conversion experiences are reported in adolescence than any other period in life. The surface memory is more vulnerable to conflict then, and it is more likely that we would be responsive to a conflict within the deep memory at this time than in any subsequent period in life. Two illustrations are to the point.

The vocational crisis can be the occasion for an awareness of conversion. What am I to do with my life? The common sense of understanding is that we are called to be "successful," meaning materially well-off. But what if in the deep memory there is a concern for the poor? If that image is powerful enough, it will continually call into question the sensitive person who chooses to pursue wealth over moral values. My experience with late vocations in seminary—the average age of the student body is 37 in the school I serve—is that the decision to come to seminary is the result of a surrender to a constant, nagging call deep within the person's soul that was unresolved in adolescence.

Another focus of adolescent crisis is sexuality. Here it can be a struggle within the deep memory, where eros is fed both by lust and love. The "playmate" in the April, 1980, *Playboy* reported that she knew three reasons for sexual intercourse: lust, love, and making babies. She reported that she could tell us all about the first two, but not the third. It is regrettable that she was not sensitive enough to discover the difference in values between lust and love. There is a conflict there to which each of us must make a choice, sometimes over and over. The choice is a conversion decision; otherwise, we live with a contradiction within the deep memory.

Conversion itself is an act of surrender, God's solicitation of us in the deep memory. This is something akin to falling in love. We surrender to the love we encounter in the other. We solve the tension by giving up what we turn from and committing ourselves to what we turn to. We are no longer double-minded. This is why there is in conversion an integration of the self, a sense of having it together, with a resultant clarity of action. The intentionality becomes "pure." Some have called this self-discovery.

The postconversion experience is then a freedom from tension, which is often translated into assurance. In the words of the familiar hymn:

> Blessed assurance, Jesus is mine!
> O What a foretaste of glory divine!

But in authentic conversion—and I introduce this adjective at this point in anticipation of a discussion of pseudo conversion— we need to be careful about the notion of "assurance."

Bernard Lonergan, the Jesuit philosophical theologian, says that conversion has three aspects: religious, intellectual, and moral. Religious conversion is being in love with God. We live for God as we live for our wife or husband, out of a passion that springs from our depths. It consumes us. A new power is released in us. An American missionary in Tanzania explained to me why she was able to leave friends and the sophisticated life in New York City to live for three years without the theater, restaurants, and air conditioning simply because she was in love with God. But this power needs to be channeled, as it is in my missionary friend.

Intellectual conversion, which provides the channel, is as readily understood as being in love with God. Such conversion is the ability to *distinguish between* the personal experience of God and the meaning we make of that experience. It is quite different from biblical literalism, which may arise from an understandable, but confused, discovery of the remarkable cogency of the Scriptures. Intellectual conversion enables us to affirm that cogency and still recognize the need for biblical criticism and interpretation. Conversion is not just an emotional experience. When we turn to God and his impending Kingdom, he reigns in our minds as well. We are freed by God to think about God as human beings think about anything else that matters; insightfully, testing images and concepts for their ability to represent what is ultimately inexpressible: the mystery of God's ways with people. Only the truly converted can be in faith and question belief.

I think of seminarians who discover biblical criticism as an act of faith. What can be more grace-ful than to discover the layers of oral and written tradition that make up the Scriptures and how they come together to record God's self-disclosure?

Moral conversion is a step beyond intellectual conversion. It is the ability to live by values and not prescriptive laws. It is characteristic of the human will as it turns from self-will to God. God does not destroy our freedom to choose, he illumines our choices. The antipode of moral conversion is moralism, the illusion that moral decision is a choice between two clearly defined alternatives, one clearly forbidden by God and the other obviously the right choice. Here again, it is all too easy for the "assured" to think that they have direct access to the will of God. One who lives by values knows, however, that all moral decisions ultimately are "difficult cases."

A real conversion for me has been the struggle to affirm the values in my children's moral commitments, which are, in some ways, manifestly different from mine. What I have discovered is that they are not nearly as different as I thought at first.

Lonergan's three aspects of conversion are essential to understanding and testing authentic conversion. It is not enough to say that conversion is preceded by tension, is accompanied by a surrender to an integrating presence, and begets assurance. We have to ask what the nature of the new vision is. Has it brought intellectual and moral insight and freedom, as well as religious passion?

There is another interesting point about the experience of conversion; there is generally in it a sense of *returning,* as in what T. S. Eliot writes:

> We shall not cease from exploration
> And the end of all our exploring
> Will be to arrive where we started
> And know the place for the first time.[1]

But there is a reason for this, which calls us back to the prior point that conversion and the sacramental life are inextricably related. Conversion is an owning of God's presence to us that has been there all along. It is a breaking-through in a convincing manner of the metaphorical coherence of our deep memory.

Rosemary Haughton, an English lay theologian, explains why. Her word for conversion is "transformation." She writes,

> The "flashpoint" of decision [i.e., the awareness we call conversion] is the moment when formation gives way to transformation. But the two have nothing in common at all,

they do not even meet. Without the long process of formation there could be no transformation, yet no amount of
careful formation can transform. Transformation is a time-
less point of decision, yet it can only operate in the possibility
formed through time-conditioned stages of development,
and its efforts can only be worked out in terms of that
formation.[2]

Formation is provided by the life in the community, particularly the sacramental life. It may also be the result of an
archetypical or primordial sense of the divine in humanity as a
whole. The transformation, conversion, or change feeds upon
the images infused or embedded within the deep memory by
the formation. We fall in love with God and we know it; and,
although transformation is not the sum of our formation, it is
the stuff of the deep memory that gives it the substance by
which we can grasp its meaning in some authentic manner.

The experience of conversion, contrary to what we may
romantically think, is reported by those who have known the
community positively or, like Paul, negatively. In transformation or conversion we discover in an entirely new way what we
have known all along. You cannot be converted to that which is
not a possibility within your formation, even though conversion
is a profound change. Authentic transformation is just this: an
emergence of the deep memory, with its symbolic power of the
divine, so that it consumes the entire self.

Emilie Griffin, an advertising executive in New York City, has
written a strange little book about her own conversion. Entitled
Turning, and published in 1980, the book evokes an odd
recollection of the early Thomas Merton, C. S. Lewis, Bede
Griffiths, and others from a time that seems so far away, and
couples this with a very up-to-date, ecumenical spirit. The
value of Griffin's testimony is its contemporary expression of
that genre of conversion accounts that call forth the complete
person to do battle with God's invitation to faith. It is a kind of
literature typical of the English-speaking intellectual, which
Anglicans would do well to remember in the face of different
traditions. Griffin is clearly a thoughtful woman who understands conversion as a process involving reason, emotion,

intuition, and will. There is a big turning, she says, followed by an unending series of turnings. One is converted again and again. She describes conversion much as Elisabeth Kübler-Ross, in her earlier writing, described the process of dying; in four steps. There is a longing, a time of reasoning, a struggle, and then a surrender. For her, conversion is a deep inner change; what I call a transformation of the deep memory.

Conversion and Nurture

Haughton's contrast between formation and transformation leads naturally to that previously postponed discussion of conversion as commonly conceived; namely, a sudden, dramatic change in point of view. Her phrase, "the flashpoint of decision," may evoke for some images of the proverbial altar call, the moment when for all time one accepts Jesus as his Lord and Savior.

Our common sense interpretation of conversion as Americans was brewed in the piety of nineteenth century American revivalism. It in turn is the heir of an evolving theological tradition formed in the sixteenth-century fascination, in both Roman Catholic and Protestant thought, with the providence of God. If God is an infinite projection of the all-powerful early modern European king, and therefore knows everything that will happen, it seems to follow that he knows who is chosen for damnation and who for salvation. This is only logical, granting the original premise. The problem for us comes in knowing in which group, those elected for hell or those elected for heaven, each of us is *already individually numbered*. It is *not* a matter of working with God in an as-yet-undetermined process toward wholeness.

A word with an honored history in Christian spirituality began about the end of the seventeenth century to take on a special meaning: the *consolation*. The consolation became the name for the experience of assurance that a person was among the elect. The experience of the consolation becomes identified with conversion: the discovery of our election by God. Increasingly, the consolation became associated with a dramatic feeling, something akin to what the late American humanistic psychologist, Abraham Maslow, called a "peak experience." John Wesley, who was very much influenced by the German Pietists among whom these ideas prevailed, reported that after attending a meeting at Aldersgate in London, his "heart was strangely warmed." This is treated by many as Wesley's experience of the consolation, although it is unlikely that he always thought it was.

Of course, profound emotional experiences of the presence of God in our lives are common to all Christian traditions and all ages. While they are not to be despised, many a Christian spiritual master (John of the Cross among them) warns us against dependence upon such emotional experiences. The problem lies in the theological expectation that leads to an interpretation of the experience. If it were true, as some people think, that all of us from before birth are predestined for heaven or hell, and if it were also true that the way we know our fate is by the experience of the consolation so defined, then such a dramatic emotional seizure of our senses would be not only desirable, it would be the *sine qua non* of Christian discipleship. The alternative would be exclusion from the elect. But the theological assumption here is that the choice of wholeness or destruction is not ours, but God's. We have no freedom of any kind—a viewpoint that is unacceptable. It is difficult, of course, in such a theology to understand what the function of the sacraments is. The church is the assembly of the elect awaiting the predetermined call home. The separation of the sheep and goats, to which Matthew's Gospel testifies, is something that took place before all time (Mt. 25:32–33). Since I mention this text, it should be noted that the Gospel is actually saying something quite different; namely, that when we look at the Lord enthroned upon the Cross *we make a choice* again and again in our life. Since we remember Christ's Passion in the sacraments, it would follow from this understanding that our choice as we participate in the sacraments has a great deal to do with our salvation.

Theological qualifications of this notion of divine providence were common from the late seventeenth up until the nineteenth centuries, and yet such qualifications still supported the quest for the consolation. But opposition to the need for such an experience has also persisted. The consolation normally interpreted as conversion has never been a part of that Christian tradition of which Anglicanism is an example. This tradition is suspicious of any exclusive dependence upon strong feeling, untempered by reason. It places more emphasis upon the value of ongoing nurture. This placed the tradition increasingly in conflict with those who insisted upon the necessity of that "blessed assurance." As the two traditions meet in the nineteenth century, a debate over nurture versus conversion flourished.

The debate perhaps posed a false dichotomy. John Westerhoff, professor of religious education at Duke University, suggests that nurture may be considered as "faith given" and conversion as "faith owned." Conversion is this understanding emerging from nurture, but is qualitatively different. It "implies the reordering of our perceptions, a radical change without which no further growth or learning is possible."[9]

Westerhoff would say that the "owning" of our faith must, of necessity, be more than an emotional experience. Conversion and consolation are *not* the same thing. They are no more alike than romantic infatuation is like an intentional marriage. One is subject to all the deceptions of feeling, while the other expresses a commitment of the total self: emotions, thoughts, and, above all, will.

But more needs to be said. A helpful illumination of Christian discipleship has been made by the correlation of models of faith development to psychosocial, cognitive, and moral developmental models that come out of psychological research. But one of the dangers of these models is to see them as a simple progression, with the implication that the Christian at some point arrives at the end in this life with a mature, owned faith. This quotation from Westerhoff runs the risk of that interpretation:

> At some point every Christian must fully internalize the faith of the church and affirm their own faith by being confronted with the choice of whether or not they accept or

reject the authority of the gospel and are brought to a
personal life transforming commitment to Christ.[4]

The language connotes the same notion as Haughton's image
of the "flashpoint of decision."

What needs to be said of Westerhoff's and Haughton's
images is that they identify turning points, which in a decisive
change in the direction of a person's life is brought to full
consciousness and owned. But a turning point is very different
from the sense of having arrived. In fact, conversion understood as an identifiable moment when our consciousness is
broadened or elevated always faces us with greater risks. We
are pushed to the edge of the life raft amid the chaos of
existence.

Conversion is a succession of "flashpoints" emerging from an
ever-continuing formation, and we must repent again and
again. We *never* "fully internalize the faith," as if to own it
without question. What may lead us to miss this point is the
dramatic experience, such as in the life of Augustine of Hippo,
Francis of Assisi, or Catherine of Genoa, which marks a radical
change in the subsequent life of the Christian convert. Augustine agreed to Baptism after reading the Scriptures at the word
of a child calling him "to take up and read." Francis gave all he
had to the poor and became a mendicant after Christ spoke to
him from the Cross while he was in prayer in a near-ruin of a
church. Catherine of Genoa devoted her life to the service of
the indigent sick after renouncing a life of sin in the face of a
deep awareness of God's love while making her Lenten confession. But all three of these holy people were deeply aware of
their sin and the need to return again and again in sorrow to
the call for repentance until the moment of their death.

It is for this reason that I have suggested in an earlier book
(*Confirmation: The Celebration of Maturity in Christ*) that we might
think of making the sacrament of Confirmation repeatable, at
least, provide a way in which we can renew our baptismal/
confirmation vows as we "own" again and again the faith given
in our Baptism. The sacrament of Reconciliation arose in the
life of the church as Christians became aware of the need to

return repeatedly in moments of repentance to the gift of God's salvation and claim it for their own. There was no question of a sudden, dramatic conversion that declared we had arrived or we were saved beyond question.

There are those who would agree with the need to own our faith repeatedly, but who would still insist there is great value in experiencing a climactic, emotional moment of ownership. If conversion were merely a matter of falling in love with God, this could be accepted without qualification. But too much emphasis upon such a dramatic moment can in fact work against full conversion in its intellectual and moral, as well as religious, implications. It would place too heavy an emphasis upon the emotional component as if it alone were sufficient. We know that a marriage is doomed that merely seeks ways of rekindling the magic of romantic love and never moves on to the hard work of identifying and sharing goals and values, which are the product of an intellectual and moral commitment between husband and wife. It is not a question of why the romance has gone out of a marriage, but what a couple are doing to build a much firmer relationship as the romance inevitably does go out of a marriage. So it is with Christian discipleship.

The church had to learn this lesson. The author of Hebrews wrote, "For if we wilfully persist in sin after receiving the knowledge of the truth, no sacrifice for sin remains: only a terrifying expectation of judgement" (Heb. 10:16–27; NEB). The writer has a simplistic idea of what it means to receive "the knowledge of the truth," and the relationship this knowledge must have to all the other levels of knowledge a person has inherited and accrued through life. The conjoining of the mind of Christ to our minds is a long process of illumination and recurring blindness. It is a much better description of this pilgrimage to speak in terms of a lifetime struggle and to pray for the purity of desire—i.e., the disposition of the whole person—rather than to suffer the illusion of the perfection of the goal.

The author of the letter to the Colossians prays that his readers "walk through life worthy of the Lord . . . increasing in the knowledge of God" (Col. 1:10; UTH). This is an understanding to be preferred to that we find in Hebrews. It is to be noted in that the word for knowledge (*epignōsis*) is the same in both passages, Hebrews and Colossians. It is used in New Testament times for a religious and moral knowledge, not just a collection of facts. There is only one kind of knowledge of God in Christ, and this is acquired through a lifetime journey of formation, marked by moments of particular awareness of its transforming power, which make the obvious occasions of our continuing ignorance and sin bearable.

Paul is making a related point when he tells the Roman Christians, "Do not let yourselves be conformed to this age, but let yourselves be transformed by the renewal of the mind" (Rom. 12:2; UTH). *Metamorphousthe*, "let yourselves be transformed," is the same word used for the transfiguration of Jesus (Mt. 19:2, Mk. 9:2). Whereas, in the case of Jesus, the inner reality becomes evident to the physical eye, Paul is calling for the conversion of the inner reality of his readers to accord with the inner reality of Jesus. He is addressing baptized Christians. It would follow that he is calling upon them to live into the promise of their Baptism, to own what was given them in that sacrament.

Conversion and Grace

Grace is the presence of God. His presence is God's free gift of himself to us. Conversion as the coming to awareness of God's solicitation of us is a growth in grace. Day by day we discover God in our lives, calling us into being more than we are already. The invitation is to live in the Kingdom.

This has some very specific implications, which Anglicanism has historically affirmed and which are appropriately remembered here.

The first of these is the practice of recollection. Recollection is a manner of meditation upon God-as-he-is-to-us that consciously looks to the images of God's presence and reflects upon them in a disciplined manner. This book is not a study in spiritual theology and practice, but much of what we say here has immediate connections with that discipline. The Benedictine tradition of prayer, which has made over the centuries such a profound influence upon the English church, begins with reading and then moves to silent meditation. This image-filled inner journey in quest of God is what we mean by recollection.

Recollection is an act that opens us daily to conversion. Because in meditating upon the images of God's presence to humanity we inevitably draw a contrast between what he calls us to be and what in fact we have been. The conflict that precedes conversion is then. The formative practice is there. The stage is set for our turning again and again to God's infinite love.

Second, this approach suggests the place that Anglicanism reserves for thoughts of our sin. Love bids us welcome. We do not turn to God because of our fear of sin, but because we respond to him as lover. Anglicans are often rebuked because we are not sufficiently moralistic. This is not, however, our weakness, but our strength. It is not out of a lack of commitment that we shy away from a hard line on sin, but out of commitment that we refuse to obscure the Gospel with a obsessive fear of the world God made and in which he became incarnate.

Julian of Norwich, a late fourteenth-century English mystic, embodies much of the Anglican spirit of conversion and grace. Her "showings," as her visions may be called, are a series of recollections of Christ's Passion. For Julian the Christian is one who constantly searches, and this pleases God greatly. We seek, we wait, and we trust in God. Our Lord comes to us assuring us that all will be well. This optimism extends even to her doctrine of sin. God lets us fall into sin, that he might lift us that much higher.

In Julian there is that Christocentricity which is typical of Anglican understanding. "I am the ground of your beseeching," says Jesus to Julian.[5] The Passion of Christ is not so much a transaction as it is a showing, an education of the person, who never totally falls into sin. "In every soul which will be saved there is a godly will which never assents to sin."[6]

There is, therefore, in this chapter a clear implication of how one lives the Christian life. We used to call it the daily practice of the presence of God. It still seems to be a pretty good way of putting it.

False Conversion

Inasmuch as conversion is a different way of talking about that renewal of consciousness also described by repentance, it would follow that any claim to conversion in which those qualities characteristic of true repentance are notably absent would be false. In the first chapter I named four such indications: a spirit of risk; the confrontation of society; an emerging new order; and a cultural renaissance. These indications reflect a community-oriented approach to conversion.

Conversion is an act of change that is over against self-inertia or the spiritual pride of individuals or society. To be converted is to be rendered vulnerable, tentative, and sensitive to the pain of the world. The converted moves to the edge of the raft of life, living in constant danger of drowning in the flood of chaos. There is no room for either self-congratulations among the transformed or easy accommodation to oppression. It is only a pseudo-piety that comforts the poor in their affliction by offering spiritual nourishment with no hope of substantial relief.

Thomas Merton speaks effectively of this point when he writes of a piety:

> that merely produces the illusion of having "arrived somewhere," of having achieved security and preserved one's familiar status by playing a part, [which] will eventually have to be unlearned in dread—or else will be confirmed in the arrogance, the impenetrable self-assurance of the Pharisee. . . . The "goodness" of such lives depends on the security afforded by relative wealth, recreation, spiritual comfort, and a solid reputation for piety. Such "goodness" is preserved by routine and the habitual avoidance of serious risk—indeed of serious challenge. In order to avoid apparent evil, this pseudo-goodness will ignore the summons of genuine good. It will prefer routine duty to courage and creativity. In the end it will be content with established procedures and safe formulas, while turning a blind eye to the greatest enormities of injustice and charity.[7]

False conversion with its pseudo-goodness attempts to escape the responsibilities of being human. That escape begins with the denial of our own deep memory and substitutes for the images of that memory the surface trivialities of sentimental, domesticated pap. The person who plays life "safe" and has no knowledge of his own dread—the awareness of the coincidence of good and evil in the same place and at the same moment within his own being—is not capable of transformation. It is like repairing a house full of termites by painting the exterior. We must expose the roots of our intentionality and discover what it means to look within ourselves and find God only to lose him and once more find him—again and again. Those who wonder why some people cannot accept the "simple Gospel" miss this vital point. Such people are only semi-conscious. The deep memory is anything but simple.

We all suffer from such semi-consciousness of the pseudo-converted. As a young university chaplain I declared from the pulpit to the young women in my congregation that she who gives her body to a man for the sake of popularity is nothing but a prostitute. For years now I have sought to repent for my sin of uncharity. The ambiguity that surrounds the image of eros deep within our memory and the behavior it evokes can hardly be dismissed, when we err, as a simple, callous transaction, a *quid pro quo*. I think that those upon whom I laid the burden of guilt may have been closer to the mind of Christ than I, who cast aimless stones into the congregation.

The difference between someone who suffers from false conversion and the person who has experienced the real thing is a question of sensibility. Sensibility in this sense means keen consciousness or awareness as opposed to a certain dullness or reduction of perception. If we can share our struggle with someone and admit that we have not only failed but enjoyed our failure, and sense understanding and support from that person in return, then we have met a convert. If this godly person knows our pain and joy—our pain in trying to be virtuous and our joy in yielding to temptation—and sees hope in our ambivalence, then we are face to face with a transformed person. Far too often when we are invited to share our struggle, we receive in return judgment from one who speaks loving words but delivers a message of condemnation. God's forgiveness, far from appearing free, has a price tag. The price is to give ourselves to a boring existence. It would appear that many who claim to be alive with God are in fact just dull people. There is a world of difference between the sensible convert and the vapid pseudo-convert.

On one occasion, a couple with whom I was very close lost their little girl at age 5 to an incurable ailment. We knew this would happen, and all of their friends rallied around them. One person, however, chose to organize the children in the neighborhood in order to teach them a "biblical fantasy," in which they were dressed as butterflies. He and the children then called on the bereaved parents and, without a "by your leave," inflicted upon them this drama accompanied by his homily. Its message was that their dead daughter was now a butterfly in Jesus' garden. The only redeeming feature of this account of this theological horror was that the parents of the little girl could laugh at it. As the mother said, "It almost made me sick to my stomach."

Yet conversion is not to be confused with being "liberated" from traditional values. One is not a more authentic Christian because he has kicked over the traces and, to mix a metaphor, shattered the sensibilities of the church like a bull in a china shop. There is a certain egotism to some people's Christian witness. I know of more than one instance where there has been great anger because "I have been poorly treated," coupled with apparently little sensitivity to the offense their behavior has created. Antinomian self-righteousness is just as false as Pharisaical self-assurance.

Some years ago I was addressing a group of clergy on the priest as a sexual person. One steely-eyed evangelical asked me if I were not justifying **LUST**! One does not justify lust, as if to embrace it as a way of expressing his freedom in Christ. Likewise, one does not deny it in himself. A general definition of lust is a passionate yearning of which sexual appetite is an example. Such lust is a fact of our deep, inner life, and it never leaves us this side of the grave. The question is what one does with it, having acknowledged its energizing forces within us. The true convert is the person who, recognizing himself as a lusty human being, by thought and will offers his lust to God. The false convert is insensitive to the power of his own lust or calls the evil good.

The primary protection against false conversion is that transformation rooted in the formation of the church and its tradition. In the baptismal rite in the Book of Common Prayer the candidate is asked, "Do you turn to Jesus Christ and accept him as your Savior?" In the early church this *turning* was not only a word, but deed as well. The candidates had faced west to renounce evil and now turned to the east to accept Jesus. It is an acting out of the fact of conversion: *a turning from and to.* The baptized person is one who has turned, is turned, and continues to turn. If we become aware of this and claim it for all it means in the context of a dramatic, emotional event, it is neither to be despised nor codified. What must be understood is the turning itself, in mind and will as well as emotion, to live in the service of God's Kingdom. It is to this end that we are called to obey the tradition's call to mission as captured in the Great Commission: "Going out make disciples of all peoples, baptizing them into the name of the Father and of the Son and of the Holy Spirit, teaching them to keep watch on all whatsoever I have commanded you" (Mt. 28:19–20). This is nothing less than a call to convert the world.

The Great Commission is an evocative text, perhaps in ways we frequently are unaware. It is marked in the Greek by three participles modifying the persons to whom it is addressed: "going out . . . baptizing . . . teaching." Participles used this way in Greek describe the ongoing quality of persons. They are more than a "general order" for behavior. All three participles point to a transformation of all people, of which Baptism is the operative action. Matthew consistently associates Jesus with the Son of Man predicted in Daniel. Earlier he hinted that Jesus was the fulfillment of the "man coming with the clouds of heaven" of which Daniel speaks (Dan. 7:13; NEB; cf. Mt. 26:64). This quotation from Daniel is followed in the very next verse with these words: "all people and nations of every

language should serve him [the Son of Man]" (Dan. 7:14;
NEB). The Great Commission is an extension of Jesus' call to
repent as the Kingdom of Heaven is closing in upon us; and
Baptism is the effective sign of God's reign, the reign that
Daniel promised: the "everlasting sovereignty which should not
pass away" (Dan. 7:14; NEB).

It should be evident that there is far more meaning to
conversion than that which we customarily attach to it; and that
if we seek to bring people to conversion it is something much
deeper, with more far-reaching implications than is conveyed
in the common sense interpretation of the individual's feeling
of consolation. Therefore, the church's mission to which the
Great Commission calls us is something that requires a clearer
definition than we often provide.

CHAPTER SIX

Mobilization for Mission

I was talking with a fellow priest, who raised the question of what the distinctively Anglican understanding of the Great Commission might be. He spoke of his experience in a parish where one of the priests dedicated to the church's mission had recruited members from a local Bible college to join him in reaching out and, as he put it, "had been trained in guerrilla warfare for Jesus." They were well-equipped and possessed the skills to wage a campaign of evangelization and renewal based upon an articulate and well-defined perception of the nature of the battle. It was Vietnam for Jesus. His problem was that he believed they misunderstood the enemy, not to mention God, and they were fighting the wrong kind of war.

In 1976 the General Convention of the Episcopal Church gave hesitant support to a program first suggested six years before and now called Venture in Mission. The intention of this program was to recall the Episcopal Church, after years of struggle over ordination of women to the priesthood and the revision of the Prayer Book, to the central purpose of the church: mission. By virtue of this campaign we were not only to raise the money to equip the church for mission, we were to educate and inspire the church to go out and do mission.

Unlike those who were trained to do "guerrilla warfare for Jesus," a basic unresolved problem was the lack of definition of the nature of mission. It appeared that for many people the word was assumed to be self-explanatory. Mission is mission, we seemed to say. Consequently, whatever images that word evokes became operative for the people of the church. Some saw the call to mission as a smoke screen for facing the real issues in the church. One of the seminary faculty suggested to me that it was a nostalgic trip into the illusion of "white man's burden" and triumphalism. Many obviously believed that it was a move in the right direction, but they lacked any consensus as to what that direction might be. As a person who was involved in the heart of the planning from 1976 on, I cannot recall much conversation, if any, as to the terrain over which we are to move and to the capacity of the enemy we are to overcome in baptizing and teaching all peoples.

The best judgment one could make as to the church's understanding of mission in the Venture in Mission program is based upon that for which dioceses' projects were diocesan conference centers—projects that some overseas dioceses found puzzling, to say the least. To people who are hungry and oppressed, millions of dollars invested in rustic, air-conditioned lodges designed for upper-middle-class Americans, nestled by lakes and babbling streams—to put it in the worst possible light—seemed a perverse notion of mission. Actually, a case can be made for the conference centers, a very good case. The problem is that neither supporter nor critic had defined the nature of mission so as to bring an articulate evaluation to bear upon, for example, the conference center as an appropriate piece of equipment for the soldiers of Christ.

When the church speaks of mission, it needs to do more than name the task: to present the Word. It must ask itself to what questions the Word comes as an answer and, therefore, how the Word may best be presented. One way of responding is to see the problem as the mobilization of the church for the union of all people in God. For example, is the church faced with a totally perverse world, whose culture is satanic, and which must be subverted, overthrown, and destroyed before a divine theocracy can be established? Is God one who achieves our commitment by any means and for whom freedom of choice is only our illusion? Is the world divided between those who are privy to the truth and others in whom there is no truth at all? If the answer to all three of these questions is "yes," then we have the beginning of a case for "guerrilla warfare for Jesus." The mobilization for mission becomes the task of equipping such missionaries to fight that kind of war for Christ. It should be clear that I do not believe this to be true.

But the issue here is the need for the clarification of content of the word *mission*. This needs to be clearly understood. An analogy would be the debate that provoked the court-martial in the United States of Billy Mitchell between World War I and World War II. Mitchell's argument was that the next war would be won by air power. Against the orders of the army and navy top commands, which thought otherwise, he proved his point by sinking an obsolete ship from the air. We now know that Mitchell was right, despite his court-martial. His call to America to mobilize for a very different war than World War I was the call of a prophet and patriot. In like manner, to what content of mission is the church today called? Who is the enemy Christians must fight? How must we be equipped? What is the nature of the terrain over which we must move? How is it that in answer to these first three questions Christ may win?

The Mission of God

It is possible that some might answer these questions by saying that since mission is of God and not the church, it is not for us to decide. When God calls us to go forth, we need only respond. While there is no doubt of the sincerity of some who think this way, it is muddy theological thinking at best. It is important, however, to reflect briefly upon the meaning of the mission of God or, as it is technically called in Latin, the *missio Dei*. The theological notion of the *missio Dei* has been central to that field of Christian thought known as missiology. (Recent literature in missiology speaks of the *missio Dei* as a technical term, which is why I begin here with the Latin.) The word *missiology*, meaning the study of the nature and implications of God-as-one-who-sends for the church and its life, arose at the turn of the century in Germany among evangelical theologians. It was adopted by the Roman Catholic Church with the creation of a chair of missiology at Münster in 1914. Its theological elaboration has been largely in Roman Catholic thinking, as in Vatican II's *Ad Gentes,* and evangelical theology. Jürgen Moltmann, a Protestant theologian, in *The Church in the*

Power of the Spirit roots the understanding of mission in the now widely accepted notion of the *missio Dei*. His theory has appeared in American Episcopal expositions of a doctrine of mission.

Jürgen Moltmann argues that because of the *missio Dei* one can say that the church is mission or that mission constitutes the church. Unless this statement is qualified, however, the church runs the danger of thinking something has been said that makes a difference, which we can appropriate. It is equally true to say that the ministry of Word and sacraments constitutes the church. It is in the sacramental life that we are formed by the God-who-is-mission. This was said in several ways in the previous chapter.

The *missio Dei* refers to two related missions: the internal one as pertains to the inner life of God and the external mission. *Missio* is a noun derived from the Latin verb, *mittare*, which means simply, "to send." It is the "sending" of God that concerns us.

In the inner life of the Godhead, Christians have believed, with some variations, that the Father *sends* forth the Son, the second person of the Trinity, to become incarnate in the person of Jesus of Nazareth. This is what is technically called the hypostatic union. We also believe that the Father *sends* forth the Holy Spirit. In the Western church, following the lead of Augustine of Hippo, we would say that the Father *and the Son* send forth the Holy Spirit, the life-giver and guide into all truth. So *sending* is a primary characteristic of the inner life of God. In some German theology, this internal mission of the Godhead is called *der Sendung* to distinguish it from the external mission, which they call *der Mission*.

The external is different from the internal mission, but it is related to it. That communication which exists within the persons of the Trinity carries a potential for communication outside to the world. It is both the inner and external nature of God to communicate himself. Therefore, a *sending* is at the heart of God's relationship to the created order, which is the medium of the divine revelation or self-disclosure. To participate in mission is in this sense to be an agent of revelation. The

external mission is the embodiment of the character of the
internal mission within the people of God. The two marks of
such mission are love and trust.

All theology today needs to be missionary and mystagogic: it
speaks from the mystery of God to the world and leads us back
into the mystery of God. This means, first, that the faith and
belief of the church are alien to the prevailing world view.
Christian thinking is over against secular thought and, consequently, the church is in the attitude of sending its message to
an unevangelized world. This refers not just to some land on
the other side of the world, but to our next-door neighbor, our
spouse, or our children. Second, there is no sense of the
mystery that surrounds our little island of knowing, and it is the
task of Christian mission to make persons aware of that mystery
and to lead them into its power.

The relation of missionary and mystagogic theology is an
important point. The image the reader might have in mind is
of the ocean tide, the ebb and flow along the shores. Mission
reaches out to draw humanity back into the mystery of God's
love. Too frequently we conceive of mission as giving people
answers to questions they ask. More accurately, our outreach
serves to provoke in people who think they have the answers
some very challenging questions. God is not so much to be
found in the "light" of contemporary knowing, but in the
darkness of our ignorance, of which we dare not ask the
questions. So a theology that provokes in contemporary humanity a sense of the mystery of God goes hand in hand with a
theology of the *missio Dei*.

The image that this evokes is of a God who sends himself
forth in the nature of a divine communication in order that he
might draw us to him. This is the imagery of Jesus' words in the
Fourth Gospel, " 'No one ever went up into heaven except the
one who came down from heaven, the Son of Man whose home
is in heaven. This Son of Man must be lifted up as the serpent
was lifted up by Moses in the wilderness, so that everyone who
has faith in him may in him possess eternal life" [i.e., return
with him to the Father] (Jn. 3:13–15; NEB). The word "to be

lifted up," *hupsōthēnai*, means in Greek both "to exalt" and "to crucify," and evoked an image related to the story of the bronze serpent in Numbers. There the Israelites were punished by God for grumbling by being bitten by poisonous snakes. If they looked upon a bronze serpent that Moses was told by God to make and erect upon a standard, they were healed. The image fascinated the Fourth Evangelist as an analogy for the crucifixion. He used the same word, *hupsōthō*, later on, but added the idea of Christ bringing people to him by the power of the Cross. "'And I shall draw all men to myself, when I am lifted up from the earth'" (Jn. 12:32; NEB). The word for "draw" is *helkusō*, which means to drag in a net of fish—not a bad image for the Gospel—or to draw a sword. It also refers to the pull on humanity's inner life, for good or evil. Plato in the *Phaedrus* used this word to say that desire drags the soul into pleasure—not a good thing in Plato's thinking. For John's Gospel it has the sense of the believer's return to the source of life.

The mission of God is the gift of himself. He is the proper subject of a missionary theology. It is theology of his Passion. It is related to God's choice of Israel, the begetting of his Son, and the gift of the Holy Scripture to the church. God is one who sends himself in love even to the death of the Cross. It informs us concerning the purpose of sacramental life of the church and our participation in the Passion, including the preaching of the Cross, and the witness (i.e., martyrdom) of prophetic Christian lives in every corner of the world. But that is only one phase of the movement. The other phase is the return to God, what the ancient church fathers called the *ascent*. God in Christ descends to us that we might ascend to him.

Another way of expressing a missionary and mystagogic theology is in the imagery of the synoptic Gospels and the Kingdom of God. The goal of creation is the Kingdom or reign of God, and the whole of the church's mission receives its focus and orientation in the Kingdom perspective. The sense of return is here: the Kingdom of God was a return to the Davidic kingdom, seen as the ideal age. The fact that Jesus is at the heart of any preaching of the Kingdom also implies the mystery of the Incarnation: of a God who, while absolute, loves us enough to send his Son that we might be as gods.

No understanding of mission is legitimate unless it takes into account the total movement: sending and return. What is the character of humanity's ascent to God? Although this book is not a text in spiritual theology, what we say about the content mission has to be said in light of our understanding of the nature of people's growth into union with God. It is my belief that some ideas concerning mission do violence to the best understanding of spiritual theology and, therefore, need to be repudiated.

Five Theories of Mission

In 1978 Frank Ponsi, a Roman Catholic missionary in Ethiopia, published a paper entitled "Contemporary Concepts of Mission."[1] It is a thoughtful essay that deserves wide reading. I am indebted to Ponsi for most of what I have to say here, although I have sought to clarify some of his concepts in order to make them more applicable to our situation in America and to relate them to my own theological understanding.

Mission as Recruitment

This is the common sense understanding of most Americans when they hear the word *mission*. It has both a Catholic (by which I mean a liturgical-sacramental interpretation, much broader than Roman Catholicism) and an evangelical dimension. The biblical precedent lies in the common interpretation of the Great Commission (Mt. 28:19–20). The enemy of this theory of mission is the seductive power of Satan, evil, and sin within the individual. Like Faust, the individual sinner sells his future for the present enjoyment. The plan of attack is in some way to convince the individual of his great peril and to get him to decide for the promise of God to him of everlasting life. This is how Christ wins. The mission of the church must, quite literally, be equipped bluntly or subtly, to "scare hell out" of people. The individual, convicted of his sin, accepts Jesus Christ as his Lord and Savior.

This acceptance in the Catholic orientation comes about in Baptism. In the Book of Common Prayer of the Episcopal Church, it is clearly spelled out. The candidate for Baptism renounces evil, he turns to Christ, and accepts him as his Lord and Savior. In evangelical thought, this acceptance comes about in the experience of the consolation. It is a much more subjective, personal occasion, rooted (as we have seen) in the emotions of the person, at which time he is moved to accept Jesus as Lord and renounce his former life.

I call this a method of recruitment because the intermediate objective—assuming the ultimate objective is the wholeness of the person or his union with God—is to get the individual's name one way or another in "the book of life" (sometimes confused with the parish register). He is to be recruited for God's side. Church Growth calls this *discipling*. Recruitment is the obvious answer in many mainline churches to the decline in church membership from 1968 on. If the numbers in the membership roles are dropping, then we need to act to reverse the trend.

But what does this assume? Recruitment is individually oriented, it identifies the human dilemma with the self-centeredness of the single person, and it understands its purpose as the assurance of everlasting life beyond the grave. I am not suggesting that there are not other concerns. The question is where the emphasis of the church's mission lies and, consequently, how it is shaped. Numbers are important because they are a measure of our effectiveness. Therefore, numbers dominate the evaluation of Christian outreach.

Cultural and historical forces in the interpretation of the experience of God tend, in this understanding, to be neglected. In fact, there can easily be a culture-denying, ahistorical set of mind in this approach that compounds a theological naïveté. What have we done when we have called the individual out of the ambiguity of his world and assured him of heaven? One thing, among others, seems possible. We have blinded him to the pervasive nature of evil. His world has become so narrowed that in some way the Incarnation is diminished.

This neglect of culture and history can have a curious echo

effect. A mission of recruitment can readily confuse the Gospel with its own culture and time in history. In effect, what it can do is call to people to serve a cultural or even a subcultural hero, trapped in our own particular history.

The effect this has upon the spiritual life is to impoverish it—unless we are very careful. The person grows by being brought into relationship with that which challenges him both within and without. Any sense of "having it made" gives us leave to turn away from the gifts of others—religious or secular—and to ignore the beckonings of our own unconscious. One of the most puzzling illustrations of this ignorance is the refusal of some professed Christians to face their own inner world, as, for example, by systematic, disciplined acts of apopathic meditation (such as the use of the Jesus Prayer in rhythm with our breathing). The effect is to produce self-righteous pseudo-converts.

Mission as Liberation

This conception is a more reflective attempt to retain the insights of the social activists of the nineteen sixties. It is particularly popular among intellectual Christians, perhaps, among other reasons, because it counters the shortcomings of mission as recruitment, which is itself often anti-intellectual. The biblical roots of mission as liberation lie in Jesus' call to care for the hungry, the thirsty, the stranger, and the imprisoned (Mt. 25:31–46). The enemy for liberation theology is the institution. Institutions, such as government, schools, the military, and industry, are considered intrinsically evil. They oppress people often without the people's knowledge. For this reason the task of the church is to make people conscious of their oppression and of the means to take control of their own destiny. The church becomes a teacher of the poor, assuring every person of his dignity. The mission must be equipped with the skills of raising consciousness by communication, comparison, and confrontation.

There is no distinction in this conception of mission between nature and supernature. The locus of salvation is the world.

The notion that the purpose of mission is to win individuals for heaven by recruiting them into the church is irrelevant to mission as liberation. The aim is to free people from what enslaves them and to establish a new society. Salvation embraces the whole of the human world. The ecclesial community is ultimately society, as there is no meaning to any claim that outside the church there is no salvation.

The Christian mission in liberation theology assumes the presence of God in all of life. The secular is not the enemy, but may in fact be the source of freedom. It enables us to work apart from the trappings and deceptions of religion. The church too easily, as this concept understands it, has become the ally of the forces of oppression and exploitation by ameliorating the pain of injustice with promises of heaven.

Wherein lies the problem with mission as liberation? For one, it is probably not so much naive as it is prone to ideological fallacy. It fails to be critical of its own explanations. Liberation theology fits too easily into its own Procrustean bed. It can romanticize the poor while taking the church to task for its failure to minister to the poor. Furthermore, without institutions, humanity is an impossibility. While institutions are sinful, it is doubtful that evil is to be identified with them. In this sense the liberal illusion—i.e., evil is a problem for right-minded people to solve—is a temptation for mission as liberation.

In fact, both this conception of mission as well as mission as recruitment have too little appreciation for the deep memory. Whereas recruitment hides from the demons that lurk within the deep structures of the human person, mission as liberation is inclined to perceive an interest in the deep memory as a luxury of the upper classes to excuse their indifference to and oppression of the poor. Actually, it is the poor who have much to teach us about the deep memory, quite apart from the ideologies of the intelligentsia, who seem particularly fond of this concept of mission. Robert Coles has taught us much about this in his studies of the religion of the poor whites of Appalachia—*Migrants, Share Croppers, Mountaineers* and *The South Goes North*—and black religion is pure deep memory.

Mission as Mutual Interdependence

At the 1963 Anglican Congress in Toronto, the Anglican Communion declared itself committed to an approach to mission that it called Mutual Responsibility and Interdependence (MRI). This conception arises out of an awareness of the paternalism of the mother church in the history of Christian mission and of the gifts that younger churches bring to the older. It values highly self-determination and the indigenous development of a Christian community. Since 1963 MRI has been the official mission policy of the Anglican hierarchy.

Obviously, this approach does not begin with an image of a hostile, pagan land to which we Christians are carrying the Gospel. It is more in the spirit of Paul's vision of the Macedonian saying to him, "Come across to Macedonia and help us" (Acts 19:9). One might ask how the Macedonians knew of the Christian Gospel in the first place. The answer lies in the hunger of the people, the preparation for the Gospel by exposure to the Jewish scriptures, and the word-of-mouth spread of the good news by nameless merchants, soldiers, and other traveling people. The mission of interdependence assumes this unselfconscious spread of the Gospel.

A case in point is a letter I received from an Episcopal missionary in Tanzania. Although she was working in the diocesan office, which, in many ways, resembles any such office in the United States, she told of someone who walked sixteen miles from an isolated village to ask that an evangelist be sent them. They wanted to know more of what they had heard only a little about. The Archbishop of the Church in Kenya once described to me a visit to a Masai village, apparently pagan, to find there a baptized woman, who became the catalyst for the creation of a school and the conversion of the people. He explained to me that the Church in Kenya has its internal MRI.

The enemy in mission as mutual interdependence is the common enemy of all people and every Christian community. It is the fear that eats at every heart, obscuring the love of God that permeates his world. Such an enemy works through ignorance and provincialism. Satan is personified irrationalism.

Evil breeds on bigotry and prejudice. We must move against it, aware of the many differences in style and sometimes content between the older and younger churches. These must not become issues that block the enactment of the responsibility we share for one another. It is by crossing over that we defeat the anti-Christian forces, inasmuch as our vision is broadened and deepened and our joy in the Common Gospel made that much richer.

There is a sweet reasonableness about the mission of mutual interdependence. I attended a partners-in-mission consultation—the heir of MRI since the meeting of the Anglican Consultative Council at Dublin in 1973—in Tanzania. Not only were church dignitaries there, but also the minister of agriculture for Tanzania and the sometime minister of education. The assumption was that as reasonable people all of us, church and government officials alike, wanted the same thing and agreed upon the same enemy. National development and evangelization work hand-in-hand. Clearly this was a church typology operating. There was no illusion as to the separation of church and state.

Mission as interdependence is optimistic and receptive. It is beautifully pastoral. There is no wonder that it is the official position of the Anglican Communion. For the same reasons it can be criticized for not taking evil seriously, for lacking an aggressive intentionality, and for confusing the God of the Gospel with good manners. Local culture and Gospel can become confused. In a sense it atones for an earlier English and American proclivity to convert people not only to Christ, but to a Western culture; yet it might be accused of a resultant lack of nerve.

Furthermore, this concept based upon the relationship between national churches, young and old, may not have the power of generalization for mission. A question can be legitimately raised as to what it tells us about the attitude of the church to the secular world. This is the danger of a church typology: to operate as if there really was such a thing as the Christian society.

Mission as Church

Ponsi explains that this theory comes out of post-World War II French thought. It was developed in the face of the de-Christianization of many European countries. Its Anglican roots reach back to F. D. Maurice, the nineteenth-century English theologian. Maurice taught that in the mind of God, the church and the world are synonymous. In its more contemporary form, the church is called to an expression of the inner dynamism of the Trinity, a perfect community. The mission of the church is the mission of God: to make actual the perfect community of the Godhead in the world.

The Christology of the Word, as found in the opening chapter of the Fourth Gospel, underlies this approach. More explicitly the following passage from Ephesians is a source for mission as church.

> In Christ he chose us before the world was founded, to be dedicated, to be without blemish in his sight, to be full of love; and he destined us—such was his will and pleasure—to be accepted as his sons through Jesus Christ, in order that the glory of his gracious gift, so graciously bestowed on us in his Beloved, might redound to his praise. (Eph. 1:4–6; NEB)

The church is the extension of Christ's incarnate presence, and its task is to call the world into becoming that body of Christ for which it was made before the beginning of time. Mission as church proceeds from a radical incarnationalism and moves to develop a doctrine of the mystical body. Such a doctrine begins with teaching that to become as a child one receives the other in innocence and, in so doing, receives Christ in the other, and in receiving Christ receives the Father. In this way the Body of Christ is built up.

The enemy of Christ in this conception is, of course, sin; but it is the sin of darkness and ignorance, rather than a sin for which Christ must pay a price to Satan. The church comes equipped with the light of Christ. "The light shines on in the dark, and the darkness has never mastered it" (Jn. 1:5; NEB). The church has to fight the stupidity and the blindness of the world. But Christ wins when the world discovers that Christ is the reason that pervades all of creation.

Although this point of view may sound optimistic, in fact, it is not. It does not hold that humanity has "come of age," but rather that we are progressively more alienated from nature, one another, and God. This makes the mission of the church, the call to community within it, and ultimately the Trinity, that much more imperative. The church's task is the process of making Christ incarnate for every age anew and gathering up humanity into the community of believers.

Mission as church is less individualistic than mission as recruitment, less ideological than mission as liberation, and less optimistic than mission as mutual interdependence. It takes the *missio Dei* as the central doctrine of its teaching. While it has a high doctrine of the church, it is ready to subordinate everything else in church life to the task of mission. The end justifies the means, which end is the reign of God.

The central problem with mission as church is also its chief virtue. It is theologically well-developed, but difficult to picture concretely. If one is asked what one *does* in the light of this conception of mission as church, the only response is: *to be the church at its best.* Emile Mersch, one of the proponents of mission as church, suggests in his exposition of "the whole Christ"—a catch phrase this school took from Augustine—that every Christian, wherever he may be, is the corporate person of the church. When you look into the eyes of a Christian you gaze in the face of Christ. This is the theory that lies behind the worker-priest movement in France after World War II, which was as notable for its failures as its successes.

The need for openness in the church as argued in this conception of mission may well have influenced the calling of Vatican II. But the theoretical base of mission as church is rejected in *Ad Gentes,* the decree of that council on mission. It is possible that the approach is too ready to subordinate all structures for the cause, while it is equally probable that the church is threatened by the willingness of mission as church to surrender those structures that provide a sense of security to its members, including the hierarchy. It is a theory that catches us in the dilemma of our hesitance to internalize all symbols of our faith and our ability to be the church in the world. With all of its problems—some of which can be ameliorated by drawing on the other four themes—it is the fundamental focus of the theology of mission in this book.

Mission as Fulfillment

To some this is a nontheory of mission. It is not primarily concerned with conversion, it is not related to interchurch structures, and it is not very interested in church extension. It bears a relationship to liberation theology, but has less of an ideological base and a greater appreciation for the deep memory. For this last-named reason, it is a helpful corrective, whatever else one may make of it, of other theories of mission.

Perhaps the father of mission as fulfillment was the second-century saint, Justin Martyr, whose apologetic for the Gospel of Christ to his fellow Romans was that it fulfilled their deepest longings. If we look to the Scriptures, sayings come to mind such as: "'You are the salt to the world'" (Mt. 5:13; NEB), "'You are light for all the world'" (Mt. 5:14; NEB), and "'The kingdom of Heaven is like yeast'" (Mt. 13:33; NEB). Paul likewise reminded his readers that the whole of creation was groaning, awaiting the fulfillment of all things in Christ (Rom. 8:22).

Some of those who have argued this position most forcefully are often Catholic (in the theological, if not the juridical, sense) thinkers, who have lived closely to persons of other faith. It is they who have become sensitive to the common deep memory shared by humanity: its longing for justice, its perception of the transcendent, and its quest for love. They have also been made aware of the narrowness of much Christian missionary activity. For example, it is increasingly saddening to confront the inability of the Anglican mission in East Africa in the first and second generation to build upon the deep religious sensitivity of the African people, instead of importing English ritual controversies into an alien land.

The American theologian, Paul Tillich, was an advocate of

mission by fulfillment; and Karl Rahner has been perhaps most notorious for this viewpoint in his theory of the "anonymous Christian." While Rahner has been misunderstood and frequently attacked for what he believes to be true in this regard, he is actually saying nothing more than Catholic theology has long held. This is that someone who believes and follows the truth as it is available to him is made whole in Christ, even though he does not explicitly profess him as Lord. Rahner is neither "baptizing" everyone against his will, even those who reject Christ, nor is he advocating an "anonymous Christianity," which is a different thing.

Mission as fulfillment clearly does reject the arrogance that so easily besets much Christian outreach. In fact, the enemy can make use of this arrogance to prevent the effective proclamation of the Gospel. This, combined with the self-centeredness that is characteristic of all people, is what we must overcome. The church needs to honor the deep memory of those who do not believe and know their longings and how they are expressed. While Christ can only be known through culture, he is above every culture and fulfills every culture. In the sixteenth century, the Jesuits followed a missionary policy summed up in the aphorism: "Go in their way, come out your way." If we changed this to read "Go in their way, come out Christ's way," it might sum up the equipment of the missionary of fulfillment. It begins with a sensitivity to the Christ implicit in the other and then calls for the skill of relating that to the cosmic Lord.

Mission as fulfillment seeks missionaries who first of all are willing to listen. One must earn the right to speak. That right is acquired as we become familiar with the deep memory of the people whom we would seek to teach Christ. In return, as we listen we will learn from them, and our own Christian faith will be deepened. John S. Dunne of the University of Notre Dame has called this process of enrichment *crossing over.*

The problem with this conception is obvious. It can easily become an excuse for indolence. There is a fine line between affirming the implicit faith of those who do not know Christ and engaging them at that point and abrogating the mission of the church altogether on the grounds that everyone has his own way to know and serve God. This becomes a particularly touchy point when considering the mission to the Jews.

Narrowing the Options

Ponsi ends his discussion of the five theories of mission with the comment that these options are likely to persist, despite the scathing criticism each makes of the others. He is probably right. Yet this book is not merely descriptive; it also aims at an evaluation from a point of view admittedly Anglican. Are we not obliged to make a choice as to which seems most in accord with the Scriptures, tradition, and reason in the light of the present sociocultural world?

It is not that simple. A major purpose in this discussion has been to lay side-by-side five theories so that the reader will not think that mission is always to be defined by one understanding in which he has been schooled—for example, mission as recruitment. Care is taken to offer some criticism of each approach, while acknowledging the viability of each particular insight.

Yet we can move beyond this, even if a simple choice is avoided. In the second chapter the biblical objectives were discussed and a common thread through most of them identified in five parts. These were: union with God; the persistence of the quest as opposed to having "arrived"; the communal stage of human wholeness; the moral component as the victory over oppression and injustice; and the necessity of suffering. A clear means of evaluating the approaches to mission lies in their consonance with this objective in all its dimensions.

It is my opinion that mission as recruitment is less likely to lead to strategies and tactics that will bring about the accomplishment of this objective than any of the five. In recent history it has been a reaction to a sterile scholasticism at a time when the common understanding of what it means to be human lacked the sophistication of the biblical period or, for that matter, practically any period previous in the history of Christian thought.

This is a controversial statement, upon which subsequent chapters will elaborate. Furthermore, none of the other four theories of mission is sufficient in itself. Probably mission as church and mission as fulfillment together offer greater promise than mission as liberation—although elements of that approach are essential to our understanding—and mission as mutual interdependence. But the problem here is in generating a sustaining enthusiasm for mission in our times under their aegis. Mission as church is more likely to do this than mission as fulfillment.

Beneath any conceptualization of mission lies those metaphors within the deep memory that provide the principal motivation. We need to be open and honest about those. Yet how do we do this? There is possibly a destructive myth that could lie behind mission as recruitment. Symtomatic of this myth are images of a deep fear of death and sex, a paranoia that breeds on a we/they dichotomy, dark corners of our life we cannot admit or share, and a need to be seen as successful or as one who wins. This is a judgment and needs only to be denied to be refuted. Yet those are very powerful images.

The same examination could be made of the other theories of mission, although they do not invite the same kind of analysis. They are not as interesting, which says something in itself. But interest is not the issue; it is the outcome that matters.

CHAPTER SEVEN

Evangelization as a Tactic

The Readiness for Ministry program of the Association of Theological Schools in the United States and Canada is an effort, originally funded by the Lilly Foundation, to evaluate the capacity of entering and graduating seminarians to function in those ways perceived by clergy and laity alike as necessary for effective ministry. The students are judged in the light of sixty-four categories, which have been positively correlated to what are considered desirable qualities in the priest or pastor. These criteria have been rated according to denominational families. In Anglicanism "assertive individual Evangelism" is rated by both the clergy and laity as less desirable for a priest than in any other denominational family except by the clergy of the United Church of Christ.[1]

To put it another way, from a sampling of clergy and laity in the Anglican Communion in the United States and Canada, it is judged that an effective Anglican priest does *not* include someone who has skills in evangelism. Without doubt, some will say that this is obvious from our action as Anglicans. But this response may make the common error of those who berate Anglicanism for a failure of commitment to evangelism and suggest it shows we are not open to the Spirit. Just as we need to know what we mean by mission, so must we first know what we mean by *evangelism* or, as I would prefer, *evangelization* before we level the accusing finger.

Why is one word to be preferred to the other? *Evangelism* is a narrower word. It often refers to a discrete function of ministry, usually set in a chronological order. There is pre-evangelism, evangelism, and then life in the church. It also can

connote a theological point of view set over against nonevange-
listic theologies. It is important to avoid reinforcing a narrow
interpretation, so the word *evangelization*, naming an ongoing
action within the total life of the church, is a happier term. The
contrast in mood and even meaning of these two words is
illustrated in two little books: David Watson's *I Believe in
Evangelism,* which is a personal and warm call to recruit
individuals for Christ, and Bernard Häring's *Evangelization
Today,* which is a clear, analytical, and judicious description of
what the church's proclamation of the good news implies for
society.

We need to remind ourselves that if God is mission and if this
mission constitutes the church, the objective of mission is to
draw all humanity to union with God. The strategy is the
renewal of the minds and hearts of humanity: *metanoia.* As the
strategy is in the service of the objective—i.e., the changing of
people's minds is to be evaluated by whether or not it brings
about union with God—the tactics are in the service of the
strategy. *A tactic of ministry is no better than the authentic renewal it
effects!*

Evangelization is a tactic. For this reason we cannot consider
it apart from the intended objective and the outcome. To say
that we "believe in evangelization" is like saying we "believe in
eating." It says nothing remarkable. It is close to affirming
existence. Eating is a tactic to stay alive, but not all eating is
equally effective. We cannot consider evangelization apart from
its place in the total picture of God, Christ, and the church. Far
too often, church people affirm or reject evangelization as if it
were only one dietary option.

Objective and Outcome

We need to recall that the objective of an intentional
process is the *projected* end of that process; the outcome is
what in fact the process *accomplishes.* The objective of the
ministerial process is a project of our theology. It is the
desired end as we picture it drawing on our understanding
of God-as-he-is-to-us.

A few examples might help to make this clear. World War

I, we may recall from history, was the war "fought to end all wars." That was the objective. The outcome was to embitter Germany, to reinforce American isolationism, and to lead us into World War II. The Vietnam War was fought to save South Vietnam and all Southeast Asia from Communism. The outcome in America was to change irrevocably the psychology of the American people. Both World War I and the Vietnam War were fought by this country in the light of our understanding at the time of the sociopolitical reality and our place within it. If we had been a bit clearer, more analytical, and sufficiently judicious in our understanding of ourselves and the world, we might have been less sanguine about our objectives.

Evangelization has the same dynamic. A sociological study of the Billy Graham Crusade in Knoxville, Tennessee, in 1970, argued that while the objective of the program was to bring the people of Knoxville to Christ, the outcome was to reinforce the old middle-class values of the people attracted to this kind of event. There may be nothing wrong with those values, but anyone with any sense of history knows that Jesus of Nazareth was not a member of the American middle class. Any relationship between the objective and the outcome is only tangential.

The activity of evangelization must, therefore, be evaluated in terms of its notion of the objective and outcome. In other words, evangelization needs to be related to its ability to effect a kind of renewal that opens people to the desired objective. If the objective is unclear or the outcome differs radically from the objective, then we need to look at the understanding of mission that begot that style of evangelization. But what we project as the desired end of evangelization, the objective, must first be capable of theological analysis; and, then, what the process accomplishes, the outcome, must be evaluated in terms of this same theological inquiry.

This process is illustrated by looking at what is known as Church Growth. Church Growth is an approach to evangelization developed over the last few decades by Donald A. McGavran and his associates. It is an articulate position, with a growing body of literature, that is well known in the churches, including the Episcopal Church. The national policy of the Episcopal Church, while not a carbon copy of this theory of evangelization, has been informed by Church Growth.

The School of World Mission in Pasadena, California—the headquarters of Church Growth—is a school of highly competent practitioners of evangelism, who need to be taken very seriously. Church Growth is not a simple-minded example of mission by recruitment. For example, their theory of ethnotheology clearly incorporates the role of culture in mission that is related to mission as fulfillment. In recent years there has been an earnest attempt to include the theology of liberation in their thinking. A brief look at both the objectives of the Church Growth people and what I suspect may be the outcome—we have no specific hard data on this— from a theological perspective is a way of exploring what is meant by evangelization in the light of a developed methodology. My intention is not a simplistic "put down," yet there are some questions that I will raise

Robert Calvin Guy, writing in *Church Growth and Christian Mission,* says: "Mission rises from theological foundations. It is a projection of basic theological beliefs. Its vigor and form reveal what it is based on."[2] It would appear Guy is proposing a relationship between "vigor" and "form" and suggesting that relationship validates a theology.

An adequate theology of mission, Guy explains, is one that gets the reader or hearer "involved with God personally and redemptively," which means that "every true theology is a theology of redemption and of church growth."[3] One would then assume that redemption is the "form." The increase in numbers alone is no evidence, *ipso facto,* that the church is "vigorous" as a redeeming community if more and more people experience redemption. Church growth *validates the form.* If this is true, it is this assumption—growth equals and validates redemption—that needs to be questioned.

Certainly the ultimate objective of evangelization and renewal for Guy is redemption. Church growth is the necessary intermediate objective (in the sense of the third chapter), meaning it is to be achieved as the *sine qua non* of redemption. But what does redemption look like? Guy says it is "eternal fellowship with God" of which Christ is the source.[4] Those who accept Jesus as Lord and Savior are brought into this fellowship, and through our total response our problems are solved.[5] Our greatest problem is, of course, the rebellion of sin. Unless we are obedient to Christ we are in sin and there is no goodness in us.[6] This is to say there is no natural good. The charitable act of a pagan is evil because it is not done in obedience to Christ.

This doctrine of sin is a classical tenet of Reformed Theology with a very high doctrine of providence in which everything happens by God's intention. Such a teaching is accompanied by a very low doctrine of human freedom. If tragedy besets us, its explanation and purpose lie in the mystery of God. If affliction makes us angry, it is because we fail to love God enough to trust him.

For Church Growth, New Testament theology reveals the objective of mission. This understanding of sin and redemption is, they believe, the clear teaching of the Bible. Arthur Glasser says, "We are under obligation to live according to Scripture (I Cor. 4:6, RSV)."[7] It is the basic assumption that this is a simple, clear, biblical theology, which transcends the pluralism of all subsequent theology. Such a scriptural understanding overcame denominational differences, which they acknowledge are often the product of historical and cultural accident.

The appeal to biblical theology is constant throughout the Church Growth movement. Consequently, their particular theological position is removed from criticism, as the Church Growth people imply, by the claim of a biblical position. Their assumption, however, is false. There is, of course, no such thing as a single biblical theology. The Bible itself has various theologies. Reginald Fuller has demonstrated three Christologies in the New Testament, and Edward Schillebeeckx has described three New Testament doctrines of the Passion. The claim that biblical theology has priority in the interpretation of the church is, in itself, a historically conditioned notion, which bespeaks a weak ecclesiology. Since there are numerous theological positions within Scripture, the Church Growth people are selecting certain ones on the basis of prior theological criteria, which is a product of their church life. Of this, the process of selection is determinative in their choice of objectives in a theology of mission.

What is the prior position? Generally, the authors of Church Growth operate from the Reformed or Evangelical tradition.[8] ("Reformed" refers to the classical theological elaboration of the thinking of John Calvin. "Evangelical" is the name for what happens to that theology as a result of the Pietist movement.) For Arthur Glasser it is the authority of Scripture, the sovereignty of God, the instrumentality of the church, and divine election.[9] The missiology that arises from such a prior theological position is mission as recruitment.

In the light of their understanding of mission as recruitment, we need to look at Church Growth's ultimate objective against the possible outcome. The ultimate objective is eternal fellowship with God. This is an understandably vague project, and to test it, we need to ask a prior question: what is the outcome of the intermediate objective of increased numbers throughout recruitment? What is the outcome of the intermediate objective of increased numbers through recruitment? Is there inconsistency between the intermediate outcome and the ultimate objective?

In 1966, Charles Glock and Rodney Stark, two sociologists, published a study in which they documented a positive correlation between religious orthodoxy, particularism (i.e., a sectarian or exclusivist understanding of religious belief), religious bigotry, and anti-Semitism.[10]

These were seen to be particularly true of "conservative" Christians, in which category the Reformed or Evangelistic traditions fall.

In 1971, Glock and Stark offered further evidence that religiosity and bigotry are associated. Since that date there has been considerable exploration of this thesis by subsequent research. The validity of their argument depends on the nature of a person's religious profession and what a researcher may examine in religion. Where religion provides a means of self-understanding in some depth—possesses an intrinsic orientation—it is accompanied by religious tolerance. The authoritarian personality, on the other hand, so lives his religion that it becomes an excuse for bigotry.

Theology, it seems, makes a difference. In all the research done on this question since Glock and Stark, the most fascinating is Walter Broughton's finding that the manner in which a person's theology resolves the theodicy question—how does God justify injustice?—is a clue to the relationship between commitment and bigotry.[11] For example, someone who holds to providentialism ("There is no need to worry about poverty, because God has a plan for the world.") or predestination ("God wills that some be born to misfortune and others to success.") is likely to be insensitive and inactive to injustice. Providentialism and predestination are historically characteristic of Reformed theology.

It is not surprising, therefore, to discover that the Church Growth movement is cautious about social issues. This caution is built upon the clear distinction in the theory between discipling and perfecting. Discipling is recruitment. It is getting people into the church. Evangelization should not, in this theory, make that unduly difficult by confronting people in their bigotry. It is for this reason that Peter Wagner says that the Christian congregation should practice social service—for instance, raising money for the world's hungry—but not social action—for example, confronting unjust housing practices.[12]

Wagner argues that it is in perfecting—something akin to growth in holiness—that moral sensitivity develops. The disciple, once confronted by the demands of the living Lord, will find his bigotry challenged and overcome. It seems true, however, that Church Growth is concerned far more with discipling than it is with perfecting. It teaches methods of discipling, but it appears naive when it comes to understanding the possibilities of perfecting.

There is no doubt that spokespersons for Church Growth

themselves possess moral sensitivity. They are not bigots. The issue is whether or not their tactics of evangelization are likely to produce a renewal that is relatively free of gross prejudice Does their life with the living Lord effect the change they suggest it does? Undoubtedly it does with a few. With the majority the evidence is that it leaves them untouched. The theology of the Evangelistic tradition, with its emphasis upon the sovereign will of God and our individual response to that will, does not provide much structure from which to challenge the cultural image of Jesus as a white, American folk-hero. Despite the insight of its leaders, the theological presupposition of Reformed or Evangelical theology works against a challenge to a bourgeois self-righteousness.

One cold February I was flying from Minneapolis to Winnipeg. Seated directly behind me was a man dressed in a white suit, wearing a white cowboy hat, and carrying a limp leather Bible. Next to him was an East Indian, who early on identified himself as a Hindu. Our white-suited companion explained for all to hear that he was going to speak for the Campus Crusade at the University of Manitoba. Throughout the flight he read to his Hindu companion selected passages from his Bible followed by interpretative comments. As we landed he asked the East Indian, "Friend, what do you think about Jesus now?" I had to cock my ear to catch the quiet reply. "I have always thought of him before," he said, "as a teacher of peace. I am somewhat surprised now to learn from you that he is more like the president of the Bank of Dallas."

The first step in questioning such cultural triumphalism as this story illustrates is to cease appealing to a nonexistent transcultural biblical theology. I am grateful to scholars such as Peter Wagner for their willingness to look at liberation theology with appreciation, and I find his criticism of this theology informative. It is unfortunate, however, that Wagner finds it necessary to pose in the face of liberation theology a sense of "oppositions." He suffers here from what a colleague of mine calls the "Chinese menu fallacy." The fallacy is the notion that theology is done by *choosing between a list of two sets of alternatives.* For example, Wagner says redemption of the individual comes before reconciliation of the group, apocalyptic comes before prophecy, nationalism comes before universalism, and covenant comes before liberation. The initial choices build a reliance upon an exclusive relation with God that easily mounts into an impenetrable self-righteousness that excludes the alternatives as possibilities. The effect is that the outcome of the intermediate objective, church growth, defeats the ultimate objective, eternal fellowship with God.

Church Growth runs a real risk of creating a situation that thwarts a perfecting consistent with biblical norms of renewal. What particularly comes to mind is the spirit of risk and cultural renaissance. It seems so important to be "right." Do we experience freedom in Christ in this approach, or spiritual smugness? There is so often a strange, dour joylessness associated with a populist piety in so many of the recruits of current Evangelical theology, which leaves no room for the rich creativity of the obscene, the orectic, and the monstrous. The deep memory is suppressed in the name of puerile goodness. Christian joy is swallowed up in the haunting fear that someone is really happy.

As a tactic, evangelization is no better or worse than the outcome it produces: intermediate and ultimate. We need to be grateful to Church Growth as an articulate movement developing a clear tactic, which can be seen as a function of its theology. There is a clear relationship between the objectives of its theology and at least the intermediate outcome. If this intermediate outcome is unacceptable for us, there is a lesson here for us. We must explore a theological alternative. But first we need to be clearer about how we got where we are.

Evangelization in America

Church Growth, despite its commendable intellectual articulation of a tactic of evangelization in the service of renewal, reflects the strong tendency in America to an homogenized religiosity. The distinction between very different Christian understandings of the objectives of mission and the resulting methods of soliciting the world for Christ has been all but washed out by the wave of nineteenth-century revivalism, now identified with American middle-class religion. The word *evangelism* conjures up for most people, including social scientists studying it, a single constellation of images born of the American frontier identified with mission as recruitment.

This was made clear to me in doing a workshop on evangelization and Christian believing. I asked the participants to bring with them to the workshop the write-up of an "act of evangelism." I was genuinely surprised to discover how difficult this was for some and how in others the request provoked anger. One woman described how when she was five years old in rural Alabama she was forced to "accept Jesus as her Savior" on the stage of a tent and, as a consequence, would have nothing to do with the church. Evangelism had had its outcome for her: it drove her from Christ.

If evangelization is appropriate to a theological position other than what we find largely implicit in Church Growth, then we need, as a prelude to exploring alternatives, to have some understanding of how it came to be associated exclusively with the American religion of the camp meeting and the revival.

American religion is more Calvinist in origin than anything else. The roots of the common sense theology of the American people, no matter what their denominational label, lie in the Reformed tradition. One explanation for this, other than pure historical chance, is that Calvinist theology—the emphasis upon the transcendence of God over against his immanence, the total depravity of humanity, the absolute authority of Scripture, and the predestination of all people—flourished where a certain kind of decision making within a social system existed. This is a possibility suggested by a sociology of religion that claims the way a people understand the relationship of God to them is a reflection of how they interact with one another in society. Reformed theology can be seen to have developed where the society provided for special interests in the society to have a part in the decision making: a parliament, the judiciary, the military, etc. In those situations, the king did not make all the decisions. The American social system, which has a high degree of multiple elements in its decision making, would appear in this theory to be both a result and breeder of Calvinist thinking.

But what gives us our narrow notion of evangelization is not Calvinism itself, but some notions out of this tradition unaccompanied by intellectual vigor. John Calvin, the author of a great architectonic system, was a disciplined man of thought. His teaching concerning election—that all persons before birth are predestined to heaven or hell—arose out of a logical analysis in the face of the overweaning concern of the sixteenth century with the providence of God. But a practical question arose out of the doctrine of election. How does one know whether he or she is elected to heaven or hell? Calvin's answer was the so-called "fruits of election," the discernible evidence of God's favor. Such evidence lay for Calvinist thinkers in, for example, modesty, thrift, devotion to work, responsibility in public affairs, and the ordering of one's life, particularly that of one's family.

There is a close relationship between the sense of destiny among the first settlers in America and their theology of election. It is this flaw in Calvinist theology that opened the door to a self-righteousness and insensitivity of conscience that justified for some the rape of the American Indians, the development of the slave trade, and the philosophy of exploitative mercantilism. Max Weber's thesis that Puritanism gave rise to capitalism is well known.

But this alone did not produce the American notion of evangelization. Calvinism was not an emotional religion nor did it advocate a missionary theology! What happened to produce a transition was the reaction among some in Germany to a sterile Protestant scholasticism (i.e., a narrow adherence to traditional doctrine) in the late seventeenth century. As is too frequently the case, the perceived cynicism of the theologians provoked a sentimental reaction. This reaction is called Pietism, after the "college of piety" of Philipp Spener, one of its early leaders. Pietism accepted the Calvinist notion of election, but wanted the evidence of election to be manifest in something more immediate than the fruits of disciplined thought and will. They found their answer in Enthusiasm, a religious outlook common to humanity in all ages, which values the overpowering emotional experience of God. (For the sake of clarity it should be noted that Enthusiasm in church history takes two forms: mystical or, as recounted here, evangelical.) The Pietists decided that if we are to know God has elected us then it will be an emotional reassurance, which they called the consolation. It would, they believed, be followed by a moral transformation. The impact of this course of behavior on American religion is immeasurable. For one trivial example, it justifies the obtrusive queries of the street-corner evangelist, "Brother, are you saved?" He is asking whether we have experienced the consolation.

Sacramental theology, with its notion of a mediated, formative grace shaping the whole person, stands over against the enthusiastic experience. Calvin had a clear sacramental theology. This was less true of his followers; and by the time of the Pietists, the central place of the sacraments had all but vanished. Baptism and the Eucharist were peripheral at best. Where the sacraments remained important, as in John and Charles Wesley, Pietism was tempered. But where the experience and maintenance of a personal experience of Jesus as Lord and Savior, commonly identified with the consolation, became all-consuming, it radically changed the pattern of Christian devotion. Sentimental worship, prayer in small groups, and "hell-fire" preaching became the rule. The moral transformation expected focused on the private, "warm" sins of the individual: drunkenness, sexual license, stealing, sloth, etc. It is much easier to preach against adultery than it is to witness against immorality of big business.

Whereas the focus of our discussion in this section is on the evolution of evangelization in America, a part of our national story is the effect of Pietism upon the "mother country" and Church of England. The restoration of the English monarchy in 1660 diminished the discipline of Puritan thought in the English church. The overthrow of James II in 1688 removed much of the committed spiritual leadership of mainstream Anglicanism. Many of those who took their oath of allegiance to James II believed this oath still obliged them, and they went into schism. What was left in the church was a theologically inept and lukewarm body of clergy, who, with notable exceptions, were lacking in imagination.

It was in this drab world that the Wesley brothers and their associates began a movement that was much influenced by the German Pietists. The movement, known for its powerful preaching, sought a simple acceptance of the gift of faith to salvation in the experience of sudden conversion. Sentimentality reacted to cynicism. The Wesleys and their associates became the impetus for both the schism from Anglicanism we known as Methodism and for the Evangelical party which remained loyal to the Anglican church. Theologically, Evangelical Anglicanism was of several kinds: extremely Calvinistic on the one hand or Arminian to the core (Arminius taught Christ died for all and not just the elect) on the other hand, or somewhere in between. This lack of theological decisiveness may have kept the Evangelicals in Anglicanism, but it contributed to the sentimentality of English Pietism.

Among the leadership of the Evangelical party there was a much-needed profound moral sensitivity. For example, it opposed the English slave trade. With Charles Simeon, the Evangelical movement in England developed an effective educational concern. The Evangelical academies, where clergy and laity were formed in Evangelical thought and manners, later became the model for some Episcopal seminaries (e.g., Episcopal Theological School in Cambridge and Virginia Theological Seminary). The Evangelical movement also developed its own missionary society in 1799, in opposition to the more broad-church Society for the Propagation of the Gospel (SPG), in which Evangelicals were not allowed membership. This society was the Church Missionary Society (CMS). But it has also retained from the beginning a curious lack of appreciation for sacramental living and the deep memory, which leaves an impression of a very "pinched" style of life.

There was a common perception of the Gospel between English Evangelicalism and the American Evangelical tradition that emerged in the nineteenth century. For this reason, the relationship of Anglicanism *as a whole* to American Pietism appears somewhat confused. Some Anglicans, for example, enthusiastically support Billy Graham, while many others find his approach quite alien to their own. This has become even more complicated since various renewal movements took hold of the Episcopal Church beginning in the early 1970s.

The simple directness of Pietist theology was ideally suited for the American colonies, where the uncertainties of frontier existence evoked a need for an emotional outlet and spiritual assurance. Pietism was embedded in our national consciousness by monumental efforts built upon the expectations of a consolation theology. The first such effort was the Great Awakening, culminating in the visit to America of the English Evangelical, George Whitefield, in 1739–40. Jonathan Edwards, the last great Puritan theologian, gave substance to what was happening in the Great Awakening by his explanation of the "religion of the heart"; but the subtlety of Edwards's thinking was all but lost in the enthusiasm of the movement. The second Great Awakening in the early 1800s had no Edwards to temper it with theology. Following in the tradition of Wesley, it lost the severity of Calvin and was now more Arminian in approach. Such optimism gave an impetus to an Evangelical outreach as exemplified in the camp meeting, the revival, and the "altar call," as well as that succession of American arch-Evangelists, who became the shepherds of the national soul: Charles Finney, Dwight Moody, Billy Sunday, and Billy Graham.

The Puritans were a thinking people, not easily seduced into sentimental assurance. They knew the ambiguity of Christian discipleship and would never let thrift be confused with greed, a sense of destiny with blind chauvinism, and the ethical life with moralism. No healthy-minded Puritan would succumb to the idiocy of thinking that an annual revival did much more than promote intemperate behavior—and the Puritans believed in temperance, not abstinence. What American religion has done since the mid-eighteenth century is drift into a form of religion untested against the tradition and unexamined by theological thought, and mostly consisting of a potpourri of cultural guilts and longings. In one sense, this explains the naïveté of subsequent prohibition, laws against teaching evolution, and the success of the "electronic church."

My great-grandfather was a Methodist circuit rider in Georgia, Florida, and Arkansas through the latter half of the nineteenth century. As a school teacher of 21, his hope was to help people get to heaven. His world was neatly divided between the Christians—those who had experienced conversion—and the non-Christians. He wrestled with God, his "carnal propensities," and Satan. His diary is filled with resolutions for self-improvement mingled with affirmations of his reliance upon grace alone.

As I reflect on my great-grandfather's story as a piece of American religious history, it strikes me how this tradition of Pietism was incapable of carrying the deep memory. In a hard life it was undoubtedly a source of comfort, but it left him "shallow." His mood is one of chronic sadness, supported by the assurance that some day his stern God would justify his inscrutable ways. Evangelization was for him the kindling and repeated fanning of an inner glow. There is a poignant honesty in his complaint:

> We had no special manifestations during our Quar[terly] Meeting exercises. Several mornings at the prayer meetings a few were blessed. The most of the church were perfectly indifferent to our efforts to obtain from the Lord a season of refreshment and revival power.

The inherent contradiction in Pietist evangelization is contained in this monumental effort to show evidence of a gift appropriated, which is already freely given and cannot be acquired by anything we do.

Asking a Prior Question

The problem with many an approach to evangelization is that we do not test the objective. What is it that we want to have happen as a result of our profession and proclamation of the good news in Christ. Since, in the last analysis, religion is always the answer to a moral question, the objective must be framed in terms of morality. What is it that God wants people to do?

Without doubt Jesus was more than a teacher of morals. Most of what we attribute to him in the way of ethical teaching was not even original with him. But he certainly believed that the impending reign of God had clear implications for the way we live our lives. The Sermon on the Mount was for Matthew a charter of freedom, the law of old covenant transformed by the impending breaking in the Kingdom (Mt. 5:1–7, 29). The Evangelist was describing what the result of hearing the Gospel would be in terms of his understanding the tradition as a first-century Jew seen through the experience of Christ. He reminds us that for Jesus and for us a call to justice can never be independent of the call of the Gospel.

Evangelization, therefore, has to begin with picturing the moral life and acting so as to accomplish this end. This is the preemptive question: does our evangelization accomplish the moral end? As Bernard Häring, a Roman Catholic moral theologian, states very succinctly: "For a Christian, a cult which does not bear fruit in love of one's neighbor and in justice directed toward the life of the world, is worth nothing."[13]

But Häring goes on to say that we must desacralize and deabsolutize morals. Morality is *not* a matter of perceiving the "plain truth of the Bible" dictated by God. It requires only a modicum of thought to understand there is no such "plain truth." Morality is the act of discerning the signs of the times in the light of the tradition and the contemporary world. It requires detachment, openness, and the willingness to listen and to give of self at great risk. Since discernment is always an act of the intuition, there is nothing "plain" about truth—moral or any other kind. Discernment is a true act of faith, hope, and love.

According to the "plain truth" of the popular Jewish law in the first century, Jesus and the disciples violated the Sabbath (Mt. 12:1–8) by "harvesting" grain. Actually, for those more learned in the Law, a case probably could have been made for what they did, although plucking ears of grain was one of the thirty-nine acts specifically forbidden by later rabbinic interpretation. On the surface, Jesus was condemned as immoral because he did not follow the black-and-white letter of the Law.

What in fact he did was an act of discernment. He gave himself and his followers space to make a judgment in the light of the tradition and the current situation and came to an ethical decision and action. At the heart of the objective of evangelization, we need the ability to discern the signs of the times.

For those who would discern the signs of the times today, it seems to me to be very clear that the American root paradigm that technology is righteousness—celebrated in "American know-how" and the naive belief that the natural resources for growth are unlimited—is bankrupt. In its place is the root paradigm that God brings judgment and justice. Any evangelization that fails to carry this message at its core obscures the Gospel. Indeed, there is mercy in God's judgment, for he seeks to save and not condemn humanity; but he also demands of us a new way of seeing that is very different from gross consumption.

The church is a community of moral reflection, consensus, and action. When a person responds to the Gospel, he accepts his responsibility to that community. He is that community, not an affiliated individual. Values prevail within the history of the Christian community that inform our ethical decisions—not so much to give binding answers as to lead to the most probable conclusions. Clearly, such a value is the freedom that is given in Christ, which condemns all forms of oppression, including the self-righteousness of the Pietist. Theories of mission and their implementation in evangelization need to honor this value.

For this reason the objective of evangelization must include all dimensions of human need at the same time. For example, Paul tells the Corinthian church: God "has enlisted us in the service of reconciliation." Reconciliation is the work of God, just as redemption is. Redemption does not come before reconciliation. Reconciliation is redemption. This is the meaning of the Incarnation. God is one to humanity in its totality: physical, social, cultural, emotional, and intellectual. Redemption is not a transaction between a solely transcendent being and an individual soul. In redemption we are reconciled to God and at the same time reconciled to all creation.

Oneness with God frees us, and to be free is to have space.

True morality requires space. By space is meant the room to explore options intelligently and with imagination, guided by the Spirit. The opposite of space is the obsessive need to be right. Space permits us a self-knowledge that begets a sensitivity to evil without and within. There is within us a God-given longing for life with him, which can only be fulfilled as we move through the darkness of evil. Moralism, which avoids the encounter, in fact works against reconciliation and provides a pseudo-redemption. The church, when she is willing to fulfill her vocation, is the institutionalization of the space to seek wholeness. Renewal is the consciousness of the space in which we are turning around to know God.

And it is here we find the mission as church. The church in all her brokenness is the primary sacrament of Christ, and all her sacraments are expressions of the reconciliating action of God in various states of life. They live out or make effective the primordial reconciling act: the life of Jesus, culminating in his Passion. There can be no evangelization without the church, which is the body of Christ. There is no evangelization that is not rooted in the sacraments making present the Passion of Christ for now. Evangelization is an event of a believing and adoring community, into which all are invited to fulfill their longing for oneness. The sacraments have necessary ethical implications and so does evangelization. Both present the person with a gospel that calls us out of the *status quo*. The Christian is always a stranger in his own country.

A Concluding Observation

Wayne Williamson, an Episcopal priest, in his book, *Growth and Decline in the Episcopal Church,* takes exception to the common view that evangelization requires us only to be present and to proclaim, and that we leave the results to God.[14] Quite apart from the fact that it is possible to argue that we are required only to be present and proclaim from Scriptures, I would agree with Williamson. Although I do not see much correspondence between his theology and mainstream Anglican theology, I think Williamson is right when he agrees with Peter Wagner's argument for a third "p": persuasion. Evangelization can be an evasion if we settle for presence and proclamation, without so intending our tactics that they effectively persuade.

But we need to go beyond Williamson. We need a fourth "p." To evangelize requires that we be present, proclaim, persuade, and *prove* our objectives by their outcome. Williamson's goal for evangelization is the increase of numbers. He wants us to "preach for a verdict" in order that we may "save souls." Williamson needs to prove that, in fact, preaching for a verdict does save souls.

My argument is that in the light of an Incarnational theology, which is central to the Book of Common Prayer and Anglicanism, as well as Roman Catholic and Eastern Christians—i.e., the vast majority of Christians—it takes more than "saving souls" in the Pietist sense to produce a Christ-intended outcome. "'Not every one who calls me "Lord, Lord" will enter the kingdom of Heaven, but only those who do the will of my heavenly Father'" (Mt. 7:21; NEB). This can be said equally well for those who say ad nauseam, "I've accepted Jesus as my Lord and Savior." This insight into the will of God and the careful cultivation of a life in accordance with that will require the church as our primary community. The proof of our evangelization is the quality of the moral life of the Christian within the community: the ability to discern the signs of the times and to act in response to what we know to be true.

Williamson quotes John Henry Cardinal Newman as saying that "growth is the only evidence of life." I am not sure what Newman meant by that statement, but I am confident he meant more than Williamson implies. (Tumors grow!) On the basis of this analogy, surely growth is not the final test of the effectiveness of our evangelization. Large numbers are admirable—but the proof comes elsewhere. What is the quality of the life of discipleship in terms of the biblical objectives? That is the crux of the matter.

CHAPTER EIGHT

The Proof of Evangelization and Renewal

The issue that the four "p's" of evangelization raises is a crucial one, which we need to pursue. If evangelization is an instrument of effecting a new consciousness (renewal) in anticipation of the impending kingdom, then it requires something more than subjective testimony for its justification. Renewal or repentance requires, as we have said repeatedly, space to turn around. The climate of renewal is marked by risk, confrontation, new order, and cultural renaissance. The proof of evangelization lies in the creation of such a climate where those marks may be evident.

Furthermore, evangelization, if it is in the service of the Gospel, must work toward the biblical objectives: union with God, the spirit of quest, the centrality of community, the passion for justice, and the time of testing. Any method of evangelization that draws us away from these as goals is not just questionable, it is in violation of every canon we can identify as to purpose of renewal. Therefore, the proof of evangelization not only lies in the climate of renewal, it is identified with the orientation of renewal.

As a contribution to the proof of renewal and its servant, evangelization, a simple model can prove helpful. I introduce it with a preliminary note. The purpose is to make some evaluation of *renewal phenomena that evangelization within a certain movement seeks to effect.* A phenomenon is an event or series of events or a representation of same that one may observe. It is not a cause or a movement. An example of a distinction between a movement and its phenomena might help. The protection of endangered species of wildlife is a movement, a very commendable movement. Some years ago this movement was able to forbid the capture or killing of alligators in those areas of Florida, Alabama, Mississippi, Louisiana, and Texas, where they used to abound and were now rapidly approaching extinction. In fact, they were so successful that within a few years the people of those regions rapidly were becoming in danger of "being knee-deep in alligators." That is a phenomenon.

I wish to make this careful distinction between movements and phenomena because I find some individuals in renewal movements—for instance, Neo-Pentecostalism, Cursillo, Faith Alive, and Marriage Encounter—take quick offense at any criticism of phenomena as a condemnation of their movement. Whereas this excessive sensitivity to criticism, met often by *ad hominem* arguments ("If you had received the Spirit you would understand!"), is worthy of examination in itself, I want to disarm if possible the offense by making clear the distinction between movements and phenomena. To criticize certain phenomena is *not* to condemn a movement, unless that movement claims a perfection to its life that exceeds all reason.

Let it be said clearly and emphatically: *we welcome all genuine renewal and the evangelization that effects it, whatever its name.* The need, however, is to get behind the rhetoric of renewal and find ways of discerning *genuine* renewal through an appreciation of the phenomenology of renewal that transcends subjective witness—"Jesus is my Lord, because I tell you he is."

An Analytical Model

The accompanying diagram is a simple model of two scales: the extrinsic–intrinsic religious orientation and the ideological–imaginal articulation of religious experience. The two scales create four quadrants or cells: extrinsic–ideological, intrinsic–ideological, extrinsic–imaginal, and intrinsic–imaginal. It is my belief that all evangelization effects renewal phenomena that generally fall within one of these quadrants.

This is a cognitive model, which is to say that it presumes that

ideological   imaginal

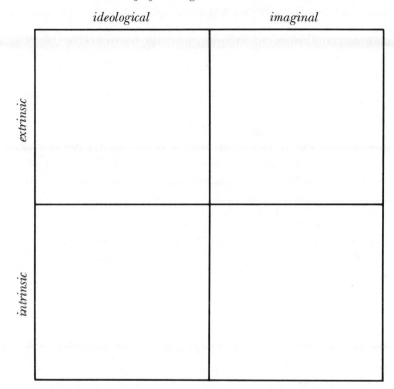

human action is a product of the manner in which we construct our world in our heads and hearts. Human action is not merely a result of how we have been programed by society. Therefore, what we make of our religion (its orientation) and how we think about our experience (its articulation) have a great deal to do with how we behave as people and as Christians.

I am also making a clear value judgment. The least desirable cell for renewal phenomena is the extrinsic–ideological. There is less possibility of such phenomena engendering a climate of risk, confrontation, new order, and cultural renaissance, which we identify with genuine renewal, than anywhere else in these scales. Certainly it is not the locus for a unity with God that is progressive, with passion and openness for testing.

It follows that the most desirable quadrant for renewal

phenomena is the intrinsic–imaginal. It is here that we must risk: confrontation is inevitable; a new order can arise; and the seeds of cultural renaissance are sown. The progressive nature of the quest for unity with God becomes most clear here, as will the existence of a community where justice is sought out and faith tried. Above all, it is here that the deep memory becomes most accessible.

The definition of these scales is as follows:

Extrinsic orientation: This term, along with *intrinsic,* was coined by the late Gordon Allport, a psychologist teaching at Harvard. In extrinsic orientation the function of religion is to provide support, protection, and assurance in the face of a world that threatens to overwhelm us. In other words, it serves a purpose extrinsic to the purpose of religion: to enable growth into the fullness of humanity, integrated within and without. An extrinsic religious orientation thwarts the development of a whole person in terms of the inner and social self as described in Ephesians 3:18–19. Because of the protective function of an extrinsic orientation, it intends to maintain religious belief at the level of the surface memory, inasmuch as the deep memory is threatening.

In an extrinsic orientation the focus is on protecting the individual from evil forces. Religion becomes a means of sophisticated divination, by which we identify and control the sources of evil. The extrinsic orientation is deeply concerned with sin and the separation of those who are sinners from those who are blessed. Consequently, it encourages us to exclude rather than to include those who are not clearly identified as one of the group. The extrinsic religious orientation is prone to correct the error of the person who rids himself of the evil spirit, but leaves his house unoccupied, swept, and tidy. The unclean spirit returns with seven spirits more wicked than himself (Lk. 11:24–26).

Intrinsic orientation: An intrinsic religious orientation understands God as calling us out of ourselves into a new order of creation. Faith is a risk without support, assurance, or protection. The assumption is, in this outlook, that what we are to be we neither have achieved nor do we understand. We are by definition incomplete and in process.

The focus in the intrinsic religious orientation is on the expanding horizon of knowing. Just as any human relationship lives off a deepening intimacy, so the relationship between the person and God is one of greater increasing knowledge of God and, as a consequence, a deeper knowledge of oneself. As Paul writes, "My knowledge now is partial; then it will be whole, like God's knowledge of me" (1 Cor. 13:12; NEB). A person in our community in whom the intrinsic orientation prevails is committed to the belief that we are the children of God, called by God into ever fuller being. It encourages an inclusive approach to people and the willingness to enrich our own faith in sharing with others.

Ideological articulation: An ideology is the doctrine of a movement, an institution, a class, or a large group. An ideology is peculiar to a particular body of people at a discrete point in history, and consequently is socially and culturally prescribed. An ideology is not bad; it is inevitable. All of us live out a particular ideological framework. For example, good manners are ideological. American males are offended by body odor. It may not be as true of European males nor was it true in this country a hundred years ago. It is a matter of ideology.

Ideology is, however, limiting. Because it is socially and culturally prescribed, it reflects the prevailing institutions within a society. Its expression values precise, clear, unambiguous language. Consequently, an ideology draws off the surface memory rather than the deep memory; when it prevails in all forms of consciousness it thwarts change.

The ideological articulation of experience is conceptual and systematic more than metaphorical and narrative. An ideologue has low tolerance for ambiguity and tends to dismiss whatever does not fit within his or her system. For example, in the first years of the women's liberation movement any notion of human personality that suggested there was more than a cultural distinction between masculinity and femininity was dismissed, despite evidence to the contrary. The advocates of women's liberation at that point were almost purely ideological.

Imaginal articulation: Imagination requires space to associate images, independent of any prescribed logical system. It is the world of metaphor and narrative, rather than concept and system. Ambiguity or apparent contradiction is a precondition of effective imaginal thinking. It provides the stimulus for new ideas and possibilities. There is minimal control in the imaginal articulation of life and high risk of threat.

The artist lives in the world of the imagination. He or she is a person of integral awareness, possessing a high degree of sensibility. Understanding and wisdom as opposed to information and factual knowledge arise from the intuitive dimensions of human thought. When the nineteenth-century Jesuit poet, Gerard Manley Hopkins, distinguished between the perception of the landscape and the grasp of the *inscape,* he was at least pointing to the function of the imagination over against a form of thinking that is more receptive to ideological thought. The inscape is how things really are "inside," and this cannot be discovered by just looking. One has to see with an inner eye.

Obviously the imagination functions within the deep memory. Such thinking opens us to and increases our consciousness of the images and their accompanying emotions that provide the major motivation and direction to our lives. If we understand renewal or repentance as a change of consciousness in heart and mind, imagination has to be something we embrace with abandon. We have to trust to the God who binds himself to us in the passion of love, a love that is fed by the imagination.

The nature of each cell within the two scales should be clear. The next step is to look at certain renewal phenomena in the light of this analytical model.

An Evaluation of Renewal Phenomena

Some years ago I criticized in print the statement of a prominent cleric as narrow-minded who was quoted as having said that within the next five or ten years all Episcopalians will either be charismatic or nothing. It is entirely possible that this priest was misquoted or that I misunderstood what he meant by "charismatic." Be that as it may, I received from a reader a stern reprimand for my narrow-mindedness.

Sometimes it appears that we live in the world of *Alice in Wonderland,* where we can make language mean whatever we want it to mean. Criticizing an idea as narrow-minded is not being narrow-minded, and it is certainly not "un-Christian." Paul tells us that discernment—the word *criticize* comes from the same Greek root—is a gift of the Spirit (1 Cor. 12:10). It seems to me that the narrow-mindedness in question is any temptation to fit all church people into one mold—"to wrap the mantle of renewal" around a single style.

There is a tendency in the church to advocate a certain cheery good will—"If they're enthusiastic, that's all we need"— in opposition to critical analysis. Those who think this way in religion could not tolerate it in business, government, or family, and for very good reason. It leads to a morass. For the same reason we cannot allow this malignant "good will" in the church. It gives permission for an expenditure of energy that in all probability will not serve the church, but only leave us possessed by our illusions.

I would like to identify some phenomena—not people or movements—*which more often than not* are characteristic of the quadrants or cells delimited by the analytical model just described as an effort toward a critical appraisal of contemporary renewal.

Extrinsic–ideological

This is the most undesirable category for the result of any effort at renewal. It is a direct contradiction to what we understand about the nature of repentance as requiring space to turn around.

On occasion I have seen a bumper sticker that reads something like this: "Jesus said it, I believe it, and that's all there is to it." It is wonderful to be certain of being so right! Of course the statement begs at least three questions: How do we know Jesus said "it"? What is the nature of "belief"? and do the "words of Jesus" answer any and all questions posed by "it"—whatever "it" may be? This bumper sticker is meaningless as a religious affirmation, but it tells us a great deal about the person who advertises his opinions on the rear of his car.

In the Episcopal Church we used to laugh about literalism. Its relation to the extrinsic needs of the believer and its inability to understand that the Bible is inevitably an ideological statement of the experience of God are self-evident. If there is a modern heresy, unknown to the ancient church, it is probably biblical literalism. The early Christian fathers certainly understood that one had to look beyond the literal meaning of the Scriptures to understand the meaning of the text. But in that strange univocal frame of mind, so common to the modern world, it is easy for us to miss the need for interpretation.

Biblical or, for that matter, doctrinal literalism is a pall of death laid over the person of faith. The Spirit is quenched in anyone who frames the experience of God within his own perception of the literal meaning of the text. It is comforting to the frightened person to think he or she has the truth in his or her control, but it leads nowhere but into an ever more narrowed existence. Such a narrowed existence is kept alive by the dull thump of the hardened heart (Mk. 6:52).

Inasmuch as literalism is the prototypical character of the extrinsic–ideological cell, it is related to the identification of cultural values as Christian. For example, an advertisement in *Logos Journal*, a slick publication of Christian renewal, asks us to "reach teens for Christ with a Bible-based, spiritually-correlated . . . Christian charm course." The contrast comes to mind between the ancient authors of the New Testament, who shared the common view that a bath a year was an indulgence, with the chapters in this "Bible-based, spiritually-correlated" course entitled: "Diet and Exercise," "A 'New Look' Within and Without," "Facial Beauty," "Your Hair—A Halo of Loveliness" (the ancient world thought the demons lived in a woman's hair), "Fashion Techniques to Flatter Your Figure," "A Girl's Guide to Etiquette," etc.[1]

Without doubt this horror is an extreme example, but there is a certain logical flow between the "Christian charm course" and some of the more subtle confusions of Christianity with social and political opinions that identify "success American style" with a biblical viewpoint. This assumption tends to seep through the rhetoric of the "electronic church" from time to time, and is even more evident in the off-camera comments and public-relations promotions of those who have made such a numerical and fiscal success out of television evangelization.

The appeal of the "electronic church" is the assurance it gives the confused and oppressed person. Like much renewal phenomena within the extrinsic–ideological cell, it comes in the form of answers to the questions of anxious people. This is true of more than the Evangelical tradition. In the early 1950s, a survey of the Episcopal Church, seeking to identify who was most likely to be active in the church, was made. It was published some years later under the title: *To Comfort or to Challenge.* The results of the survey showed that the person most likely to participate was someone whose religious needs were met by extrinsic–ideological answers. It would be a woman, divorced or widowed, over 50, who came from the lower socioeconomic classes—in other words, someone whom the system is least likely to affirm.

It is very tempting to direct evangelization tactics to this quadrant. It produces results. There are more lonely, uncertain people in our society than anything else. More than once I have found myself challenged to explain what we teach in the seminaries to enable our graduates to reach persons who think concretely and want concrete answers. My inquisitors remind me that the mainline churches are dying for lack of numbers. What are we doing, they want to know, to fill them up. The enemy of visible results is abstraction, as they put it, and equivocation. The alternative, it seems to me that they are suggesting, is to identify what they want to hear and give it to them. This is to advocate an extrinsic, ideological religious expression.

There lies behind the extrinsic–ideological phenomena a sociopsychological need, which almost compels people to express their Christian faith in this restricted manner. It is perhaps the reason why people who live this kind of religion are very successful at working with drug addicts. One may take drugs for the same reason that one expresses one's religion in this manner. There is a low tolerance for ambiguity, a need to reach a resolution in life and to know what to do. Difficult questions are reduced to simple ones. The point is that the extrinsic–ideological cell all too often reveals a commitment to a religion of comfort for the person confident of salvation. This requires a *simple* assurance, which means all ambiguity must be banished and disquiet repressed. This becomes particularly evident in the narrowing of ethical issues. I was watching a television news feature recounting the story of a man who makes handmade shoes and boots. The boots run about a thousand dollars a pair. This craftsman mentioned in passing that a prominent evangelist—his name is a household word—had recently ordered eight or ten pairs! Hunger stalks our streets, the pious condemn homosexual rights, and a preacher spends eight to ten thousand dollars on shoes!

Life is a great deal more complicated than the phenomena in this quadrant would imply. Any claim to renewal that characterizes this cell is simply untrue.

Intrinsic–ideological

In this cell there is a less obvious contradiction of the spirit of renewal and a not quite so limited space for turning about to Christ. The problem lies in the reductions of the ideological stance.

An obvious example of an ideological reduction is the Christian adoption of a Marxist philosophy. Marxism is a somewhat dated ideology, which can provide valuable insights. But it also quickly becomes a Procrustean bed. Everything for the Christian Marxist is strained through the notion of political theology. For example, Elaine Pagels in a book on the ancient Gnostics, *The Gnostic Gospels,* defends the Gnostics as a group on the basis of her political theology. The Gnostics rejected the Resurrection, she explains, because they were oppressed by the hierarchy, which taught the Resurrection. The myth of the risen Lord becomes the tool of a political struggle.

There are no surprises in such political theology. It is boring. Life is a stereotypical drama, like a "horse opera" or a Hollywood war movie. All the characters are two-dimensional and predictable. An example of the reductionist viewpoint is a notion, passed on to me, that when the Russians invaded Afghanistan in 1979 it was to protect that country from a CIA takeover. To raise any other possibility was to violate "the obvious." All imperialism was, one had to believe, necessarily capitalist. Surely life is not this simple.

Ideological religion is not limited to Marxist political theology. Other cultural patterns are confused with the Gospel, become dislocated from the logic of time or place, and end up appearing as strange affectations. In an earlier generation Episcopal seminarians with disciplined devotion had "high tea" in their rooms in order to prove their commitment to the Gospel of Jesus Christ. Somehow an English style of life was confused with the service of the Palestinian messiah. That distinctive dotty Anglican air, which Hollywood enjoys ridiculing with considerable humor from time to time, is more than just a benign confusion of the Gospel.

What happens to the excitement of hearing the good news in the intrinsic–ideological cell? Philosophical orthodoxy or good manners quell the possibility of anything untoward evoking the deep memory, with its possibilities of incongruity and vulgarity. Proclaiming the good news of Jesus became akin to selling the party line or sending fraternity bids. It is predictable and not very compelling because it is insensitive to incongruity.

I remember once sitting at a very formal dinner party in my honor in which everyone was a "card-carrying liberal." Throughout dinner the conversation fluctuated between extolling the behavior of our host, who had recently committed what some considered high treason, and discounting everyone who disagreed with their doctrinaire position. Meanwhile I became progressively more and more concerned with the disagreeable flavor of my coffee. It was only when after the third cup—I found drinking the stuff one way to soothe my dis-ease—that my dinner companion politely and quietly observed that she had never known anyone who used salt in their coffee. I had mistaken a large salt dish for the sugar! But my gastronomic gaffe did nothing to break the rhythm of that totally predictable social interaction. It was ignored. Indeed, I felt like an imperfection in a ritual, which is quickly overlooked lest it disturb the comforting predictability of the liturgy. It is so easy for us to become mesmerized by the self-evident truth of our own ideas that no surprise can break through to the deep memory.

Theological orthodoxy is another expression of this same intrinsic–ideological quadrant. It can be the imposition of a bygone cultural ideology in the name of the divine Father. This is not to suggest dogma is unimportant. The problem arises when we fail to take into account the historical nature of theology and avoid the hard task of testing in every age the ability of Christian dogma to express the experience of God in terms of contemporary reality. Theological orthodoxy ceases to be more ideology only when it espouses plausibility.

Much of the banter between Jesus and the Pharisees in the Fourth Gospel is an example of a people caught in the intrinsic–ideological cell. Jesus shows them signs: the changing of the water into wine at Cana; the curing of the crippled man on the Sabbath; the feeding of the five thousand; the healing of the man born blind; and the raising of Lazarus. One would consider these rather earth-shaking occurrences. But the Pharisees, in turn, ignore what happened and reject his teaching, because it does not fit their categories. This is ideological blindness.

Extrinsic–imaginal

It perhaps seems strange that the imagination can be employed for extrinsic purposes, but in fact it can. It is not unlike the use of psychoanalysis to avoid responsibility rather than as a tool for becoming better integrated. The current fascination with the thought of C. G. Jung can become a refuge for those unwilling to make a commitment and act on it.

In the more overtly religious vein, the "turn to the East," or the rise of the cults, or the dabbling in the occult, all of which requires an exercise of our intuitive side, becomes cluttered with hidden agendas. People rebel against society, the church, their parents, the West, or something else by becoming receptive to new insight. They become vulnerable, but also exploitable. If those coming to this quadrant of our model do not have ulterior motives, those who seek to use the innocent for their own ends find the extrinsic–imaginative quadrant a rich hunting ground. James Jones and the tragedy in Guyana is a clear case in point, where people rejecting their past and open to the Spirit were led into hell.

This may seem esoteric to most of us, but a corrupting imagination can operate within traditional Christianity as well. Paul wrote the church in Colossae:

> You are not to be disqualified by the decision of people who go in for self-mortification and angel-worship, and try to enter into some vision of their own. Such people, bursting with the futile conceit of worldly minds, lose hold upon the Head. . . . (Col. 2:18–19; NEB)

The Apostle is describing a spirituality that is reminiscent of a discussion in the early 1970s I had with a high-school student. He was what we knew then as a "Jesus freak." He came to a seminar I was leading at his school carrying his Bible. We spoke together of his "mountaintop experience," and I asked him what he was going to do when he came down from the mountain. "That's the point," he replied, "I'm never going to come down. Everyone down there is evil. It's beautiful up here." He somehow missed the point that Jesus went down, he went down to Jerusalem to die.

In some people's minds *spiritual* means "spooky." Although I reject this equation, there are those who call themselves spiritual and evangelize others that they might become spiritual, who give spirituality a bad name. By their demeanor it is evident that spiritual for them *does* mean spooky. It serves their extrinsic needs for such things as escape or a sense of superiority, by an exercise of the imagination that is disconnected from the past. Such fantasy is wishful thinking. Bishop James Pike, who in his grief over his son's suicide ended up consulting mediums, comes to mind.

People drowning in this quadrant, drown in their deep memory, unable to relate that memory to the Gospel of Jesus Christ, its rootedness in the tradition and its service of a broken world.

Intrinsic–imaginal

St. Paul in the letter to the Galatians was angry. Having evangelized these people, he learned that someone had followed him there and convinced at least some that they must obey the Jewish Law, particularly circumcision. He assured his readers that slavery to the Law does them no good since God has revealed himself in Christ. "Christ set us free," he says, "to be free men" (Gal. 5:1; NEB).

Paul's letter to the Galatians is one of his earliest efforts. In some ways his theology is very conventional. He explained sin as the lower, physical nature of a person warring against the higher spiritual nature. His doctrine of humanity was dualist. He provided his readers with a list of sins and virtues, which did not differ from the common practice or content of the Hellenistic moralists of his day. What is unique about Paul was that he grounded the Christian ethic in neither the Jewish Law nor the Hellenistic education in virtue. It was the Spirit's gift of freedom!

Freedom is space. It is imaginal space unencumbered by fear; for freedom by definition is the release from the fear of the Law or of our lower nature. It is the space of redemption, where one may turn and see as he or she has never seen before.

The Greek verb that in our English New Testament is translated "to save" and from which the Greek noun (which it translates "savior") is derived, is *sōsō*. It is the same word that is used in the Greek version of the Old Testament and Apocrypha to translate the Hebrew word *yashah*. The fundamental meaning of the Hebrew word is "to make spacious" or "to make roomy, broad." A random example from over a hundred such translations in the Old Testament is this verse: "For the Lord our judge, the Lord our law-giver, the Lord our king—he himself will save us [Hebrew: *yoshiyehnu;* Greek: *sōsei hēmas*]" (Is. 33:22; NEB). It could just as well be translated: "He himself will give us space." In this Hebrew sense the savior is the space-giver.

In the New Testament the savior as space-giver is exemplified in Jesus' treatment of sinners. For example, Mary

Magdalene was a prostitute. Society had placed her in a very narrow, oppressed place, even while making generous use of her profession. Jesus saved her, he gave her space. She was lifted out of the narrow categories of ideology and prejudice and given room to grow as a human being.

Space is always defined, or it is not space, but an empty void. The beautiful space within a cathedral exists because of the sweep of the stone arches. My family and I once lived on the edge of a mountain with a view that looked out over a plain. It was beautiful, but a few hundred yards out there was a large maple tree that obstructed a bit of view. "Why not cut it down?" someone asked. "Don't do it," an artist-friend replied, "it defines the space."

Jesus defines the space that I have called the intrinsic–imaginal quadrant. This quadrant is devoid of ideology, as well as our own agenda. It is the shape of the freedom that he has given us by his Incarnation and Passion. For this reason, the deep memory is laid bare; we are vulnerable, but not exploited. We are led by the Spirit that we might have in us the mind of Christ.

It has been suggested that all this sounds something like the euphoric last third of *The Greening of America* with its call for a new consciousness. But this criticism misses the point of a *defined* space, a space which we are addressed at the point of our innermost questions by God. The very possibility of repentance, because it inevitably demands a theology, requires an expanding horizon of humanity's knowledge of God. The invitation and movement of this expansion is shaped by God's presence in Christ given to us, and yet there has to be this space for humanity's heart and mind to wrestle, like Jacob at the ford of Jabbok, with God (Gen. 32:22–31). I suspect the remnants of the counterculture of the late sixties belong in the extrinsic–imaginal or ideological-intrinsic quadrants.

Jesus' definition of the intrinsic–imaginal space is expressed in the constants or the intermediate objectives of renewal. These are the extraordinary within the ordinary, the institutional carrier, parabolic language, theological development, an ascesis with a purpose, moral seriousness, and appropriate leadership. It is these intermediate objectives that hold us on course within this quadrant.

The tactic of evangelization can be approved as it leads us into this dimension of Christian living. Anything else is unfaithful to the witness of the Lord whose disciples we are and who to know is freedom (Jn. 8:31–32). Bernard Häring has described this authentic evangelization as establishing the ground of the moral life: the ability to discern the signs of the times. Inasmuch as there is this necessary moral component to the intrinsic–imaginal space, the fact becomes apparent that knowing in the Christian sense always includes loving. Love is an act of the will, which means that it is an affective part of humanity. Reason has been attributed to the cognitive realm of humanity. In this study, knowing is believed to be both a cognitive and an affective perception of experience. Consequently, the Gospel that we preach must not set the cognitive against the affective, or the other way around. The Gospel calls us both to think and to love.

The intrinsic–imaginal space is, as well, a place to which God speaks to us from the future. The Kingdom of God is approaching. The Gospel is a statement about the future, and this quadrant is by definition open to the future. A people who are truly evangelized are called into an anticipation of the impending Word of God, which is only partially or proleptically understood. This is to say that we have a taste of what to expect, but only a taste. This is why no one can live here and support the status quo.

No denomination or movement has a corner on the intrinsic–imaginal quadrant. I have heard a testimony to its existence in persons who called themselves "charismatic" or who have spent their professional careers in clinical pastoral education. I, myself, would justify my commitment to Anglicanism, amid all its stormy life, on the grounds that it enables the Spirit's gift of imaginal space; yet I have learned about it from Baptist preachers and Roman Catholic scholars.

What is of concern here is that evangelization never be justified for its own sake. It is an essential tactic in the church's ministry, but like any tactic or strategy, has to be tested. The accumulation of numbers is no justification by itself. It is the ability to bring people into a space where they can turn and grow up in Christ that justifies what we do under the name of evangelization.

But that leads us to the question of what it means to grow up in Christ.

CHAPTER NINE

Growing Up In Christ

One of the fascinating recent recoveries in theological research has been the thought of John Wesley. Wesley was the source of much that American religion identifies with renewal and evangelization. His theology stimulated the organized enthusiasm that shaped the Evangelical movement within Anglicanism and gave birth to a free-church movement that was the focus for the evangelization of the American frontier. A Jesuit, Michael Hurley, has written that Wesley provided:

> a reforming and missionary agency by means of which a deep and widespread religious revival took place in Great Britain and Ireland, and in America such a rapid expansion of Christianity as "had not been equalled in Christendom since the Apostolic Era."[1]

But regretfully, it appears that Wesley's thinking is often forgotten even as we live in the shadow of the enthusiasm of his followers. He developed a fascinating compromise between the forensic notions of attributed righteousness characteristic of Western Christianity, particularly as taught in the Reformed tradition, and the ideas of forgiveness and participation in God dear to Eastern Christianity. He rejected the either/or of justification by faith or holy living of the previous century, and argued in an Anglican compromise at its best. For him *justification* and *holy* are a "both/and."

Justification, the pardon of the sinner, and sanctification, his growth toward holiness, were in Wesley's thinking the two gifts of faith. Regeneration, God's renewal of our fallen nature, was the middle term between the two, forming the Wesleyan syndrome of justification-regeneration-sanctification. All people, he taught, are capable of salvation. He went on to explore the meaning of Christian perfection, teaching that in one sense it is attainable even in this life, and in another sense something that never ceases to develop within us.

Wesley believed we are pardoned by grace through faith alone that we may participate in God, do the works of love, and grow in holiness. Sanctification is always evidenced both in the vertical dimension of saving souls and in the horizontal dimension of saving society. Consequently, one does not divide the private, social, and public spheres of life in our growth toward holiness. This is in spite of his apparent belief that the Kingdom of Heaven is formed within. The narrow-mindedness that is often associated with American revivalism—its concern for the certainty of individual salvation—is not attributable to Wesley's thought.

Wesley's doctrine of assurance must be seen in the light of his understanding of salvation. His reflection upon his experience at Aldersgate, where he received the assurance of the Holy Spirit's presence in his life, shaped the rest of his ministry. It was the evidence of regeneration, the process of ongoing renewal, but it was not proof that a person had arrived at perfection. Wesley protected himself from the charge of being an enthusiast by insisting that the assurance of the Holy Spirit must always be followed by the fruits of the Spirit. The experimental base of his faith, the heartwork as he called it, was consequently more intentional than emotional. Wesley was an intellectual. The world of feeling was the marriage of desire and will, not the frenzy of ecstatic experience. This helps us understand his break with those Moravians whose experience of the consolation led them into Quietism. Wesley makes a succinct contrast between "the light wherewith the Son of Righteousness shines upon our heart" and "that glimmering light which arises from 'sparks of our own kindling.'"

A friend of mine, who professes to be a charismatic, describes what that means to him in words very much like these I have used to indicate what assurance meant to Wesley. If the charismatic movement has recovered for the church the Holy

Spirit's marriage of desire and will for a holy life, then we can only thank God.

I have begun this chapter with an extended reflection upon the thought of John Wesley, because as a source of so much in contemporary popular thought about renewal and evangelization, it is helpful to ponder the implications of his thought as we examine what it means to grow in Christ.

First, Wesley suggests a logical sequence to justification, regeneration, and sanctification, but there is no chronological sequence. Justification is pardon, regeneration is renewal, and sanctification is growth in holiness; but there is no pardon without growth, no renewal without the forgiveness of sins and the promise of eternity, and no growth with continual trust in God's pardon and rebirth by the saving action of Jesus Christ. "The more we grow in grace," says Wesley in one voice with the great saints of the undivided church, "the more do we see the desperate wickedness of our heart." Woven through all the movement of justification, regeneration, and sanctification is the moral call to perfection, which cannot be separated from any of them.

Second, Wesley teaches that one does not "arrive" in Christ, but one grows in Christ. He does not see his own experience of assurance as a guarantee of his personal election, but as an evidence of God's solicitation of him into perfection. Here again, he stands within the mainstream of Christian understanding of the process of salvation, and reveals his own fascination with the church fathers, where God's salvific activity draws the willing Christian along a steep ascent to participation in him. "From the moment we are justified, there may be a gradual sanctification, a growing in grace, a daily advance in the knowledge and love of God."

Finally, Wesley's refusal to polarize faith and holy living anticipates Vatican II on evangelization by 200 years and offers the teaching of both a solution to a vexed problem within Protestantism. He rejects George Whitefield, who believed exclusively in salvation by faith, and William Law, who overemphasized holy living. The result is a healthy tension, where both enrich the understanding of the other as we seek to grow in Christ.

It is on this theological foundation that I wish to build the meaning of growth in Christ within the intrinsic–imaginal space. Renewal is in this light an ongoing strategy for the lifetime of the person, and, as a consequence, evangelization is a tactic that continues within the process of renewal. Growth is dynamic, not static, and this is equally true of renewal and evangelization. Therefore, any notion of renewal as being identified with a single moment in time, once for all, and of evangelization as an act of recruitment without a continuing "re-recruitment" is to be avoided.

It is for this reason that my own focus upon mission is that of church as an imaginal space, where the possibility of growth in Christ—with all that means for renewal and evangelization—is supported and enriched. This is not to exclude the other four approaches to mission—liberation, mutual interdependence, recruitment, and fulfillment—as contributions toward this central conceptualization.

A Theory of Christian Growth

It is natural to think of persons as growing in their relationship to God. Paul writes the Corinthian church:

> I have been unable to speak to you, brothers, as persons living according to the Spirit, [but I have had to speak to you] as to persons living according to the flesh, as infants in Christ. I have given you milk to drink and not solid food [to eat]; for you have not been able [to eat solid food], nor are you able now, for you still live according to the flesh. (1 Cor. 3:1–2; UTH)

In this passage he does not contrast Christians and non-Christians, but mature and immature Christians. The implication is that one grows as he is led by the Spirit *from* living according to the lower nature to the life in the Spirit. This growth from immaturity to maturity is a movement, as Paul says earlier (1 Cor. 2:15), where the person in the Spirit is able

to discern the signs of the times. We need to recall that that is
Häring's description of true evangelization.

The author of Ephesians expressed the same notion as Paul,
saying that Christ is the measure of the mature Christian who
has realized—the Greek says "arrived at"—what is implicit in
the faith and knowledge of the Son of God (Eph. 4:13). The
author of Hebrews upbraided his readers, saying that they are
still infants in need of milk rather than solid food (Heb. 5:11–
14). He went on to explain that it is their lack of moral
sensitivity that reveals their immaturity—an idea that is implied
in Paul's distinction between those who live according to the
flesh and those who live according to the Spirit.

The church never lost a step from New Testament times in
picking up on the expectation that the life in Christ was a life of
growth with moral implications. This is even true to those, like
the author of Hebrews, who taught that there was no forgiveness of sins committed after Baptism. Justification by faith went
hand in hand with holy living. As God drew the person to him
by power of his love, that person was illumined by the divine
wisdom—the Holy Spirit—which illumination showed itself in
the life of virtue. This ascent was a process that many believed
could be described step-by-step. The task was to find the place
where such growth could happen. This is why a great many
ancient and medieval Christians went out in the desert or
entered the religious orders in search of such a place.

Modern Christians have had trouble finding the place for
growth in Christ, much to our detriment. There has been the
heroic witness of some like John Wesley, who have refused to
accede to oppression in any form within the church. But the
ecclesial structure has been confining, particularly since the
sixteenth century, in the name of orthodoxy, enthusiasm,
practicality, or civil religion. We will not understand renewal
and evangelization until we overcome this proclivity to extrinsic
and ideological expression of the religious life and provide a
space to grow in sanctity.

In any theory of Christian growth the value is placed on the
process of growth, not on the comparison of one stage to
another. In other words, if a person is immature in faith, that is

not to be despised unless there is no movement. Psychologists would say unless a person is fixated. Any form of evangelization that inhibits growth as it proclaims the Gospel—which encourages a fixation—is to be rejected. Maturity can only come from immaturity. The apple must first be a flower and then a green fruit, before it turns red and ripe and can be eaten. In like manner, the Christian must crawl before he walks and walk before he runs.

The metaphor of space is not a category for those who are only mature Christians. It is a metaphor for a place of growth. In the words of Scripture, it is the "good soil" on which to cast the seed (Lk. 8:4–8). In proving the tactic of evangelization we need to perceive whether or not it calls the immature person to that space so that a person might grow. It is not sufficient that evangelization promise that sometime in the future he or she might shed his or her ideological and/or extrinsic shackles and move into the intrinsic–imaginal space. The three cells other than the intrinsic–imaginal are the places of fixation to one degree or another and thwart growth or movement.

In recent decades, developmental psychology has led research into the meaning of the growth of the person. Erik Frikson, Jean Piaget, and Lawrence Kohlberg have done a great deal to deepen our understanding. Central to their theories is the epigenetic theory of human development. By epigenetic is meant that turning points or crises arise naturally and in a discernible sequence at chronological points in people's lives. One cannot move on to another stage until the previous crisis is resolved. Furthermore, each stage is carried in the light of the subsequent stage, which is called sublation. Sublation is like the nest of boxes I used to get at Christmas. The big box has a smaller box inside, which in turn has a still smaller, and so on until there are five or six boxes, each inside the other.

A discernible sequence of stages in Christian growth has been argued throughout most of the history of Christian thought. Even the reality of sublation has been implicitly suggested. This has been incorporated into notions of contemporary developmental thought, with the significant addition of epigenetic

theory. Prior to the last century or so, adolescence was unknown and children were considered "little adults." Aside from
a notion of the "age of reason," which we now know is not one
identifiable time in life, there was little sense that people's
relationship to one another, their cognitive abilities, and their
moral sensitivity differed according to age. Any contemporary
idea of growth in Christ now must make a decision in regard to
the epigenetic theory of human development.

Without question, epigenetic theory related to sanctification
causes problems. Is sanctification governed by our age and
circumstances? It is not simply a question of egalitarian ideology. The person's growth in God is ultimately a mystery, and
God is not limited by our psychology any more than by our
theology. If developmental psychology and epigenetic theory is
a shortsighted, unproductive paradigm of human growth, then
we do not want to tie holy living too closely to its principles. But
at the same time we do not want to divorce the experience of
the Spirit from what we can determine about the nature of
human existence. The Preacher wrote, "For everything its
season, and for every activity under heaven its time" (Eccles.
3:1; NEB). Obviously he was not referring to developmental
theory, but he does suggest that God "has made everything to
suit its time" (Eccles. 3:11; NEB), which may imply far more
than the original author ever conceived.

As a way of summarizing what has been said in this section, it
needs to be noted that much understanding of evangelization
and renewal does not take a systematic look at the question of
growth in Christ. This can be because evangelization is
identified with justification, or because justification and
sanctification are seen as simultaneous, or because the analysis
of developmental stages is considered a cognitive activity and
the interest is in the heart. But the point is that if we are going
to do justice to the theology of sanctification for our times as
exemplified in someone like John Wesley, we need to take
account of the theories of growth as they may relate to our
union in Christ. At the same time, we must know the mystery of
grace. What is said here has historical precedent, as well as
support from the human sciences.

Stages of Christian Growth

In the analysis of the stages of growth in Christ I want to attempt something of a tour de force. The intention is not to offer a concise and indisputable theory, but to provide a suggestive association of ideas with the hope that they will open up further possibilities in our understanding of the process of sanctification, particularly as it relates to evangelization and renewal.

The source of these descriptions begins with a twelfth-century account by Richard of St. Victor. I have spoken of the evangelical awakening of the twelfth and thirteenth centuries as a particularly successful expression of the mission of the church. Richard of St. Victor contributed substantially to the understanding of what it means to be a person seeking union with God as he experienced that awakening. Even as Wesley, Richard will not provide a developmental model of sanctification that fits with contemporary epigenetic theory.

Then to Richard's description the analysis of C. G. Jung can be joined in a helpful manner. This can be expanded at the adult level by the research of Daniel Levinson and his associates, which was the basis for Gail Sheely's popular book, *Passages*. Finally, all this can become a setting for a look at James Fowler's theory of faith development.

We can begin by dividing human life into three stages and then within each of those stages identify two more. This will make a total of six stages: a paradigm common to Richard of St. Victor and James Fowler today.

The Age of Imagination

C. G. Jung speaks of the age of infancy and childhood (for those familiar with the models of Erik Erikson and Jean Piaget, it corresponds to the first four stages of Erikson's psychosocial theory and the first three of Piaget's cognitive theory). It begins with a unitary reality in which the person perceives no difference between himself or herself and the external environment. The world, including the self, is undifferentiated. The life task is one of *de*integration (*not* disintegration), which means the differentiation of the world. The "I" emerges. We divide the world into subjects and objects. We become conscious of ourselves.

The principal cognitive style by which a person begins to relate to the world is the *imagination*. The imagination plays with the possibility of what might be. It is the source of new insights and the artistic capacity to picture the future and then live into it. It functions by the association of images, not by arranging them in any logical sequence. The imagination depends upon the deep memory and is a source of its enrichment; consequently, it provokes an awareness of the mystery of life.

Richard says that imagination is the contemplation of God in the world of the senses. He speaks of giving attention, amazement, wonder, and veneration to the diversity, beauty, and joy of corporeal things. Imagination is not the same thing as sensation, however. Sensation feeds the affections, and the affections lead to virtue. Imagination is properly related to reason, from which follows Richard's distinction between two kinds of imagination: undisciplined ("bestial") and intentional ("rational"). Bestial imagination fails to discipline the sensations, but intentional imagination shapes the affections toward virtue.

The two stages of imagination are, first, "imagination according to imagination only," and, second, "imagination according to reason." The first is the free contemplation of the world, without the augmentation of an agenda—free play, if you will. The second emerges as we begin to ask ourselves what those experiences and images our imaginations present to us may mean. We address our contemplation of the world with a fundamental concern for how it works.

Richard was, of course, writing for adults. But the capacity of imagination that he calls his readers to exercise is a cognitive ability that emerges in the human person at about age 3 and that, we may hope, we never loose. We can look at Fowler's discussion of that age in this light, reflecting upon its implication for us as adults.

Fowler begins with what he calls (1) the *intuitive–projective* stage of faith. It is not dependent upon logical thought. Its conception of morality is one where behavior is shaped by the anticipation of reward and punishment. It is a magical, numinous world, in which symbols function as identical with what they represent. Fairy tales are as "real" as today's newspaper. Epigenetically, this stage is characteristic of children ages 3 to 6. But, as Richard implies, it is the bedrock upon which adult commitment is formed. The problem comes when this stage lacks space to grow and faith never grows. As in Richard's bestial imagination, we become mired in a fantasy life, undisciplined by reason.

Fowler's next stage is (2) the *mythic–literal,* in which the first hint of reason begins to function, but not in a developed manner. Epigenetically, it is related to ages 7 to 14. The imagination is tempered by the question of concrete reality and the way in which things work. The stories of heroes who have mastered the evil of life, particularly in the Bible, become the meat of faith development. Our moral life is guided by what will bring us and our friends pleasure. Because of the fascination with the concrete, there is a demand for specificity in our symbols which evoke a one-dimensional, literal view of life. When a Christian does not have the space to grow, he becomes fixated at this level and cannot move to a deeper level of spiritual perception. In Richard's language, the person does not move beyond the "sensibles" to the "intelligibles."

The commentary in the Gospels on the parable of the sower is an example of the mythic-literal stage of faith development. A parable is not an allegory. It is intended to subvert our common sense world and lead us deeper into the understanding of God's ways. But it is apparent that the early church could not rest content with this and, in the case of the parable of the sower, had to specify what each kind of soil meant in the attitudes of the people to whom the Word is preached (Lk. 8:9–15).

Richard insists that, without imagination, there can be no reason. But he makes the point as well that imagination must never withdraw itself from the service of reason. In Richard's meaning, imagination is the faculty of mind with which we read the Scriptures or attend the liturgy, as well as walk in the streets

of the world. To take what we see through the eyes of
imagination literally and not subject it to the scrutiny of reason
is for him a sinful misuse of the gift of imagination.

The Age of Reason

Jung calls this age adulthood, although it more accurately is
adolescence and early adulthood. (It roughly corresponds to
Erikson's fifth through seventh states.) On charts where church
attendance is plotted by age, it is the time when people are less
likely to attend worship services. The sense of the numinous is
largely lost. Rationality and control are values, and the "I" over
against the other "I's" prevails. The principal task becomes one
of adaptation to the external reality, and we easily fall into the
illusion that we are the masters of our fate. We meet our own
deep memory reflected in other people, which has effect on
whom we marry and whom we hate. The early adult is not very
self-conscious.

Richard's perception of reason is not one of unqualified
praise. He shares the suspicions of some contemporary critics
of the intellectual in that it is easy for reason to be seduced by
praise. A virtuoso intellectual performance often serves its own
end and is not a means to spiritual growth. Secularism is
particularly given to this sin of pride. As a true medieval man,
Richard attributed the adulteration of reason to the power of
the senses and prescribed their tempering through patience
and mortification.

The two stages of reason within his system are "reason
according to imagination," and "reason according to reason."
The first stage grasps the basic rudiments of abstract thought,
in which one may generalize in the light of the observable data.
The second stage is the awareness that meaning is conveyed
through concepts and systems of thought and that they can be
explored independently from the data, as in symbolic logic or
mathematics.

Bonaventure, a thirteenth-century theologian, who developed Richard's ideas, says of this same category of reason that
the first stage under reason is one of making distinctions and
comparisons. In Fowler's approach, this more appropriately

belongs to the next stage. It appears that there is a different perception here between the twelfth and twentieth centuries.

Fowler's corresponding stage to Richard's "reason according to imagination" is (3) the *synthetic–conventional* level. No negative evaluation is intended in relating people to this stage unless they are stuck here in their growth in Christ. At this stage, people understand the function of metaphor as opposed to a literal interpretation of the Bible, dogma, and liturgy, but there is not much that they do with the understanding. Their approach is precritical or naive. Analogies about God are taken as conveying an immediate knowledge of the being of God. There is no awareness of the historical nature of all statements—biblical and traditional—about God. Furthermore, there is still a fusion of thinking and feeling, with the result that if one feels a certain way he is still liable to think something is true because he feels it is. We are all fideists in some dimension of our being, but we do not want to let fideism consume us. *Fideism* is the confusion of subjective feelings with objective truth. It is possible that for Richard fideism is the result of the bestial imagination infecting reason.

In John Westerhoff's four styles of faith development, this third stage of Fowler's fits in the *affiliative style.* I mention this because it helps us perceive both the positive nature of this stage and its negative threat. In Westerhoff's system, the affiliative style precedes searching faith. If someone is fixated at this level, any challenge to move on is seen as very threatening. He or she lives in a world of law and order, in which interpersonal concord is highly valued. To question that naive perception of a world neatly put together will meet strong resistance.

This is why it is again important for the Christian pilgrim to be in a space that gives support while, at the same time, insisting on the ambiguity of any generalization about God as he is to us. In such a climate the pilgrim will be led on to test his faith, just as in other ways that person tests his vocation and sexual identity.

The following stage in Fowler is the (4) *individuating–reflexive,* which is associated with Richard's "reason according to reason."

The self now is no longer dependent on others and has a reciprocal relationship with a particular world view, including a given system of belief. A self-autonomy now begins to develop that is crucial for growth in Christ. For example, spiritual direction becomes a possibility for someone in this stage, whereas before they probably could not make appropriate use of it. The positive resolution of the transition from the synthetic–conventional stage to the individuating-reflexive stage is most desirable because it signifies the ability now to differentiate between the experience of God and the meaning we give that experience. This is the threshold of Christian maturity.

This is not to suggest that one has "arrived" at this point, but it implies one is "teachable." In moral development there is an understanding of the "grays" of ethical decisions and the need for casuistry. Symbols are perceived as symbols. On the negative side there is an obsessive need for usable concepts. This leads to what Paul Ricoeur, a French philosopher, has called the "reductive hermeneutic." This can become very tiring when people cry for "practical religion" and accuse those who are more sensitive to the deep memory as being on "head trips." The fact of the matter is that the opposite is true. This level of development is very given to "head trips."

The Age of Understanding
Understanding according to Jung is a function of the turn within and, consequently, only comes when we are ready to make that turn—about age 40 to 45, at least in men. Daniel Levinson, who with his associates, has studied the transition to middle adulthood in males, agrees. Fowler is only slightly more optimistic about the possibilities of an earlier movement. This is the bad news that epigenetic theory conveys. There are very few wise or spiritually mature people in their twenties and thirties. It would seem there could be social settings and circumstances where this rule does not always prevail.

Someone might say that Jesus was only 33 when he was crucified and ask if he was spiritually immature. It hardly follows, however, that the epigenetic theory for humankind can be challenged by the example of him who is the fulfillment of all humankind. It is intriguing to speculate, on the other hand, why the Jews challenged Jesus' claim by pointing out that he was not yet 50 (Jn. 8:57), an age in their minds, perhaps, at which one comes to a certain level of understanding.

Levinson states that when a man reaches 40 he is faced with three major tasks as he makes the transition from early adulthood to middle adulthood. The first is deillusionment (once again, not dis-illusionment). He must cease to live under the illusion that he is master of his fate. The second task is to make and test new choices in his style of life. The third task is to confront and integrate into his life certain polarities: young vs. old, destructive actions vs. creative actions, masculine vs. feminine, and attachment vs. separation. There is no resolution one way or the other of these polarities within himself. He has to learn to live with them. Wisdom may be defined as doing that. As Erik Erikson suggested, the wise man is he who knows what his parents made him and forgives them.

How does all this fit in with what Richard calls understanding? Understanding is God's self-disclosure to the person who is open to him. It is not a knowledge we achieve, it is a knowledge given to us. But it becomes a possibility for us through self-knowledge. Richard uses the image of the mirror to explain what he means, which is an image consistent with Paul's words: "Now we see only puzzling reflections in a mirror, but then we shall see face to face" (1 Cor. 13:12, NEB). He said that in the quest of self-knowledge we wipe the mirror of our inner self again and again. As one does this and gazes upon that mirror a long time "a kind of splendor of divine light begins to shine in it and a great beam of unexpected vision appears to his eyes." This is a different kind of knowledge than is identified with the accumulation of facts. It is knowledge that God gives and we often call wisdom.

Evangelization and renewal must take into account that the knowledge of God requires a continuing self-exploration and understanding. It is not enough to be an extrovert; we have to practice introversion. These are hard words for those who think that evangelization is like selling cars. Evangelization is a very different process, requiring an honesty that would destroy the stereotypical salesman.

The two significant works in Richard's discussion of the journey of the soul to God are sometimes called *Benjamin Major* and *Benjamin Minor*. The reason for the titles is that they are both based upon a verse from Psalm 68 (67): 28, found only in the Latin version of the Scriptures. In English it translates: "Benjamin a young man in ecstasy of mind." Benjamin is for Richard the type of the human mind longing for a vision of God. Ecstasy of mind is what Richard means by the soul illumined by God or understanding: the mind drawn outside itself by the God's revelation.

As before, there are two stages in understanding. The first stage is "above but not beyond reason." The second stage is "above reason and seems to be beyond reason." The first stage is to acknowledge that one cannot know God by reason. It is a form of the "cloud of unknowing," as described by the anonymous fourteenth-century English mystic. The second stage is the ecstasy of mind, the transfiguration experience, when one sees the glorified Christ.

Fowler's last two stages fit nicely into what Richard describes. In the (5) *paradoxical–consolidative* stage there is movement beyond our prejudices, personal myths, and norms to a deep self-knowledge. Thought and feeling, reason and passion, and cognition and commitment are held in a creative polarity. There is a moral commitment to a principled higher law. Richard points out that a person at this level discovers discretion, the ability to make judgments in accord with the divine will. "The intention of the mind," he says, "is guided by discretion," which shapes the life of virtue. Fowler concurs.

In the fifth stage of Fowler, there is a postcritical participation in both symbolic reality and conceptual and systematic meaning. What Ricouer has called the second naïveté, a conscious recommitment to the acceptance of symbols as symbols, emerges. Liturgy, the Scriptures, and the tradition take on a very powerful symbolic meaning. Consequently, envisioning becomes a way of seeing. One would hope that Fowler is wrong when he says that very few people reach this stage.

His sixth stage is (6) *universalizing.* The person moves beyond paradox to the incarnation of absolute love and justice. There is oneness to the consciousness of the world, begotten of a loyalty to being and a transparency of symbols. There is a profound transformation of the deep memory, made possible by the intrinsic–imaginal space in which the person has been allowed to grow in Christ. This is the moment when, as Richard says, "The rational soul especially rejoices and dances when from the irradiation of divine light it learns and considers those things against which all human reason cries out."

Space for Grace

The process of sanctification outlined in this chapter can be misunderstood. One accusation is elitism, another is Pelagianism.

It is easy to read Richard of St. Victor, C. G. Jung, and James Fowler and accuse each one of them or all of them of being elitist. In its most crass form, elitism is the belief that there is a particularly gifted group who are superior to everyone else because of their ability to advance farther intellectually, morally, emotionally, or spiritually. Models of faith development are open to this kind of charge.

The response to the charge of elitism begins with two observations. The first is that growth in holiness is an observable fact. There have been those who discounted what they saw on the grounds of their theological presuppositions; namely, that humans are beasts and that all appearances of good are illusions. People are totally worthless, they would continue to say, and their only hope is a righteousness imputed to them in spite of their total depravity. Wesley rejects this, because the idea of an incurable total depravity does not correspond to our experience. There is always something contradictory in this pessimistic theory, since it is invariably accompanied by exhortations for the faithful to strive for the good.

A more optimistic objection to theories of faith development comes from egalitarianism. Like its theological cousin, egalitarianism reduces everyone to the lowest common denominator, which amounts to saying that we are all equally bad. It confuses descriptive statements—some people are more intelligent or more spiritually advanced than others—with evaluative statements—some people are worth more than others.

One way in which Richard's discussion of the six steps provides some assistance in tempering the charge of elitism is to remember that Richard is a mystic writing for mystics. Everyone has the capacity for the mystical contemplation of God, but certainly not everyone has the opportunity or chooses to exercise the option to fulfill that capacity. Fowler's sixth stage is not, therefore, very crowded; and, in fact, the fifth stage does not bring to mind myriad examples. Therefore, there is value in emphasizing the importance of the fourth stage, which is a real possibility for contemporary Christians and, if achieved, exemplifies a creative, mature Christian life. It may be possible that elements of the last two stages can in some way be incorporated into their lives, as long as we understand the unfinished nature of our pilgrimage.

My second observation is that justifying faith is present at all stages. We need to keep justification and sanctification separate in our minds and realize that faith is an absolute; that is, either we have it or we do not. Furthermore, faith is our posture to the future, not some*thing* that we accept or do not accept. *What* we hold to be true is our belief. Faith is the expectation that God will speak to us from the future; and, consequently, what it requires is space. As long as we are in the intrinsic–imaginal space, we are people of faith.

Theologically speaking, since the process of sanctification is constructed in dialogue with human science, it may either appear or, in fact, *be* a plan for secular self-improvement. If this were true—which in fact it is not—it would be Pelagianism, the belief that we do not need God's grace to become whole. Yet there are those for whom *any* notion of a capacity within humanity for cooperation with divine grace is Pelagian. I disagree.

John Wesley was a believer in *prevenient grace,* the doctrine that God is universally and already present to us before we ever are aware of his presence. God nurtures us, and when we are in a space where that feeding can elicit our response and cooperation, we will *naturally* grow in grace. The reader needs to be aware of the implications of the word "naturally." I am speaking of a tradition of Christian humanism with a long and distinguished list of theologians—Irenaeus, Origen, Augustine, Bonaventure, Thomas Aquinas, John Donne, F. D. Maurice, Charles Gore, William Temple, Bernard Lonergan, Karl Rahner, to name just a very few—who believed that there was no radical discontinuity between nature and supernature. This is the position of mainstream Anglicanism.

The belief that when human nature is infused by the divine, it grows naturally, also repudiates forensic or legal notions of the Passion of Christ. It was Anselm at the beginning of the twelfth century who systematized the forensic concept of the Passion, although notions of Christ's death as a sanctification for our sins go back to the third century; the Western church has been frequently given to the teaching that, in his death, Christ paid a price for our souls to the devil and that we were not made righteous, but imputed or treated as if righteous. This teaching developed alongside the growing fascination with law in Western civilization. While historically understandable, it does not accord much insight with understanding God today, as compatible with the idea of the good. A more Eastern approach, expressed in the growth of the person by the power of Christ's incarnation into the likeness of God, speaks more effectively to our vision of a God who calls us into the relationship of a father with his daughters and sons to complete the work of creation.

The intrinsic–imaginal space is, therefore, the place of grace. Grace is nothing less than the presence of God himself. God's presence to us is not that of a despot, but of a lover. Love must have space in which to move and invite the beloved. There can be no sharing of love where there is compulsion or preconditions or victimization. There has to be room for us to turn and grow in relationship to one another.

CHAPTER TEN

A Theological Reflection

In these last two chapters the intention is to draw together, first, the implications of what has been previously discussed for systematic theology, and, second, to speak to the consequences of this study for ministerial action. It has been my experience that these are two general questions of principle that arise in any discussion of mission, renewal, and evangelization.

The intention is to provide reflection upon the subject of renewal and evangelization from a different angle in order to form an extended summary. Some themes presented in the previous nine chapters will be considered anew from a consciously theological or pastoral perspective. My desire is to draw together a somewhat complex phenomenological consideration of the mission of the church with the more familiar categories of the theological and pastoral disciplines.

I recall an occasion on which I had been speaking on theological education and the mission of the church. In the dialogue that followed my talk, two persons stood out. One wanted to know what the seminaries were doing about "functional universalism" and the other wanted to know how the seminaries were teaching the future priests of the Episcopal church to reach all people in their concrete situations. I could never get the second inquirer to see that he was asking a question that demanded we deal initially with the implications of the first inquirer's question. It is vital that we understand just how this is true. For a start we have to ask ourselves what the theological presuppositions are that suggest the Episcopal church *should* "reach all people in their concrete situations."

What the first inquirer was saying is that our actions are a function of our theology. If we are going to understand someone's ministry or if we are going to shape someone's ministry, we must first raise the theological question: What is God-as-he-is-to-us? The previous nine chapters have been neither systematic nor programmatic; they have been phenomenological. We have discussed, in the light of Scripture, what mission, renewal, and evangelization look like, with occasional theological and programmatic implications stated. But now it is time to be less occasional or *ad hoc,* and to touch upon some important themes within systematic theology. In this way the previous discussion may be seen reflected against the outline of certain theological assumptions. In this light the programmatic issues will be discussed in a sharper manner.

Functional universalism is a description of what is assumed by what people do. As they are not concerned with bringing people into the life of the church, it is assumed that they believe God will make all people whole, no matter what they profess or do not profess. Universalism is the belief that everyone will be saved. The problem with a functional universalism is that we are deducing a theological position on the basis of observable behavior. We do not, in fact, know the theological commitment. It could be, for example, that the observed action is the result of a simple not-caring for others regardless of the future implications. It is better, therefore, that our theology be expressed.

Creation

What is the fundamental belief about God upon which everything else is built? We can say that God *is*—an affirmation of his existence. But moving beyond that, it is that in Christ "everything in heaven and on earth was created, not only things visible but also the invisible . . . : the whole universe has been created through him and for him" by God (Col. 1:16; NEB). This is an unqualified statement: the totality of the world is of God's making. Nothing that is exists except by the express will of God. We cannot separate any part of creation from God, such as matter or the so-called lower nature of humanity.

The author of Colossians goes on to relate the creative action of God to the Incarnation of Christ. The fact that God becomes man in every sense, except that Jesus did not sin (Heb. 4:15), is more than an affirmation of the goodness of human existence. The Incarnation is the pivotal moment in the history of creation. God did not create the world in one "big bang." Creation is a process that is not yet finished. The Incarnation is the prolepsis, the foretaste or anticipatory event, of the consummation of the history of creation, which is not yet come. This is what the preaching of the Kingdom promises.

Everything is in God. This is what it means for God to have created all that is. Yet God is infinitely more than this. In one sense we can say there is an incompleteness in God in that the intention of his creative action has not yet been fulfilled. But in another sense God is complete because all being is in him. He has a vision of what shall be; that being is in God's mind.

The distinction that is important to make here is between a God who creates a dynamic universe and one that creates a static universe. The ancient Greek or Hellenistic world expressed its understanding of experience in static terms. God is the unmoved mover. There is no motion in God; he does not change. God is without feeling. The most important thing to the Hellenistic mind was predictability—permanence. It withstood the chaos that always threatened the ancient world. Therefore, God is the unchanging source of ordered motion.

The contemporary world perceives its experience through a more dynamic model of reality. The center of the world is not a cosmos, an ordered system, but the self. However we understand the self, the self is at least a constellation and patterning of energy. God becomes the ultimate self and yet infinitely more than any self we have known. It is the nature of the self to project into the future a vision of what might be and to act to fulfill that vision. God is for us one who does this on an unqualified scale. The world exists for God's self-communication to it.

We are created and invited to share with God in that process of creation as the receivers of this self-communication of the transcendent. This is what it means to be in the image of God.

The author of Colossians says that Christ is "the image of the invisible God" (Col. 1:15; NEB), which is revealed by the fact that the world is created by and for him. Jesus' death and resurrection are acts of creation, and we who are also made in the image of God are called, as the author says of himself, "to complete . . . the full tale of Christ's afflictions" (Col. 1:24; NEB). The Cross of Christ, in which we share, is a creative act. It is the condition of the new life.

It is on the basis of this belief that mission, renewal, and evangelization is seen, first of all, *as an act of creation*. The God who sends is he who sends in order to create in the light of his vision of what might be. At the root the church's mission is to share in God's vision and act in its light. This is the nature of love. The essence of love is not emotion; it is an informed will. It is no accident that the "to know" is a euphemism for sexual relations in the Old Testament (Gen. 4:1). The act of love is an act of knowing and issues in creation. Mission draws upon the fecundity of the divine will.

Humanity

To be human is to be capable of self transcendence. What does that signify? It signifies that we have an incurable need for meaning. To make meaning of our existence, humanity has the ability to remember the past and project the future, and act in terms of the world of our meaning. Only human beings wonder where we were before we were born and where we will be when we die. We stand outside of ourselves by virtue of abstract thinking and understand and make value judgments about ourselves and our actions. By virtue of this fact we are responsible.

People who work with apes, such as chimpanzees, have in recent years claimed that the boundary between humanity and our primate cousins is not as clear as we once thought. Our hominid line went its singular way from the rest of the evolutionary process only perhaps ten million years ago, and this is a short time in the history of the world. This should not cause us any problem. The glory of humanity is, on the one hand, that we are firmly rooted in the remarkable unfolding of

creation in the evolutionary process. This process is a testimony
to the divine vision. On the other hand, however, there came
that time when the hominid creature realized that he was
thinking—"I think that I am thinking"—and humanity was
born.

Although Paul certainly had no knowledge of evolutionary
theory, he struggled with this same amphibian character of
humanity as he explained the resurrection of the body. He
appropriated the philosophical vocabulary of the time to
explain that humankind has its feet rooted in the earth and its
head in the heavens.

> The first man was made "of the dust of the earth": the
> second man is from heaven. The man made of dust is
> the pattern of all men of dust, and the heavenly man is the
> pattern of all the heavenly. As we have worn the likeness of
> the man made of dust, so we shall wear the likeness of the
> heavenly man. (1 Cor. 15:47–49; NEB)

The only problem with this is that the concept sets the man of
dust in opposition to the heavenly man, which was the common
understanding in the first century. What is more accurate is
that humanity is at the same time of the dust and of the
heavens.

This ability to think about thinking gives birth to culture. I
mean more by culture than the ability to make tools. Apes can
make tools, as did our hominid ancestors. Perhaps a sign of
cultures is when we make *beautiful* tools, not just ones that get
the job done. Beauty points beyond utility to a sense of order
and, perhaps by implication, a source of order. Other animals
than humanity behave in a largely instinctual manner, but our
actions express our values embedded in our culture, learned
there, and chosen even at the most simple level by a reflective
process. This is why humans live by principles and apes do not.

The capacity for self-transcendence implies that human
beings are in some sense free. It is probably ill-advised to speak
loosely of free will. We cannot do anything we want to do. We
are limited by our biology and our history. We cannot by an act
of will see x-rays with the naked eye or live as someone in

eighteenth-century Japan. It is better to say that we have
limited free choice. There are within the context of our
genuine and particular humanity options from which we can
select. I can choose whether to give money to feed the hungry
or to buy a new suit. Our choices are significant for whom we
may become, for our future.

If this were not so, it would not be possible to speak of
cooperation with God's creative purpose, and the call to
mission would be as meaningless as every other moral summons. The alternative to free choice is absolute determinism. I
have suggested an understanding of humanity grounded in
moderate determinism (i.e., we are limited); but any theory—
biological, sociological, philosophical, or theological—that says
that persons are what they are *only* as a result of what is external
to them is immoral. It leaves us without the freedom to make
any kind of responsible choice.

Like creation as a whole, however, humanity is incomplete.
But we have a purpose, which is to be whole. Christ is the
embodiment of that wholeness, the sacrament of God's union
with humankind. The metaphors for the end of humanity
abound: the Kingdom of God, eternal life, the heavenly city,
the peaceable kingdom, and the messianic banquet. The central fact is that to be human is to be invited into wholeness.

The yearning to become a whole human is fundamental to
humanity. We naturally long for God, even when we are unable
to name God or claim that he does not exist. It is rooted in the
questioning that arises in the midst of our self-transcendence.
Without God, however, that yearning cannot be fulfilled. It
simply becomes a source of frustration for us. This means that
by nature humanity is open to God. We are called to listen to
the transcendent Word and we have the capacity, by virtue of
God's abiding presence within us, to hear that Word. This is
what theologians mean by prevenient grace—the presence of
God moving us before we ever acknowledge that presence.

Renewal and evangelization are possible because of the
capacity of persons to hear the Word of God. No one is so deaf
or blind as to be beyond hope of hearing and seeing the
Gospel. Some are more readily than others, it should be noted,

and all of us must be continually evangelized in order that we may turn to God again and again. The world is not divided between those who "have it" and those who do not. All people are pilgrims along the way. Mission is the call to enter on the pilgrimage to share what we as Christians have, which is the path we travel in Christ. After all, it was Christ who said of himself, "I am the road" (Jn. 14:6; UTH).

Knowing

There are two kinds of theology: that which understands the person's relationship to God as *internal*, and that which thinks of it as *external*. The Eastern church has leaned toward the internal. It often speaks of the movement in humanity from mortality to immortality or becoming like God. Irenaeus, writing about A.D. 180, says that God became human in order that we might become God. The Western church is usually external in its description of the relationship between God and humanity. It speaks of sin and redemption, not mortality and immortality. Beginning with Tertullian in the early third century, it had often spoken of Christ making satisfaction for the sins of us all, as if the Passion were a legal transaction.

Each approach has its own appeal. The values of the internal approach over the external approach, other than the fact that God comes off better as a loving creator in the internal approach, is that it makes more sense in the contemporary anthrocentric understanding of theology. Over the last 200 years it has become increasingly difficult to defend a theological position that begins with God and moves to humanity. This is called a cosmocentric approach. It is a bit like building a house beginning with the roof. Theology begins where we are, with ourselves, whether or not we wish to admit it. This is what Kierkegaard meant when he said that subjectivity is truth.

This means that the metaphor for the point of relationship between humanity and God is consciousness or the fact of knowing. In the story of Adam and Eve in the Garden of Eden, Yahweh says, "'The man has become like one of us [i.e., he is in our image], knowing good and evil'" (Gen. 3:22; NEB). The image of God in humanity is described as our knowing. The tree of knowledge of whose fruit Adam and Eve ate symbolizes that joining of heaven and earth, the union of God and humankind.

The first attribute that we bestow upon God is mentality. Some might argue that it is love. But one cannot love unless we also know. Actually, there is no knowing in the sense we use the word here without loving; for knowing is more than having information about someone or something. It is coming into a relationship, participation in what or whom is known.

Furthermore, for most of the history of Christian theology, the identifiable core of the human spirit—what Paul mentions when he speaks of the heavenly or spiritual person (1 Cor. 15:46–49)—is the mind. For him, God joins himself to humanity as Spirit calls to spirit; the mind of God forms the mind of humanity. The result is consciousness. This is what John of the Cross, the sixteenth-century Spanish mystic, understood when he said that the Word of God is the effect upon the soul or spirit.

There is a historical problem with this line of argument, which makes some people feel "safer" in an external notion of the divine–human relationship. Briefly, it begins with the fact that the Greek word for knowledge is *gnosis,* from which the word "gnostic" is derived. Gnosticism is a classical heresy or false teaching. But Gnosticism, with a capital "G," and gnosticism, with a little "g," are not the same things.

The heresy of Gnosticism, which arose with great strength in the second century, is characterized by at least these three errors. First of all, Gnosticism separates humanity by nature into three kinds of people: spiritual, natural, and material. The Gnostics attributed these divisions to the nature of humanity by virtue of creation and claimed for themselves, the spiritual people, a special, secret knowledge to which others could not be privy. The second characteristic of Gnosticism is that it either advocated a world-denying asceticism or divorced morality from perfection altogether. Some Gnostics practiced self-mutilation; others were promiscuous, arguing that the behavior of the body had no impact on the spirit. The third feature of

Gnosticism was that it created a cosmology in which the material world was not created by God, but by some lesser, semidivine being. The creation of the physical world was, at best, accidental. In effect, the Incarnation was compromised.

The centrality of knowing to the divine–human encounter implies none of the above. Authentic knowing is characteristic of humanity as a whole—there is no secret knowledge, unavailable by nature to a class of people. Knowing demands a relation between insight and action, consciousness and morality; yet it involves the totality of existence, the material and the spiritual. We know with both our bodies and our minds.

What the internal approach does require is that evangelization engage persons in order that they be brought into a deeper consciousness of God in their lives. Such an awareness, as countless Christian spiritual masters through the centuries have told us, requires self-knowledge. Richard of St. Victor, for one, writes, "The soul that has not been practiced over a long time and educated fully in knowledge of self is not raised up to knowledge of God."[1]

Evangelization that is true to the Gospel is a tactic, therefore, that leads to a deeper self-consciousness in those evangelized. The apparent fact that those who claim to have experienced God are often those who seem most close to the need for a deeper self-understanding presents evangelization with a particular challenge. It must confront these people with God's promise that the inevitable pain of self-knowledge is not to be compared with the glory of what shall follow (Rom. 8:18, 1 Pet. 4:12–13).

There is nothing very remarkable or different in this understanding of the centrality of knowing in the relationship between God and humankind. What is perhaps unusual is the bald statement of this point of view. Since the Middle Ages, Western Christians are more likely to speak of love rather than knowledge as the point of contact between humanity and the transcendent. This can easily become a way to avoid the truth that knowledge and love go hand in hand. Authentic love in its many dimensions is ultimately a form of knowing, deciding, and acting. It is without content save as possessing a *structure* of meaning or intention.

Furthermore, lest someone imply otherwise, a formal education has no necessary positive correlation to the depth of the God–humanity relationship. A Ph.D. is no assurance of sanctity. Anyone who would conclude this from the discussion has not yet understood that knowledge as discussed in this book is not a matter of knowing facts or being able to develop sophisticated systems. It is a matter of consciousness, the ability to perceive the difference between experience and meaning, and consequently to be able to enter into an experience with depth and freedom to discover the possibilities for a new life.

Sin

Evil is an internal, destructive power. It is internal to the cosmos, and we call it Satan. It is internal to institutions, and we call it the corrupt powers. It is internal to each of us, and we call it sinful desires. Actually Satan, corrupt powers, and sinful desires are the same thing, perceived in different manifestations. They are all evil, which thwarts and tears apart in us God's vision of consummate unity for his creation.

I would not pretend to be able to explain the existence of evil. All efforts to do that end up either putting a piece of creation outside God or else making evil an absence, rather than the very present, corrosive force many of us experience it to be. It is, as I have said, both internal and a power. I can only conclude that in some sense we experience evil within God's creation, within institutions, and within persons, and that there appears to be a dark side to God, to society, and to you and me.

Jakob Boehme, the seventeenth-century Lutheran mystic, wrote:

> God is all. He is darkness and light, love and wrath, fire and light. He calls Himself only God according to the light of His love. There is an eternal *contrarium* [opposition] between darkness and light. Neither grasps the other, and neither is the other. And yet there is only one being, but separated by the source and by the will. Yet it is not a divided being, but one *principium* [first principle] divides it so that each is in the other as a nothing. But it is there, although not revealed in the characteristic of that which it is.[2]

The opposition of good and evil is the very nature of creation, and we have to live with that apparent contradiction. In fact, the Christian witness is that goodness is experienced most deeply within evil. This is the message of Good Friday. But where this becomes difficult for us, who wish to affirm God as creator, is that the darkness of the Cross is as much a part of his creation as the light.

The images of darkness and light find a parallel in the notions of ignorance and knowledge. This correspondence will not hold if we think of knowledge as information. But if knowledge is the result of the participation in the being of God and consequently the sharing of *his* knowledge, then we can say that sin is ignorance. It is whatever draws us away from the knowledge that comes of and through God. Everyone desires his own good. Even the suicide does himself harm out of the belief that this is for him the greatest good. But he does not achieve his own good because he cannot participate on his own in God, know God, and know himself as God knows him.

Inasmuch as knowledge, which is the participation of the total person in the other person or thing, opens us to God's life, so does ignorance destroy us. Its gift is death. The biblical notion of sin begins within the consciousness of the person, moves to the deed, and ends in ruin. The intention, the act, and the judgment are all coterminous. This is the implication of the Fourth Evangelist when he writes, "The one not believing has already been judged forever" (Jn. 3:18; UTH).

The Greek word in the New Testament for sin sometimes comes under criticism. It means "to miss the mark." This may seem weak if we do not understand the Greek mind. The Hellenist world had a very high vision of what it meant to be human, in which virtue—much the same virtue the New Testament touts—was expected. This vision, which is called in Greek the *skopos* (as in the English word "scope"), was the mark that was missed. Paul says, "I press towards the goal [*skopon*] to win the prize which is God's call to the life above, in Christ Jesus" (Phil. 3:14; NEB). To miss that mark is to sin. If to the Greek mind we missed the goal, it meant that we were less than human, no better than the beasts. Hence, ignorance was feared and despised, for it led to the wrong intention, the immoral deed, and the destruction of the person.

Paul tells us that sin pervades the world, but it is only the knowledge of what should be that makes us aware of this sin (Rom. 5:12–13). But our own knowledge is not sufficient to enable us to overcome the sin of the world. ("Sin of the world" is a more theologically and biblically accurate phrase than the more common term for this reality, "original sin.") The law only makes us feel guilty. Guilt is one of two fundamental human experiences. The other is the hope for forgiveness. But we cannot forgive ourselves. Such knowledge is not available to us. So we look to the Word of God.

Knowledge is, therefore, both a curse and a blessing. It renders us guilty. But knowledge is also the propaedeutic of Christ, the hope of our forgiveness. Paul writes, "The law has become our slave-who-leads-the-child to Christ, in order that from out of faith we might be justified, and where faith has come we will no longer be under the slave-who-leads-the-child (Gal. 3:24–25; UTH). The implications of this familiar passage sometimes miss us. Paul is drawing on the educational model of his times. The "slave-who-leads-the-child" is not the teacher, but the attendant who makes sure he gets to the teacher and behaves while he is there. Christ is the teacher, and the knowledge he imparts is faith. Paul understood faith to be openness to God, our understanding of God, hope, and confidence. Furthermore, he says that when we have learned from Christ we will become adult and no longer need the "slave-who-leads-the-child." There is the sense of growth in Christ in which morality is internalized.

The relationship between forgiveness and consciousness is implied in all of this. The mind of God cannot illumine the human mind as long as it is in rebellion to God. Forgiveness becomes the gift of knowledge perceived as love, which lifts the darkness of rebellion from our minds and unites our spirit to the mind of Christ. Forgiveness is, therefore, an act of creation because it is the prerequisite of our sharing in God's vision for his world.

In 1 Timothy there is a curious passage—in part because the Greek is so convoluted—that reads:

> Preach and teach these following things. If someone teaches otherwise and does not preach the words-which-give-whole-ness of our Lord Jesus Christ and the teaching pertaining to our duty to God [i.e., piety], he has become stupid. . . . Whenever men have dry rot in the mind and have been robbed of the truth, they reckon there is a payoff in piety. Depart from such men. But there is a great payoff in piety after self-sufficiency. (1 Tim. 6:2–3, 5–6; UTH)

A number of things fascinate us in this passage. It reflects the Hellenistic culture of the day, including a list of vices that I omitted in verse 4. I will reserve a discussion of the words of Jesus until the next section. The author described a false piety, which we call pietism. Pietism is a sentimental approach to our duty toward God. False piety in his day as well as ours expects an immediate payoff (e.g., the consolation). Such thinking is a sure sign, the author said, that we have become stupid, suffering from dry rot—the original Greek refers to what happens to a ship that lies unused and untended in its slip—of the mind and a loss of the truth. All these are images of ignorance and knowledge, of mental blindness and consciousness. But there can be a payoff, the author said, that comes only after we are free of dependence upon others, or self-sufficient. The Greek word for self-sufficiency is a technical term from Stoic philosophy, which means the person who has the knowledge that comes from the eternal logos or reason. Self-sufficiency is one way to describe an intrinsic religious orientation.

If we think of the hope for forgiveness of sin in light of this passage, what happens? Repentance or renewal—*metanoia*—confronts sin. Sin is rebellion, saying "No" to God. As previously explained, some moral theologians today make a distinction between objective sin, which is the occasional act of rebellion common to everyone, and subjective sin, which is the continuing intentional movement of the person away from God. The call to renewal is directed toward subjective sin.

Repentance requires a new consciousness, in which we overcome the dry rot of our minds and have renewed in us a love of the truth. It is characterized by the openness to the Gospel, the words of wholeness of our Lord, Jesus Christ. It is one way of understanding the unforgivable sin against the Holy Spirit—otherwise known as Holy Wisdom—as the refusal to become conscious of the divine knowledge.

Good evangelization directs itself to a renewal of consciousness. To promise immediate payoffs is contrary to Scripture, reason, and the tradition. It is a redirecting of our minds through our lifetime, in the hope that we may become self-sufficient in Christ. Self-sufficiency is rooted in the deep memory. If the inner self is shaped by the wisdom of God, then we possess the freedom to become instruments of God's purpose. This demands a far-reaching forgiveness, which absolves each of us of subjective sin.

Christ

The New Testament interprets the experience of Jesus in a number of ways, sometimes incompatible one with the other. What speaks most effectively to our times is Logos Christology. This is an interpretation of the place of the historical Jesus derived from at least two streams of prior thought: Jewish and Stoic.

If we examine the Old Testament and the Apocrypha, we find there both the notion of the creative power of God's speech and the personification of wisdom. "God *said,* 'Let there be light,' and there was light" (Gen. 1:3; NEB). The power of language fascinated ancient humanity, particularly as a tool of thought that it knew as wisdom. "I am Wisdom, I bestow shrewdness and show the way to knowledge and prudence" (Prov. 8:12; NEB).

> Hear the praise of wisdom from her own mouth, . . . "I am the word which was spoken by the Most High; it was I who covered the earth like a mist. . . ." Then the Creator of the universe laid a command upon me; my Creator decreed where I should dwell. He said, "Make your home in Jacob;

find your heritage in Israel." Before time began he created
me, and I shall remain forever. (Ecclesiasticus 24:1, 3, 8–9;
NEB)

There is a clearly implied relationship between the Word and
Wisdom. "God of our fathers, merciful Lord, who hast made all
things by thy word, and in thy wisdom hast fashioned man, to ·
be the master of thy whole creation" (Wisdom 9:1–2; NEB).

Alongside the Jewish speculation concerning wisdom there
developed the Hellenistic notion of reason, for which the Greek
word is *logos*. It is translated "word," but it is actually what
language makes possible: reason. The Stoics, a school of
philosophy beginning in the fourth century B.C., taught that
reason is what holds the world together, creating order (*cosmos*,
in Greek). Every person, they said, has a "seed of reason" within
him, which is the explanation of our capacity for the divine
reason.

The idea of wisdom and reason as the eternal creative
presence in God and coming from God to humanity was a
ready-made concept for the Fourth Evangelist as he explained
our experience of Jesus. "So the Word [*logos*] became flesh; he
came to dwell among us, and we saw his glory, such glory as
befits the Father's only Son, full of grace and truth" (Jn. 1:14;
NEB). The eternal wisdom (which is *sophia* in Greek) takes on
the meaning of *logos*, but dwells in the "home of Jacob" as Jesus
ben Sirach says. He leads us, as the author of Proverbs
promises, to "knowledge and prudence." Jesus, the Word of
God, becomes the incarnate presence of Wisdom. (Matthew
25:34 implies this.) But every Hellenistic schoolboy could make
the connection. The illumining reason that glues together the
cosmos is now present in Jesus to humanity, informing our
minds and uniting us to the divine order.

The Fourth Evangelist is deeply indebted to the Jewish
sapiential tradition for his understanding of Christ. The association of Word to Wisdom brings out all that tradition's association with Wisdom. Wisdom is more than conceptual knowledge.
She is the revealer of God and, consequently, both mystical and
practical. Wisdom gives immortality (Wisdom 6:18–19) and

pursues persons for God (Prov. 8:1–4, Wisdom 6:16). The pictures of Jesus in the Fourth Gospel are an incarnation of Jewish Wisdom.

What is added by the Evangelist is, of course, the historical context of the historical Jesus, which gives to the Word and to Wisdom a personal warmth. "The Word-become-flesh," the Wisdom of God, is the self-disclosure of God to the world as a supremely compassionate self. In Christianity, *logos* is the word we use for God's offering of himself to humanity in history. The knowledge that comes from God's *logos* is that derived from the participation in a person, not a collection of concepts or a system. Christ is the sacrament of God, who is personal.

This understanding of the experience of Jesus is often spoken of as incarnational, and so it is. It looks back to the centrality of God as creator and forward to the church as the sacrament of Christ. The Cross is the pivotal point in the flow of history. God's offering of himself reaches fulfillment in Jesus' free acceptance of his death, and can be appropriated by us only in his Resurrection. There is a very appealing suggestion that the heart of the Resurrection is the knowledge by Jesus' followers that they were forgiven for their apostasy of Good Friday and their awareness that forgiveness can only come from a *living* Lord. (For example, there is the juxtaposition of a resurrection appearance and forgiveness in Jn. 20:19–23.)

There is little question that some early Christians, Paul for instance, thought of the knowledge that is Christ as cultivating the seed of reason that is within the spirit of humankind. "Think this same thing in yourselves," Paul says, "which also [is] in Christ Jesus" (Phil. 2:5). He is admonishing his readers to act as Jesus and, to that end, to think like Jesus. But if that knowledge is to transform our lives, it can only be received by faith. We have to trust in Christ, and be open to his call. For this reason Paul ends the invitation to the Philippians to think as Christ thinks with a call to faith, saying "'Jesus Christ is Lord'" (Phil. 2:11; NEB).

In our culture many who evangelize speak of "getting decisions for Christ," inviting people to accept "Jesus as Lord."

But this decision has to be made over and over as we struggle by God's prevenient grace to live the life of faith. Furthermore, while some intellectual grasp of the meaning of Jesus is not a necessary prerequisite to this decision, the test of its authenticity is found in the presence of the transforming power of Christ in not only our feelings, but our thinking and action. Logos Christology requires that the effect of our discipleship be the inner transformation of the person, evidenced in the conformity of his or her mind to the mind of Christ. We must become wise as Christ is wise.

Holy Spirit and Church

Dennis Bennett, an Episcopal priest who was an early leader in the charismatic movement, has said that the Holy Spirit does not speak to groups, but only to individuals.[3] Other than the fact that I wonder how he would interpret the Pentecost experience of a 120 disciples (Acts 2:1–4), Bennett is undoubtedly speaking out of his own experience misinterpreted by a cultural bias.

It is not any more accurate to say that the Holy Spirit speaks only to groups than it is to agree with Bennett. In fact, it is not accurate to say that the Holy Spirit speaks *both* to groups *and* individuals. A biblical insight that we need very much to recover is the notion of the corporate person. It is the underlying assumption about human existence informing Paul's account of the church as the Body of Christ, and is an explication of a long Hebrew tradition (1 Cor. 12:12–31). Simply put, the conception of the corporate is that every person is *by nature* a part of his community. We *are* our communities. When we meet another person, we meet his community, and the community is responsible for that person. The Holy Spirit then speaks to the corporate person, which manifests itself in the life of the community and its individual members.

The Holy Spirit not only speaks to the corporate person, he is the life of the corporate person of Christ, which is the church. The Fourth Evangelist describes the Holy Spirit as "the Spirit of truth" (Jn. 14:16, 15:26, 16:13); he guides us into all truth

(Jn. 16:13; cf. Ps. 143:40, translation in the Book of Common Prayer). Truth is a particularly popular word in the Johannine literature. It belongs to the same Jewish tradition as Word and Wisdom, upon which the Fourth Evangelist is so dependent. Jesus ben Sirach, for example, writes,

> Never remain silent when a word might put things right,
> for wisdom shows itself by speech,
> and a man's education must find expression in words.
> Do not argue against the truth,
> and have a proper sense of your own ignorance. . . .
> Fight to the death for truth,
> and the Lord God will fight on your side.
> (Ecclesiasticus 4:23–25, 28; NEB)

Truth is divine reality, but as shaping the person to whom truth has been revealed. Christ is also truth (Jn. 14:6), which is the source of moral action and simplicity of heart or piety. Truth is at home to the deep memory.

The Fourth Evangelist also speaks of the Holy Spirit as the Paraclete (e.g., Jn. 14:16). It is an obscure title, but in part the Paraclete is the personal presence of Jesus in the Christian while Jesus is with the Father. This confuses the second and third persons of the Trinity, but the Evangelist was not privy to the debates 200 or more years later about the nature of the Holy Spirit vis-à-vis the Trinity. Here the Paraclete and Jesus share the identity of Word, Wisdom, and Truth. Both have the same function to form the disciple that he might inherit eternal life. The Fourth Evangelist is answering the question of the early church; namely, since Jesus has ascended to the Father, who will be their guide. The answer was that Jesus is still present as Spirit–Paraclete.

The Spirit works to make known the mind of Christ through the life of the church. Christ and the church form a corporate person; like Yahweh and Israel, they are husband and wife. The author of Ephesians plays with two metaphors—head and body, husband and wife—which become symbols for the mystical union between Jesus and the people of God (Eph. 5:30–32).

The church is the sacrament of Christ, it is the means by which we come to know the Lord. The head or mind is known through the body, and the wife serves and obeys the husband. The Holy Spirit, who is the personal presence of Christ among the disciples, is given to the church that this wonderful mystery may be a reality.

Evangelization is, therefore, to be carried out in the knowledge that the Holy Spirit and the people of God, the church, go together. The church is not a like-minded gathering of believers, after the fact of someone's conversion. Even as an individual evangelist, one proclaims the Gospel as a personal embodiment of the church. The Holy Spirit acts through the church to call people into the life of the church. The community announces the Good News of the Kingdom and nourishes us in anticipation of eternal life. This is why mission as church is the fundamental precept of missiology.

Without doubt the presence of the church in God's salvific plan bothers some people. They complain about "churchianity" and grumble about the institution. The brokenness of the church, like the sin of each of us, is a reality. But there can be neither worship nor belief without community. God works through the fallible gathering of his people just as he does through each of its fallible members. We do not experience the Holy Spirit by denying that very community that constitutes our identity as members of Christ.

The Sacraments

The sacraments are a window upon the presence of God's grace everywhere in his creation. They are not some rite, magical or moral, in which for an isolated moment the faithful encounter the divine amid a world bereft of God. Quite the contrary, God's salvific plan goes to the very roots of his creation. The Greek word for reconciliation—the central New Testament word for what God did in Christ—means to overcome disharmony and to restore unity to the totality of the cosmos. Sacraments are an access to that divine grace, working for harmony and unity within God's world.

A highly linguistic age, which admires rational discourse, such as the sixteenth century to the present time, thinks of the Word of God as words that speak of concept and system or that arouse sentiment. Think, if you will, of the traditional Anglican pulpit "essay" or the popular homiletic principle, "Make 'em laugh, make 'em cry, make 'em feel religious." We have been inclined as a consequence, to speak of word and sacrament with particular vigor over the last 400 years. The distinction originates in Augustine. It is difficult for us to perceive a ritual, which is a liturgical drama appealing to all five senses, as a communication of the Word. But the sacraments are an event of the Word made manifest, just as is preaching. They are a way to know.

The particular power of the sacraments, all of which enact the meaning of Christ's Passion, is that they employ our complete sensorium and consequently are better able to reach the deep memory. Because the sacraments possess power and power threatens, our inclination is to lessen the risk by domesticating the ritual. This is done by reducing the effect upon the senses. Yet the sacraments constitute the church in that they are instruments of the Spirit in illumining our lives with the knowledge within God. They are the symbolic means to make present the memory of what God has done in Christ (1 Cor. 11:28, Rom. 6:1-11). What we need to do is enrich our sacramental life, not make it more palatable.

Language readily lapses into argument or sentimentality. If evangelization is to escape the external, manipulative qualities of either argument or sentimentality, it has to ground itself in more than the church talking. Sacramental living, the church enacting the mysteries, creates more naturally the space for grace to nourish the people of God. It is riskier and less predictable, but it moves the imagination and makes room for God.

The church has always believed that the Holy Spirit is not limited by the sacraments. This is not our problem today. The opposite danger prevails: the belief that the Holy Spirit is experienced privately and individually, and the church and its sacraments are subject to personal feelings or emotions. This is enthusiasm at its very worst, and will obscure without hope the witness of the Holy Spirit within a morass of subjective claims.

Universalism

The question that was posed to introduce this chapter concerned functional universalism, Christian behavior implying that everyone will be saved no matter what he does. This is an important question in any discussion of mission.

We cannot know the future; it is ineffable. So what we do is to project our present condition into the future. In the present, humanity understands his experience in terms of time and space. Historically, Christianity has spoken of the end of things in reference to everlasting life in heaven or hell, drawing upon the syncretistic imagery of the Near East. This implies time and space after death, which is a metaphor that raises more questions than it answers. For when we think about it, apart from finite matter, there is no time or space.

We can say, however, this much. The Christian understanding of history is that it shall end beyond time in eternity. God's intention is that corporate humanity shall be joined to him. We believe that this shall come to pass. But parallel to this belief is a commitment to individual freedom, which is absolute in the sense that it is not relative to anything. Freedom requires that we entertain the possibility for the individual of the absolute loss of God. This is not to speak in any sense but metaphorically of a *place* of *everlasting* punishment (space and time); it is only to claim the absolute nature of the individual's freedom.

There is a tradition within Christianity that teaches the restoration of all people to God in the end, which is classical universalism. Origen and Gregory of Nyssa were among the early church fathers who believed this. In recent times, the Swiss German theologian, Karl Barth, taught the same thing. If we place a high premium on individual freedom, however, I am more inclined to say that someone may choose against God for eternity. Furthermore, if the all is in God, who is also infinitely more, it would seem logical that by the choice against him by a given person God himself is to that extent diminished by the loss.

Mission is an action outside of the Godhead on our part as Christians, patterned upon the very nature of the divine mission within the Godhead. We carry out the mission of the church in order that the world may be more in God's image and in turn that God might be more fully God, the one who sends.

CHAPTER ELEVEN

A Pastoral Reflection

Only when we clarify the theological presuppositions of renewal and evangelization can we reflect intelligently upon the concrete questions of mission. Yet the call for discussion of evangelization and renewal as a specific pattern of ministry is a legitimate request of the church's pastoral theology. The church is called to be responsible in this fundamental function of its ministry.

The intention of this study has not been to ask the reader to "do evangelism" in a last-ditch effort for the church to survive. Instead, we need to reflect carefully on the meaning of the church's mission illumined by the tradition. There is a temptation in mission studies to pose mutually exclusive alternatives, which, while intended to challenge the church, obscure the issues. Several of those alternatives will be discussed here.

The mainline churches have lost membership since 1968, including the Episcopal Church, which has dropped 20 percent in membership in twelve years. The alternative is that either one realizes this loss is an unqualified disaster requiring its reversal as the top priority of the church, or one is not in favor of evangelization. This alternative, stated here in an extreme form, requires qualification.

Is the drop in membership in the church the result of a prophetic witness, such as unpopular social programs from 1967 on, or the ordination of women to the priesthood and, in the future, the episcopate? Is it the reaction to the revision of the Prayer Book? Is it a function of our culture? Is it a part of a natural fluctuation in church membership? The evidence is that the decline in church membership is not the result of any one thing. It could be all these things and many more.

Certainly a 20-percent drop in membership in twelve years is to be considered a cause for concern. But it is not a repudiation of mission to resist sacrificing everything else to church growth. It is possible that there is some health in that decline *if* we act responsibly in the face of a shifting church population.

Another false alternative is that either the church leaders are persons devoted to social action, whom we call "liberals," or they are in favor of the salvation of souls, and we call them "conservatives and traditionalists." These two mutually exclusive options are a pernicious deception. The narrowest possible assumption is being made about both the nature of salvation and of the soul.

Salvation is only secondarily a movement *away* from sin, and sin is not a private matter. Salvation is a movement *toward* the Kingdom of God, and the Kingdom of God is a social reality. Anyone concerned for salvation is a social activist. Furthermore, the soul is not a discrete, spiritual monad, unrelated to society. The self, which is a better term than soul, *is* its community. Mission as liberation, for example, is one approach to the salvation of souls.

We need to declare a moratorium in the church on the use of the terms "liberal" and "conservative." They are meaningless in theological discussion, unless they are very carefully defined. They have been particularly abused in the sociology of religion over the last twenty years, with little effort at intelligent definition. When such a definition is made, "liberal" and "conservative" will have minimal correspondence to what they usually evoke in the mind of church people.

Still another frequently assumed alternative is that theology is opposed to evangelization and religious experience. Therefore, either one is a theologian or one is an evangelist. This opposition of theologian to evangelist is often grounded in the misapprehension of the passion or enthusiasm in theology. There is, undoubtedly, such a thing as emotionally sterile rational thought, just as there are religious enthusiasts who are charlatans. But both are relatively rare. The church is not divided between people without feeling, called theologians, and people with feeling, called evangelists. It has all kinds of peoples whose enthusiasms take different forms.

Everyone courts and makes love in his own way. It is hard to comprehend the method of another, if we are so unfortunate to be in the position of a voyeur. But as the saying goes, "Don't knock it if you haven't tried it." It is simply not true that what sets theologians off as a class from other Christians is the lack of commitment to evangelization and renewal.

The intention is that this discussion set the stage for points in method for evangelization and renewal. Nothing definitive is claimed in what follows, but it is a logical extension of the theological reflections summarizing this study. It would be pointless to clutter the discussion that follows with constant references to earlier material, except when it particularly pertains. I will assume the reader has in mind the evidence of renewal, the biblical goals, and the intermediate objectives. The importance of the intrinsic–imaginal space will undergird everything that follows. As I have indicated before, my own theological orientation leads me to believe that mission as church is the pivotal understanding of missiology, but the four other viewpoints—mission as recruitment, mutual interdependence, liberation, and fulfillment—are by no means excluded from what they do contribute to the practice of evangelization.

Invitation, Not Rape

A friend related this version of the familiar anecdote, which probably corresponds to actual events on only rare occasions. A self-appointed evangelist confronted him on the subway with the persistent question, "Brother, are you saved?" "Have you accepted Jesus Christ as your Lord and Savior?" His answer was typically Episcopalian. "I'd like to say 'yes,' but your actions put in jeopardy my chances." Such a smart reply, whether true or fictitious, is undoubtedly lacking in charity, but its theology is accurate. Spiritual rape does incapacitate our ability for genuine response to the Word, just as sexual rape inhibits the sexual response of the victim in subsequent, loving relationships.

Evangelization is not an act of rape in which we rob the other person of a choice. Manipulative techniques of any kind come under this category. It is no better to force a decision for Christ

by involving fear than it is at the point of a sword. It is true that
the end justifies the means, but only when the end is desirable
and the means does not inhibit that end. The argument of this
entire book has been that evangelization viewed apart from the
objective and outcome often violates the Gospel.

I use the word *invitation* as the alternative. The invitation is
like a proposition of marriage. Evangelization is the art of
beguiling, charming, or luring people into relationship with
God and on pilgrimage with the church to his Kingdom. Truly,
God solicits us into being, and his church is the messenger. All
these words have the same feeling-tone. No one loves another
against his or her will; at some level we are caught in our
longing for union with the other and we are beguiled into
response. There is in some evangelization an excitement, a
mystery, and a sense of enrichment, which reaches deep into
the memory.

The church is the evangelist. The individual only represents
her. The people of God are to the world as a lover, not a
salesperson. Our task is to be present to persons in their
yearning for a richer life, not to play upon their insecurities.
Evangelization that builds upon people's fears, be they of "hell
fire" or of being inferior, only narrows their world and prevents spiritual growth. It is a matter of telling people there
is no death; it is living in their presence the conviction that in
the midst of death is life.

How is the church present as lover? Its worship invites those
who come in to a sense of mystery, a place of inner discovery.
Its membership is open, accepting people in their uniqueness.
It is more a place of relationship, with the possibility of genuine
intimacy, than a program center, looking for new workers. It
solicits persons into its life, but it does not press them for
decisions they are not ready to make. I realize this runs
contrary to much popular advice about pressing people for a
decision. It is my experience that pressure does not initiate
inner growth in Christ.

Bennetta Jules-Rosette tells in an anthropological study,
African Apostles, of her conversion to the Church of John
Maranke, a native African Christian sect. She came to study

this sect as an observer and through participation found herself open, as she describes it, to a new reality. Yet at no time did she believe herself consciously recruited by the people in the Church of John Maranke. Their liturgy worked itself into her world of meaning and transformed the shape of her memory.

Authentic evangelization is not the confirmation of our old world of values, but is a turning upside down of that world. There are more accounts than that of Jules-Rosette where someone out of a secular perspective becomes vulnerable to a more primitive—in the sense of being underived or being elemental—culture and discovers himself transformed. If the person had been put on the defensive, rather than courted, it never would have happened. Our modern Western notions of persuasion are often very crude.

This is not to argue against intentional acts of evangelization. It is to say that they need to give people room. It is one thing to invite someone to accompany you to church; it is another thing to ask for that person's financial pledge as he leaves the first Sunday. Most of us are more subtle than this, but there is a genre of evangelization that leaves people thinking we are more interested in the statistic or in the maintenance of the institution than in them. This is ecclesiastical scalp hunting.

There is a curious story about an old Jesuit missionary in the sixteenth century who has been in Japan forty years. Finally the Society sent someone out to visit him. When he found him in a remote village, he asked him how it has gone for these forty years. The old priest described how the Holy Spirit has used him in countless ways and how he looked back over a life of rich reward. "Yes, Father," the young Jesuit said, "but how many have been baptized." Puzzled by the question, the old man pondered for a few moments and then replied, "One person, maybe two."

It has been said before, but it is true. The church is called to be faithful, not successful. We must not despise numbers, but a climate for transformation comes first. The church must be an active lover, not hiding in the bushes. But we cannot make people fall in love.

Some of the People, Some of the Time

The Episcopal Church is often criticized for seeing itself as the church for the intellectuals or the upper middle class. Other denominations have their own self-determined target areas, which is rightly called into question by missiologists. Such target areas can be excuses for laziness, disbelief, or a lack of trust.

But the alternative is equally false. No expression of the church can expect to be able to reach all of the people all of the time. There is the appropriate time. Bruce Reed of the Grubb Institute in England has made the point that people are open to evangelization when the secular values are being questioned, when there is a "crack" in the social veneer. At this juncture, people fall back on the deep memory and live out of a more primordial understanding of existence. They become vulnerable to what may speak to them at that deeper level of meaning.

At such a point, persons can either retreat into the nostalgia of a past golden age or they can take this occasion to move on into the future. Vulnerability is no guarantee of health in spirit. It is a question of who reaches out at those moments and for what end. What is desirable is the support of Christian community in moving deeper as the person turns to the future. The risk, the sense of sin, the pain never completely disappears, but there is an even deeper sense of the promise.

There is also the matter of space. We need to acknowledge that we will never reach some people because of whom *we* are. The possibility of communication is not there. Some people we will never reach because of whom *they* are. The price is too great or they choose not to listen for various reasons. Some people we will never reach because *our resources* are limited. The task is to determine whom we may reach and at what time. As in the early church, our most available candidates are the "God-fearers"—those questioning, but not yet committed.

Carl Dudley in his book *Where Have All the People Gone?* describes the new and young believer, who does not belong to the institutional church. They believe in God, they have a deep moral sense (which may not be the same as ours), and they want to have a relationship with God (that is, they have a piety). They often exhibit a simpler life style than many church people and possess a reverence for creation and a tolerance for differences with others. I know these people. My children are among them.

Dudley says of the new and young believers that belonging comes last in their order of development. The apparent order for them is experience, believing, and only then belonging. I think he is wrong. It is community that opens to us the possibility of experience; but for the new and young believers it is not community as Dudley defines it, organized and oriented toward program. What has happened with the new and young believers is that they have consciously cultivated the receptive mode of consciousness as opposed to the action mode. I have described this distinction in detail in two of my books, *Ministry and Imagination* and *The Priest in Community*. Very briefly, the receptive mode of consciousness draws deliberately on the deep memory. It thinks associatively, rather than logically, and consequently is more intuitive than rational. It places a higher value upon symbol and story. Ambiguity is desirable. Receptive consciousness is sometimes called feminine consciousness.

The community of the receptive consciousness is *communitas,* which is the name for a form of being together where roles and statuses are reduced to a minimum, and people relate not over against one another but in their common humanness. *Being* together is valued far more than *doing* together. Plato's saying that to be is to be in relation is taken with the utmost seriousness. What characterizes *communitas* is the symbolic life, of which true ritual and open story are the purest expression.

The community of the new and young believers, which has been the context for their experience of God, is this kind of primordial togetherness that the church has often lost. *Communitas* is not automatic paradise; it can be demonic, puerile, or artificial. But within such community a new expectation of life can emerge. The church has often lost *communitas,* perhaps because such community is not supportive of our secular values of control and prediction. It works against establishment norms. Contrast the church's sponsorship of the exploitation over the centuries of creation in all its human, animal, and inorganic forms, with the genuine sense of the oneness with all creation in the new or young believers. Think of the moral strictures we have placed about human sexuality. We can only mourn our blindness. More and better programs are not going to solve this myopia.

There has to be a new consciousness—the biblical term is repentance, *metanoia*—if we are to reach those people who probably believe more immediately in God than most of us who occupy the church pews every Sunday.

If this change of consciousness would happen, we might not get great numbers of people. We would without doubt frighten some people away, just as our Lord did. But the issue is whether the church would reach people with the Gospel, which calls us to be co-creators with God, instruments of his love and purpose.

The Dangers of Feeling Good

Evangelization that seeks to meet people's needs for assurance in a time of anxiety is bad news. Evangelization should be designed to stretch people beyond their limits where God can take over. Many people need to feel comforted, accepted, secure, successful, entertained, and better than other people. If evangelization only promotes such feelings, it is very likely leading nowhere. If Jesus had done this he would have agreed to be made ruler over Palestine. This was the self-perceived need of the people of his day for the Messiah.

I recently was sent a series of stratagems for a renewed parish. Some were good, some were obvious, and a few were simply horrible. In the last named category came one that said, "Assure people that Jesus is the solution in all counseling problems." Aside from the heretical notion that Christians should look to their faith for "solutions," there is an implication that anxiety is always bad. Jesus appears to be the divine tranquilizer. Did it ever occur to us that if we took Jesus seriously we would feel ourselves very much on the edge of the life raft? This is the feeling of dread, and dread is not a sign of unfaith, but the healthy accompaniment of one standing naked before God. Abraham about to sacrifice his son, Isaac, was filled with dread. The depth of his faith is evidenced in that he still raised the knife to slay his son.

The Gospel needs to engage people at the edge of their growth. The knowledge that comes from God may very well be heard because we are in dread by which I mean we are moving in the direction of the unknown, *which is the direction of God.* Dread is a more authentic reaction to the presence of the living God than good feelings.

A by-product of attempting to meet people's recognized needs is the stereotypical expectation of the effects of renewal. It is the common idea that evangelization seeks to effect "a personal relationship with Jesus Christ." This is an aspiration for Christian piety that was made popular by Bernard of Clairvaux, the great twelfth-century spiritual master. Devotion to the humanity of Jesus arose in the High Middle Ages for complex cultural reasons. After Bernard, it was developed in the thirteenth century by the Franciscans and later by several pious groups that influenced the Reformation. It is not the only authentic, affective reaction of the Christian to renewal.

Just as clear in the Christian tradition is a deep sense of mourning, evidenced by tears. The notion of the darkness, sometimes called the "luminous darkness," as a sign of renewal is a recurring theme. This is related to a divine emptiness, a spiritual nakedness, which some spiritual masters describe as the focus of a new consciousness. The word *piety* itself denotes an obedient devotion to God as Father, which is several steps removed from a personal relationship with Jesus. The ecstatic experience of the Holy Spirit, best known in the experience of "speaking in tongues," has an authenticity of its own. The New Testament indicates as well that the Holy Spirit can be recognized in clarity of thought.

The American religious experience has typically placed a high value on the immediately observable results of evangelization. It is almost as if we are operating from a medical model, where the person is seen as sick and in need of a cure. Our expectation is that we meet people's needs by an instantaneous restoration of their physical ailments. It may be that our sickness is unto death, and that the task of evangelization is to speak the Gospel to that situation.

One of the great spiritual giants of the twentieth century was Simone Weil. She was a committed Christian, but was never baptized. She believed that to "join" the church was to lose her identity with all those who are oppressed by institutions, such as the church. But more important, she argued that Christian awareness is accompanied by a deep sense of affliction, and that the love of God lies at the bottom of this well of suffering. Evangelization and renewal has to take Simone Weil seriously, as it does Martin Luther King, Thomas Merton, and Dag Hammarskjöld—all of whom were Christians both of great depth and of intense suffering.

Reaching Out

The ministry of evangelization and renewal is not a function of the laity alone, much less of the clergy. It is the ministry of the church as church, in which all baptized persons join to make evident the call to all people to be members of the Kingdom of God. It is the witness of the community in the world that is the heart of evangelization's outreach. The contrast between the shabby aspirations of the secular world and the character of the Christian community is what is needed.

Everything in the New Testament illustrates the incompatibility of the Gospel to the sociopolitical notions of the right or the left. The moralism of the Pharisees, in their "white-washed tombs" (Mt. 23:27), was subverted, as well as the simplistic solutions of the zealots, who would force the hand of Jesus (Jn. 6:15). The Christian proclamation in the word and deed of the church serves as a shock to the consciousness of persons, awakening in them the imagination that is receptive to the future. A Christian is subversive of any secular party line, particularly when it drapes about its shoulders the cloak of piety. It is as blasphemous for the Christian guided by the Holy Spirit to wear political buttons announcing that he or she is a "Christian for [the candidate-of-your-choice]" as it was for the German soldiers in World War I to enter battle with the words engraved on their belt buckles: *Gott mit uns* ["God (is) with us"].

There is among all peoples an effervescence of life that eludes all efforts to confine our existence to the definitions of the social order. What is this effervescence? It is the consciousness of humanity that rises above the strait jacket of institutional definitions of life and its values. There is a spirit to humankind that transcends the moralist in the pulpit, the dogmatist in the study, and the canonist in the bishop's office. This effervescent transcendent aspiration is a symptom of the intimation of the Kingdom, the invitation into a new life. It is what gives rise to women's liberation in the Soviet Union; it is the hope of the prostitute stumbling into church like Mary Magdalene; it is what encourages a faithful scholar such as the Dutch Roman Catholic genius, Edward Schillebeeckx; and it is the inspiration of the faithful remarried church person, who refuses to believe that he or she is living in sin.

As the Christian community reaches out in witness it gives substantial meaning to the tenuous aspirations of people, which I have described as a transcendent effervescence, never acceding to the banal routinization of society. This may be a difficult idea for some to grasp. But for the church to evangelize the world it will first have to confound the world's notion of what it conceives the church to be. Jesus shocked the religious establishment and ate with sinners. The church will have to do the same thing.

We often hear the suggestion that we must beware of "scandalizing the faithful." Without doubt it is dangerous to engage in scandal for its own sake. Not all scandal is of God; but yet the Gospel is always a scandal, a stumbling block for those who identify the will of God with their own way of life. Paul said this very clearly when he wrote, "We proclaim the crucified Christ, a scandal to the Jews and foolishness to the gentiles" (1 Cor. 1:22; UTH). It is the scandal that calls us into question, lifts the oppression of our minds and hearts, and opens us to a new vision. The effervescent hope of the people takes on form.

Simone Weil in *Waiting for God* described a pivotal moment in her own turning to Christ as occurring during a vacation with her family in a Portugese fishing village. They were there during the patronal festival of the village, and in the evening the wives of the fishermen walked along the shore, singing in petition to their saint for the safety of those who went out to sea. The song was incredibly mournful. It was then, Weil says, that she realized that Christianity is a religion of slaves, longing for freedom. We are all slaves to the oppression of our external and inner certainties. Not one of us has lived very long without a nagging longing to kick over the traces and to risk God in the dark.

The people of the church have to be trained carefully for such an evangelization of themselves and the world. We have to know ourselves and to have internalized the Gospel. The ability is essential to interpret the tradition, including the Scriptures, and the world about us and to draw together these meanings to inform our lives. It is because this is true that it is necessary that there be an institutional carrier for renewal in the church that is beyond the gathering of enthusiasts. It is also because this is true that the only institutional carrier available today, which meets the specifications, is the theological seminaries of the church. This claim may surprise some, but I believe it to be true. We cannot be reactive Christians, solving complex problems with simplistic answers; but we have to be intentional Christians, thoughtfully and confidently pondering life as prayerful servants of the Spirit.

If this sounds strange it is because there are not a great many such people around. A friend of mine has said that the only vital witnessing congregations are those where either the laity and the clergy share ministry or where there is a sense of the Holy Spirit working within the congregation. Preferably both should be present. I would agree with him, as long as the proofs be present of that response to the Gospel that I have claimed in this book.

Reaching Deep

It is reasonable to conclude this pastoral reflection with *how* they can be present. Again, it is important to return to the notion of the deep memory. Bruce Reed in *The Dynamics of Religion* speaks of functional and dysfunctional religion.

Functional religion is that which enables a person to approach the abyss or chaos without cloaking the pain in the illusions of literalism or moralism, and to return better able to engage the world. Dysfunctional religion would be, of course, anything that contributes to a retreat from this process. It is the deep memory that informs us and is informed in the awesome territory that borders the abyss.

There are without doubt those who find mention of chaos or the abyss a vestige of some dark nineteenth-century romanticism, and there are others who believe it has the odor of hell. The point here is that the abyss or chaos is a fact of human existence, often successfully dismissed from our consciousness, but only to our ultimate peril. The abyss is neither good nor bad; it is raw potential for both that can only be guided by God's grace working through images deeply embedded in our memories.

The ministry of the Christian community is to the deep memory. The most significant acts of ministry are those that reach to that level. Liturgy, preaching, prayer, and community life reach far within our memory to invite us to live as members of God's Kingdom present now and to come.

The Liturgy

In the early church Baptism was called the illumination. "Remember the days gone by," writes the author of Hebrews, "when, newly enlightened [*phōtisthentes*], you met the challenge of great sufferings and held firm" (Heb. 10:32; NEB). The author of Ephesians uses a form of the same word, *phōtisai*, to state that the Gospel illumines God's hidden purpose or mystery. The symbol of light was present throughout the baptismal rite itself. It and the other liturgies of the church fulfilled the requirements of performance as specified earlier in this book. The illumination was of the deep memory.

What make liturgy a true performance? Subtlety is needed above all, in the sense of inviting discernment. Liturgy is not a didactic exercise, and clarity is an enemy of its power. Churches should not be lighted like operating theaters, the participants should call attention beyond themselves, and the music ought not to be obvious in feeling. A friend of mine was visiting the Church of the Redeemer in Houston, Texas, a distinguished congregation in the charismatic tradition, and was struck by the serene beauty of the music. He commented about this to the organist, who spoke of the growing maturity of the parish. "We can no longer sing," he said, "the ditties of the early 1970s."

Perhaps one of the greatest errors of the Reformed tradition was to design liturgy as if cleanliness is next to godliness. It is not. I am told that G. K. Chesterton once said that a saint can afford to be filthy, but a seducer must always be clean. Smell is our most symbolic sense, and Lysol lacks the odor of sanctity. Worship needs most of all to engage us at the point of our noses. It is worth remembering that John the Elder identifies corporate prayer with the smell of incense (Rev. 5:8). People will remember what they have smelled. Begin liturgy there and we probably will assure the deepest impact.

It is said on occasion that Morning Prayer is the best service for evangelizing people, because it is the most easily understood and resembles the worship in other churches. If liturgy were an intellectual exercise and our goal were to make everyone comfortable, a case might be made for this argument. Even less excusable are prayer services that are alien to the tradition and express only the sentimentalism of populist piety. If we wish to engage ourselves and others at the effervescent edge of consciousness, where an undomesticated God still lies outside the expectations of civil religion, then the Eucharist has the greatest possibility of providing that point of contact.

Liturgy is in the service of mystery. It is our deepest self that is most immediately available to the mystery of God, his Incarnation and his abiding presence in the Spirit. There is no place in authentic performance for sentimentality or "drawing the moral." It is the evangelization of the twilight of our minds and hearts, which lies beyond platitudes of behavior or emotion.

Preaching

The sermon or homily—the first name comes from Latin meaning "word" and the second name from Greek meaning "confession"—has as its object the inscape of existence, not the landscape. Preaching is not teaching. As an act of evangelizing the deep memory, it needs to reveal to us the inner person, not describe the externals (Eph. 3:16). If one agrees with the Jesuit poet, Gerard Manley Hopkins, preaching and poetry have this in common.

Effective preaching, in this light, requires strong language, which produces vivid imagery and awakens the imagination. It needs to engage the hearer where the weighty thoughts and feelings lie. The powerful homily will evoke a consciousness that is fraught with possibility and danger and offers the good news of Jesus Christ as a way of living with hope in that place. Like folk tales or fairy tales, a sermon is in the oral tradition and allows the primordial aspirations and fears of the people to emerge into consciousness. It is in the territory bordering the abyss where these images of hope and fear lie.

This is why good sermons make poor reading. The personality of the preacher is essential to the entire gestalt of the event. The words spoken render the preacher transparent to the congregation and, in turn, invite their vulnerability. When this happens, we move beyond mere social interaction and recount the drama of God's love for humanity and share in his vision. Faith is called forth and belief formed. The homily itself no longer belongs to the preacher, but becomes the context for the inner journey of discovery for all present.

Prayer

Evangelization is an invitation to prayer, and prayer is to the spiritual nature of humanity as dining is to hunger. It is what we do with an innate quality of the person that reaches far beyond physiological requirements. Prayer is the enactment of the personal relationship between God and humanity. It presumes the possibility of an intimate level of sharing that moves past the surface amenities.

Among these surface amenities is included the shopping-list approach to God. Such an understanding puts our wants at the heart of our prayer life. There is no doubt that the New Testament sometimes described prayer as registering our needs (e.g., Lk. 11:5–10, Jas. 4:2–3). Yet we need to remember that in the first century genuine relationships existed for years in a patronage system. The parable of the poor beggar, Lazarus, illustrates the point (Lk. 16:20–31). In our culture such patronage does not exist, and genuine relationships begin with less tangible, mutual expressions of vulnerability.

We are called first of all to *be* with God, and this requires a style of prayer that allows that to happen. At its center is silence, not just external silence, but internal silence. It is significant that the psalmist identifies silence with speaking within the heart. "Speak to your heart in silence upon your bed" (Psalm 4:4B, Book of Common Prayer translation). Prayer is an inward movement; and meditation, the reflection upon the Scripture or the emptying of our minds and hearts as in the Jesus prayer ("Jesus Christ, Son of God, have mercy upon men," repeated in rhythm with our breathing), is the ground of all prayer.

If people wish to hear the good news, they must begin by listening. It is not a simple listening, but requires an inner hearing. It is akin to what psychotherapists mean when they speak of "listening with the third ear." It is like attending to the sound *between* other sounds. This is what it is to pray, to reach deep within ourselves to know what God is saying to us.

Life in the Community

If prayer is an inner journey, with all the risk of self-deception, the safeguard is our life together. The New Testament frequently speaks of the *koinōnia* that Christians have with one another (Acts 2:42), with the Gospel (Phil. 1:5), and with the Holy Spirit (1 Cor. 13:13). It means an intimate relationship, the root verb meaning "to share." It is noteworthy that the author of Hebrews speaks of Christ sharing our human flesh and blood as children have shared (*kekoinōnēken*) flesh and blood (Heb. 2:14). He is the Incarnation and the means of our *koinōnia* with God. Our sharing in the sacramental body and blood of Christ—what we call Communion, a transliteration of *koinōnia*—becomes the enactment of this union with God and one another by virtue of Christ's Incarnation.

Evangelization is an invitation into this life, a life of intimacy where Christ is found in the other. There is support here, but there is also confrontation. A favorite word for marriage in the Greek-speaking ancient world was *koinōnia*. All that constitutes a healthy, life-giving marriage characterizes the Christian community. The deep memory is exposed, called into question, and shaped. Our joy turns into pain, and our pain, if we have the courage, leads to growth and the joy of new life.

Evangelization as a ministry reaching deep within the lives of people needs to recover a feminine mode of consciousness. I spoke earlier of the emergence of the feminine in the twelfth-century evangelical awakening in the cult of the Blessed Virgin and in the celebration of romantic love. We need a recovery of this spirit.

What do I mean? This example might help explain the possibilities. A female graduate student of mine told of her work with an aphasic man. He had been in the hospital and the time came for him to go home. His mother came for him in a taxi, which was to take them to the airport. When he got to the car, he grabbed hold of the door handles, and nothing was able to loosen his grip. The taxi driver, a man of large build, tried to pry his fingers from the door, along with a nurse and two male chaplains. All efforts at assault, a masculine solution, failed.

My student, a woman Baptist minister, turned to prayer and then found herself led to ask the man, looking into his face, "Harold, do you like music?" He heard her and grunted assent. And then she began to sing an old Baptist hymn, "Take my hand, take my hand; and follow me, follow me." Harold muttered, "Jesus," and fell into her arms.

Somehow a very different act of ministry touched Harold deep within his memory and evoked a trust. He followed. This is what the ministry of evangelization must do.

Conclusion

The rapid spread of Christianity in the Roman Empire can only be understood if we remember that it arose from the spontaneous witness of a community of faith, who hoped to find in Jesus the fulfillment of their expectation. New vision met inchoate longing. For across the Empire there were groups of people for whom the order of the *Pax Romana* was a banal substitute for the resurrected life. They were unwilling to settle for what the satirist Martial called "bread and circuses" in return for following the accepted norms of a citizen of the Empire. The effervescence of the time expressed itself in earnest moral discourse, in philosophical speculation, and in the worship of gods imported from Egypt, Persia, and Greece. The synagogues of the Diaspora collected about them "God-fearers," persons who admired Jewish theology without subscribing to the Jewish Law.

If authentic evangelization has a possibility in our age, it will be among those for whom the *Pax Americana*, the *Pax Europa*, the *Pax Africana*, or whatever human order there may be is recognized as pap, thin gruel in comparison to the promise of the hidden God who calls us out of our security into the great pilgrimage. The unwillingness to retire from the spiritual quest and settle for cheap grace is the preparation for the Gospel or pre-evangelization.

Anglicanism has not always been noted for its evangelistic zeal. It is the curse of the established church, be it "established" in legal fact or mental fiction, to assume that everyone who counts is already a Christian and an Anglican. We are a people who find it very easy to accept good order and to succumb to "bread and circuses." When in our guilt we rouse ourselves to fulfill the Great Commission, our response can be an unthinking imitation of the model of evangelization that is nearest at hand. We are too ready to repudiate what is our greatest gift in mission when faced with the charge that it appeals only to certain classes of people.

In fact, Christianity is always going to appeal to only certain classes of people—those who are ready to risk faith. Conversion requires a prior discontent, a restlessness of spirit, which leaves us open and eager to give ourselves to the mystery of God's love. There are no guarantees, only a promise of things hoped for that lies beyond the suffering of our cross. The Gospel can only be heard if we are so disgusted with the slavery in Egypt that we are willing to wander in the wilderness in anticipation of the Promised Land.

Notes

INTRODUCTION

1. Robert Penn Warren, *A Place to Come To* (New York: Random House, 1977), p. 339.

CHAPTER 1

1. Léon Joseph Suenens, *Your God?* (New York: Seabury Press, 1978), p. 99.

CHAPTER 2

1. Gregory of Nyssa, *Life of Moses,* 239.
2. Ibid., p. 10.

CHAPTER 3

1. Richard of St. Victor, *Twelve Patriarchs,* v.
2. Ibid., xxxviii.

CHAPTER 4

1. Jeremy Rifkin, with Ted Howard, *The Emerging Order* (New York: Putnam, 1979), p. 232.
2. Richard Bandler and John Grinder, *The Structure about Magic I* (Palo Alto, Calif.: Service and Behavior Books, 1975), p. 45.
3. Victor Turner, "Performance and Reflexive Anthropology," an unpublished paper, p. 4.
4. Walter Bruggesmann, *The Prophetic Imagination* (Philadelphia: Fortress Press, 1978), p. 45.

CHAPTER 5

1. T. S. Eliot, *Four Quartets* (New York: Harcourt, Brace & Co., 1943), p. 39.
2. Rosemary Haughton, *The Transformation of Man* (Springfield, Ill: Templegate, 1967), pp. 31–32.
3. John H. Westerhoff, "A Necessary Paradox: Catechesis and Evangelism, Nurture and Conversion," *Religious Education* 73 (1978): 413.
4. Ibid.
5. Julian of Norwich, *Showings,* 41 (long text).
6. Ibid., 37 (long text).
7. Thomas Merton, *Contemplative Prayer* (Garden City, N.Y.: Image Books, 1971), pp. 103–104.

CHAPTER 6

1. Frank Ponsi, "Contemporary Concepts of Mission," *Missiology: An International Review* 6, no. 2 (April 1978): 139–151.

CHAPTER 7

1. David S. Schuller, Merton B. Strommen, and Mils L. Brekke, eds., *Ministry in America* (San Francisco: Harper & Row, 1980), p. 127.
2. Donald A. McGavran, ed., *Church Growth and World Mission* (New York: Harper & Row, 1965), p. 56.
3. Ibid., p. 43.
4. Ibid., p. 48.
5. Ibid., p. 43.
6. Ibid., p. 52.
7. A. R. Tippett, ed., *God, Man, and Church Growth* (Grand Rapids: William B. Eerdmans, 1973), p. 53.
8. C. Peter Wagner, *Our Kind of People* (Atlanta: John Knox Press, 1978), pp. 1–3.
9. A. R. Tippett, ed., *God, Man, and Church Growth*, pp. 52–58.
10. Charles Y. Glock and Rodney Stark, *Christian Beliefs and Anti-Semitism* (New York: Harper & Row, 1966).
11. Walter Broughton, "Religiosity and Opposition to Church Social Action: A Test of a Weberian Hypothesis," *Review of Religious Research* 19, no. 2 (Winter 1978): 154–166.
12. C. Peter Wagner, *Your Church Can Grow* (Glendale, Calif.: G/L Publications, 1976), pp. 155–159.
13. Bernhard Häring, *Evangelization Today*, trans. Albert Kuuire (Notre Dame: Fides Press, 1974), p. 2.
14. Wayne Williamson, *Growth and Desire in the Episcopal Church* (Pasadena, Calif.: William Carey Library, 1979), pp. 56–57.

CHAPTER 8

1. *Logos Journal* 9, no. 3 (May–June 1979): 64.

CHAPTER 9

1. Kenneth E. Rowe, ed., *The Place of Wesley in the Christian Tradition* (Metuchen, N.J.: The Scarecrow Press, 1976), p. 95.

CHAPTER 10

1. Richard of St. Victor, *Twelve Patriarchs*, lxxi.
2. Jakob Boehme, *The Way to Christ*, IV, ii, 9–10.
3. *Logos Journal* 9, no. 4 (June–July 1979): 48.